Heal Us, Emmanuel

Heal Us, Emmanuel

A Call for Racial Reconciliation, Representation, and Unity in the Church

GENERAL EDITOR: REV. DOUG SERVEN

White Blackbird
BOOKS

Unless otherwise indicated, Scripture quotations are from the ESV Bible (The Holy Bible, English Standard Version), copyright 2001 by Crossway, a publishing ministry of Good News Publishers. 2011 Text Edition. All rights reserved.

Julie Serven edited the publication.
Sean Benesh designed the cover.

Printed in the United States of America.
ISBN 13: 978-0-9973984-0-3

About White Blackbird Books

White blackbirds are extremely rare, but they are real. They are blackbirds that have turned white over the years as their feathers have come in and out over and over again. They are a redemptive picture of something you would never expect to see but that has slowly come into existence over time.

There is plenty of hurt and brokenness in the world. There is the hopelessness that comes in the midst of lost jobs, lost health, lost homes, lost marriages, lost children, lost parents, lost dreams, loss.

But there also are many white blackbirds. There are healed marriages, children who come home, friends who are reconciled. There are hurts healed, children fostered and adopted, communities restored. Some would call these events entirely natural, but really they are unexpected miracles.

The books in this series are not commentaries, nor are they crammed with unique insights. They are a collage of biblical truth applied to current times and places. The authors share their poverty and trust the Lord to use their words to strengthen and encourage his people.

May this series help you in your quest to know Christ as he is found in the Gospel through the Scriptures. May you look for and even expect the rare white blackbirds of God's redemption through Christ in your midst. May you be thankful when you look down and see your feathers have turned. May you also rejoice when you see that others have been unexpectedly transformed by Jesus.

Other books in the White Blackbird Book series include:

The Organized Pastor
Everything Is Meaningless? Ecclesiastes
Birth of Joy: Philippians

Praise for Heal Us, Emmanuel

Heal Us, Emmanuel is a tremendous resource on racial reconciliation that powerfully serves many of us who need to be quicker to listen and learn and slower to speak and self-justify. This book displays a diverse, multi-voiced expression of the Gospel, yet with glorious harmony and unity. May God use this resource to increase our faith, hope, and love and to heal our deep wounds so the Gospel of Christ's kingdom advances more and more!

> **Dr. Mark Dalbey**, President and Associate Professor of Applied Theology at Covenant Theological Seminary, St. Louis, MO

Heal Us, Emmanuel offers a provocative and challenging biblical, theological, and practical call to all Christians to fight against all forms of racism and monoethnicity with the Gospel and urges its readers to pursue reconciliation with all people in Christ. Readers will likely not agree with everything here, but they will certainly be challenged to consider how their churches can do their parts in living out the one new man in Christ in both church and society.

> **Dr. Jarvis J. Williams**, Associate Professor of New Testament Interpretation at The Southern Baptist Theological Seminary, Louisville, KY

Our nation is in desperate need of repentance and healing when it comes to the legacy of racial supremacy that has pervaded every sphere of life, including the church. While called to be a voice of reconciliation, unfortunately many in the church—past and present—have either been silent in the face of racism or just as worse active in its perpetuation. *Heal Us, Emmanuel* is a much needed cry to turn away from complicity with evil and instead turn toward participation in building the kingdom of God, for truly the Lord is with us in this ministry.

> **Dr. Todd Allen**, Professor of Communication Studies, Grove City College, Grove City, PA

Heal Us, Emmanuel is a tremendous work by pastors and elders, and this diverse work should be read by everyone willing to be persuaded of the image of God in all people. Each chapter connects into a persuasive argument of thoughtful, convicting guidance, yet in a warm and winsome way. It will help us be a better church, a better people in a hurting world that needs Jesus.

Dr. John Sowers, Author and President of The Mentoring Project, Oklahoma City, OK

This book is dedicated to everyone in our world th
everyone. We reach out to the pastors, elders, o
attenders, and visitors in our churches who have be
Presbyterian Church in America.

Emmanuel, God With Us, brings us togetl
reconciliation and love.

Heal Us, Emmanuel[1]

Our faith is feeble, we confess
We faintly trust Thy word;
But will you pity us the less?
Be that far from You Lord!

Chorus: Heal us, Emmanuel, here we stand
Waiting to feel Thy touch
To deep wounded souls reach forth
Thy hand O Savior, we are such

Remember him who once applied
With trembling for relief;
"Lord, I believe," with tears he cried;
"O help my unbelief!"
(Chorus)

She, too, who touched you in the press
And healing virtue stole,
Was answered, "Daughter, go in peace;
Thy faith has made thee whole."
(Chorus)

Like her, with hopes and fears we come
To touch You if we may;
O send us not despairing home;
Send none unhealed away.
(Chorus)

1 Text by William Cowper. Music by Kevin Twit and Lucas Morton. © 2015 Kevin Twit Music (ASCAP) and Lucas Morton Music (BMI). Used by permission. All rights reserved.

Table of Contents

Foreword

In the mid-1960s, I was a high school student in Gary, Indiana. Since this was in the day of *de facto* segregation in the North, my contact with Whites was limited and usually tinged with racism. However, I often heard many of my friends mention the "Hills sisters." Though they were White, they stood out in the minds of my peers because they were known for "not being prejudiced." Having been jaded by many racist encounters, I was skeptical about such a possibility among White folk.

Soon after coming to Christ, I met the Hills sisters and found out why they were so highly regarded for defying the traditional conventions of racism—they and their family followed Christ. That convinced me of the transforming power of the Gospel message, and it changed my outlook. In meeting Christ in them, I was healed.

However, through my developing years as a Christ-follower, I was often disappointed by people who claimed to be Christians but didn't seem to have been transformed by the Gospel in the area of race. I encountered this so often that my old jadedness about the possibility of rising above American racism began to return with a vengeance. Each time this doubt welled up in my heart, the Lord sent a reminder that he has many in the body of Christ who have "not bowed the knee to Baal"—in this case, the bad politics of race-based discrimination.

Heal Us, Emmanuel is a welcome balm—a reminder that the transforming power I saw in the Hills sisters so many years ago is still operating today.

It is one thing to condemn racist attitudes and behaviors, it is another thing to reveal the "dis-ease" that helps drive those attitudes and behaviors; namely, the aberrant theology that was developed to justify American chattel slavery and Jim Crow. The American Church continues to limp about with this festering wound today because the infection has not been disinfected by the light of Christ. It is not enough to admonish American Christians to have biblical attitudes and behaviors regarding race without dissecting and putting to death the dis-eased theology that plagued American Christianity—a theology that gave credence to race-based oppression. Anything short of this radical approach, coupled with repentance, will allow similar sinful and destructive attitudes to flare up again, producing more harmful history and culture.

Theological dis-ease happens when we seek to make the Bible conform to man-made philosophies and ideologies. For centuries, the Bible-believing community has identified and condemned this as heresy. *Heal Us, Emmanuel* lays a needed foundation for rising above the heresy and history that made it easy for Black militants and Marxist thinkers alike to label Christianity as "the White Man's Religion," or simply as useless in today's modern context.

These militant thinkers, however, overlooked an important fact; namely, that no sane person would embrace the religion of his or her oppressor. Yet our African American ancestors, along with those who opposed the racist culture and boldly proclaimed their dignity, encountered Christ in spite of the aberrant theology that surrounded them. When they met Christ, they discovered something about Christianity that defied the heresy their oppressors tried to impose on them. This gave them a powerful affirmation of human dignity, enabling them to resist the forces of dehumanization.

Theology is a two-sided coin; side A is doctrine, and side B is ethics. A robust system of doctrine can be discredited if we use it to justify unbiblical ethics. By identifying what went wrong theologically, the contributors to this valuable book have laid a foundation for a reformation and revival—something so many of us have fervently prayed for. The beautiful brothers in *Heal Us, Emmanuel* "get it." Their open hearts are a valuable and precious resource for the body of Christ, and these are the voices we need to hear to facilitate healing.

Today, there are many who claim to be biblical and yet seek to address the current racial issues with the same political and social ideologies employed by the fomenters of gratuitous racial unrest. These well-meaning activist Christians don't seem to realize that these ideologies often mask nefarious agendas. As my wife Karen teaches, "These ideologies are based ultimately in principles of destruction, not in building up men and women to good works; therefore, such ideologies have no place in the body of Christ."

Heal Us, Emmanuel reminds us that no matter how sophisticated our theology may be, it is always in need of being disciplined, corrected, and expanded by Scripture (2 Tim. 3:16), not by man-made ideologies. It challenges us to get busy doing theology that addresses current issues while being faithful to Scripture. Doing so will enable us to walk in biblical wisdom—a wisdom that far surpasses the power and scope of today's prevailing short-sighted ideologies. All who accept this loving challenge will discover new ways that God's Word "does not return void" (Isa. 55:11), and the implications will affect generations to come.

Heal Us, Emmanuel is a must-read and a must-have in the library of anyone who is serious about honoring God in this age of polarization.

Rev. Dr. Carl F. Ellis Jr.

Introduction

No doubt, churches in America continue to be largely monoethnic, without much mingling of races either within or between churches. This book is written by church leaders who would like to see that changed. It is a way for those in the church to hopefully wake up and speak up so we may more fully be God's ambassadors of the Gospel on earth.

Many of the contributors to this book are Caucasian, theologically conservative, Presbyterian pastors and church leaders. Their stories are of their eyes being opened to what their brothers and sisters of color experience every day. How could they not see the inequity before? How could they be so behind in such a basic concept? It is the essence of White privilege. They are asking God to help them listen better to the experiences of others.

To that end, this book also includes stories from African American, Asian American, and Latino pastors and leaders from the same theologically conservative denomination, the Presbyterian Church in America. Many of them are tired of talking about racial issues without seeming to get anywhere and wonder why it has taken so many Caucasian Christians so long to wake up. Some have considered retreating to churches and denominations where more people look like them and think like them. Yet they remain faithful to stand in the uncomfortable role of speaking up and speaking into the need to break down dividing walls, of which race is the most substantial and enduring in the United States. These brothers do not give a comprehensive voice to the issue, but they do provide valuable perspectives.

Waking up is painful and difficult. It is startling. Many times, it rubs people the wrong way. But it is important. The hope of the contributors to this book—whatever their race—is that racial reconciliation would occur not only in their own denomination but in all the churches of Christ. They realize their union with Christ compels them to pursue reunion and reconciliation across the ethnic lines that divide us outside of Christ.

This book was originally born out of discussions among a group of pastors and elders in the Presbyterian Church in America who desired reconciliation, representation, and unity in their individual churches and in their denomination as a whole. Many of them supported a call for their denomination to repent of its churches' inaction in standing for the rights of African Americans during the Civil Rights Movement. Though they write from their context, their words apply to any monoethnic church or denomination seeking to become more representative of the body of Christ, welcoming the sojourner among them and seeking justice for all of God's children.

The Pew Research Center reports that Protestant churches—whether in the mainline tradition, the Evangelical tradition, or in the historically Black tradition—are not ethnically diverse in any substantive way. Their 2007 survey indicates that 81 percent of Evangelical Protestant church members are White, 91 percent of mainline Protestant church members are White, and 92 percent of historically Black Protestant church members are Black.[1]

The 2014 LifeWay Research survey, *American Views on Church Segregation*, found that 66 percent of Americans have never regularly attended a place of worship where they were an ethnic minority.[2] Korie Edwards, in her book on interracial churches, calls religious racial integration a dubious enterprise.[3] She notes that, "Churches are most successful within the American context (where 'success' is measured by the number of attendees) when they appeal to one group."[4]

---

1 The Pew Forum on Religion & Public Life, *U.S. Religious Landscape Survey* (Washington, DC: Pew Research Forum, 2008), 75. Accessed March 26, 2015. http://religions.pewforum.org/pdf/report-religious-landscape-study-full.pdf: 2008.

2 LifeWay Research, *American Views on Church Segregation* (Nashville: LifeWay Research, 2014), 4. http://www.lifewayresearch.com/files/2015/01/American-Views-on-Church-Segregation.pdf.

3 Korie L. Edwards, *The Elusive Dream: The Power of Race in Interracial Churches* (New York: Oxford University Press, 2008), location 59, Kindle.

4 Ibid., location 72.

While people may prefer sameness, "God apparently loves difference; he created so much of it."[5] The abundance of human differences can become a source of difficulty because we have to navigate our differences in the context of relationships with others. Thus, our comfort with God's preference can only occur when we desire to embrace and understand difference.

We all have much to confess. We all have much to be thankful for. It is all grace and mercy. None of us would be anything or anyone or anywhere without the grace of our Lord and Savior Jesus Christ, to whom all things work for his glory and honor.

Jesus says the dividing wall is coming down. It's been up far too long. We grieve that we are so late to the party. We have finally arrived at the troubling conclusion that there is brokenness in the way that we value and treat one another on the basis of skin color. We praise God that he is patient and gracious with us as we slowly come around to the reality that so many of our neighbors, brothers, and sisters have known their entire lives. We pray they would forgive our blindness to their suffering as we move forward, seeking to learn and grow toward racial reconciliation.

Rev. Dr. Irwyn Ince and Rev. Doug Serven

---

5 Duane Elmer, *Cross Cultural Connections: Stepping Out and Fitting In Around the World* (Downers Grove, IL: InterVarsity Press, 2002), 64.

An Invitation to Listen

Chapter 1

A Familiar Conversation

Rev. Lance Lewis

Lance Lewis serves as Senior Pastor of Soaring Oaks Presbyterian Church (PCA) in Elk Grove, California. Previous to that he served as the church planter of Christ Liberation Fellowship (PCA), a multiethnic church in West Philadelphia. Lance has contributed to Glory Road: The Journey of 10 African-Americans into Reformed Christianity *and* Aliens in The Promised Land: Why Minority Leadership is Overlooked in White Christian Churches and Institutions. *Lance has degrees from Temple University (BA) and Chesapeake Theological Training Center (MATS). He and his wife, Sharon, have two children.*

I've had versions of this conversation a few dozen times. It goes this way:

"You see, Lance, we've gotten past all this race stuff, and the country has moved on and so should Black people. Blacks have just as much chance to succeed as everyone else if you're willing to work hard and not use race as an excuse. In fact, our supposed 'race' problem only exists because self-serving politicians and the liberal media just want to use race to keep us divided and maintain the loyalty of the Black community. I mean Barack Obama is the president, you know."

I respond, "I hear you and agree with you that many things and attitudes have changed in America since I was born in 1964. But I think you're missing the point regarding the issue of race and ethnicity."

"Excuse me? Isn't the point to become a color-blind society where people are viewed as individuals and judged by the content of their character and not the color of their skin?"

It was a question I'd heard many times. I knew what to say: "Well, yes and no. The actual point has much more to do with what the living God is doing through the Gospel of our Lord Jesus Christ."

"Exactly, Lance, which is why I wonder why all this fuss about race/ethnicity? Wouldn't all this be solved if we just viewed ourselves as Christians first and foremost and not as members of diverse ethnic groups? It seems to me that this so-called pursuit of ethnic unity is little more than a liberal scheme to take our focus off of the Gospel and place it onto one of the newly cherished values of the world. Besides, I've been through the mandated diversity training at work, and it was a woeful waste of time."

And I had to answer him in what becomes an extended monologue: "Those are valid questions, and I'd like to have some time and space to address them. Let me begin by acknowledging your concerns and assuring you that I don't think they arise out of an attitude of hostility toward Black people. I honestly believe that we can disagree about the issue of race and ethnicity and still enjoy genuine fellowship in our Lord Jesus Christ.

"However, you should know a couple of things before we go on. First, I am passionate about the issue of race and ethnicity, and not just because I've been blessed to be born and raised as a Black man in America. I'm passionate about this issue because as I read Scripture it's one of the core concerns of the living God and intimately connected to what he's doing through the Gospel. Now, there are times when my passion may appear to come off as anger but please, please don't take it that way. Instead, try to view it as the outgrowth of a deep frustration and pain.

"Here's an example that might be helpful. Imagine the most painful thing or incident that has ever happened to you or someone very close to you. Try as you may, you just can't shake off all the effects of the trauma. Everything within you would like nothing more than to be miraculously healed and whole. In fact, there are times you find yourself daydreaming and wishing you could just go back in time and undo what happened.

"But you can't. You have to live with this, and even though it doesn't dominate your life, it's still present and it hurts. Consequently, when you speak about it (which you hesitate to do because often the conversations don't end well and just reinforce the effects of the trauma), what comes off as anger is more accurately the expression of your deep frustration, pain, and longing for the total healing and redemption promised by our Lord upon his second return.

"Second, in my view, the Evangelical church has never gotten the doctrine of race and ethnicity correct. For the most part, it is in error about it today. This is why I pray you're willing to hear what I have to say, think through it, pray through it, and search the Scriptures about it. Lord willing, our gracious Father will use this to enrich our fellowship as together we purpose to promote the saving and unifying Gospel of our Lord Jesus Christ deeper into our lives and our society."

My friend then answers, "Thanks, Lance, for approaching the topic in this way. I have to admit I'm a bit less defensive and willing to hear what you have to say. We may not agree, but I can appreciate where you're coming from."

To which I say, "Amen. Then let's get started."

Politically minded thinking

In my view, many brothers and sisters in Christ are in doctrinal error regarding the issue of race and ethnicity because they've embraced what I call a political mindset about it. A political mindset views the issue of race and ethnicity as primarily or exclusively a social problem that for the most part was solved through the political process in the mid to late '60s. Consequently, this country does not have a problem with race, and Blacks now have as much chance to succeed in their life endeavors as anyone else. Moreover, any focus on race, even if that focus simply consists in discussing it, works against the unity we've achieved and highlights make-believe divisions.

Viewing the issue of race from a political mindset is faulty and unfruitful for a number of reasons. First of all, doing so can lead us to place the temporary country of America over the eternal kingdom of God concerning the critical work of Gospel-focused ethnic unity. Instead of going about the work of pursuing unity across ethnic lines within Christ's church, we take pride in the efforts this country has made to achieve a "color-blind" society, and in so doing absolve ourselves of any responsibility to follow the commands of our Lord in this area.

3

Maintaining a political mindset further damages our witness by actually preventing us from talking about race and ethnicity. I can't count how many times I've been told that we mustn't talk about these things because doing so is what causes the division in the first place. That's similar to saying, "Don't talk to me about smoking because we all know that talking about smoking leads to cancer." I realize that discussing race and ethnicity is difficult and uncomfortable for many. For some, it's like wading through a minefield with a blindfold on. But it's an issue the church must address since God has called us to diligently maintain and pursue unity across ethnic lines (see Eph. 2:11–4:32, especially 2:11–22–3:1–7 and 4:1–7).

Thinking politically robs us of the opportunity to show genuine concern and love for the Black community, some of whom worship with us on a regular basis. It does so by essentially negating our history, the cultural heritage God has given us, and our present experience with acts of racism within this country.

The fact is the vast majority of Black people don't immediately believe that every negative interaction with a White person is an act of racism. But some are. Do all of these acts present a significant hindrance to our obtaining the kind of lifestyle most Americans desire? No, they do not. What's the big deal then, you ask? The big deal is that among other things, acts of racism serve as a statement that we're not valued, welcomed, or wanted. They are the reminder that we are viewed as different, we are "the other," and that though we may be tolerated, we're not truly accepted.

Thinking politically discounts this reality by merely focusing on the bottom line. It does so by expressing the view that though an act of racism may be unpleasant, it's not debilitating and therefore should be ignored. It therefore robs Evangelicals of the opportunity to show love to Blacks in a way that declares, "You are valued, welcomed, and wanted. We do see your difference and thank God for it. We will more than tolerate you—we will joyfully accept you, along with your history, culture, and present struggles attributed to race."

Finally, holding onto political thinking leads us to embrace American values such as merit, fairness, and individual rights as opposed to biblical virtues such as mercy, grace, sacrifice, and humility.

Redemptively minded thinking

Which brings me to why you should embrace a biblically grounded, redemptive mindset regarding the issue of race and ethnicity. A redemptive mindset views race and ethnicity as a theological issue stemming from the truth that by his sovereign will the living God created people of various ethnicities for his own good purpose. According to Scripture, that purpose is to gather people from every ethnicity and through faith in Christ form them into one, eternal, multiethnic worshipping community (see Rev. 5:9–11; 7:9–17).

What's crucial for us to understand now is that the process of unifying believers of various ethnic groups not only began on the day of Pentecost, but is one of Christ's top priorities for his church and a key component to our witness (see John 17:20–23). It's imperative therefore that believers joyfully pursue redemptive ethnic unity not because it's the latest fad that's sweeping the church, nor as a cave-in to political correctness, but in obedience to God's express command. Beyond that, I believe it's important for us to see the beauty, wisdom, and power God displays through his multiethnic worshipping community, as together we express the tangible unity that is our present calling and settled destiny.

Thinking redemptively about the issue of race and ethnicity corrects the functional way we view God's ultimate purpose for African Americans (and for that matter, people from all ethnic groups) in America. It does so by stopping us from measuring success in this area by the number or percentage of African Americans who assimilate into the middle-class and obtain a share of the American dream (along with the attitude that our success is almost wholly due to our taking personal responsibility for it). It's this kind of politically focused mindset that helps many Evangelicals distance ourselves from the lives, issues, and challenges of many African Americans.

A redemptive mindset recognizes that God's ultimate purpose for Blacks in America (as well as all the other people groups) is that we repent of our sins, believe in his Son, the Lord Jesus Christ, and be vitally, visibly, and tangibly joined to his church. And the work of promoting the Gospel to African Americans (as well as other people groups) is the responsibility of Christ's church.

To put this another way, among the first thoughts Evangelicals must have regarding Blacks in America shouldn't be whether we're doing our part to improve our lives and achieve the American dream, but whether or not the Evangelical church in general—and my local church in particular—is following God's command to pursue redemptive unity with those who are already in Christ and promoting the Gospel to those who are not.

Considering the issue of race and ethnicity from a redemptive as opposed to political mindset opens us up to the grace of practicing many of the biblical virtues we prize and often talk about. My guess is that given a test, most Evangelicals would heartily affirm their belief in and support for virtues like humility, mercy, peacemaking, meekness, kindness, grace, sacrifice, and love. Yet concerning the issue of race and ethnicity, it appears that far too many of us actually practice the American values of individualism, individual rights, individual merit, and strict fairness.

Viewing race and ethnicity through a redemptive lens will afford us the blessing of relating to the Black community as servants who employ biblical virtues for their overall well-being. We can be a witness of God's love for them, with the chief aim of highlighting the character and Gospel of our Lord Jesus Christ. At the very least, this will give Evangelicals an opportunity to resist knee-jerk reactions to issues that concern the greater Black community, reflect upon them a bit more deeply, consider developing a dialogue with an African American to gain a different perspective, and even seek to partner with the community to work toward solutions.

The supreme value of love

Connected to this is the supreme value of love. Redemptive thinking fuels our desire to walk in love toward the African American community rather than walking in indifference. And though that might seem self-evident, it's both an important and often overlooked point.

You're probably aware of the history between Evangelicals and the Black community. If not, I need to let you know that for almost all of its existence in this country, the Evangelical church purposely and blatantly fought against the unity of Christ's body. For much of the twentieth century, many Evangelical churches and denominations maintained a policy that forbade Blacks from participating in communion and becoming members of the church.

It was this kind of active hostility toward African Americans that emboldened our society to maintain their stance of ethnic separation and segregation for as long as it did. More troubling is how much damage this did to the Gospel of our Lord Jesus Christ then and its residual effects in our society now. On the one hand, Evangelical churches preached that the living God loved and accepted all of his people in Christ, while at the very same time they practiced the opposite.

Following the period of active hostility against Blacks, the Evangelical church retreated into a time of silent apathy as it accepted our society's change concerning enforced segregation. But apathy and indifference aren't virtues to which our Lord calls us, especially with respect to the command to pursue redemptive unity. From my perspective, it seems that up until the late 1960s, Evangelicals held the same kind of contempt for and malice toward the Black community as did the rest of this country. That was followed by a period of casual indifference in which Blacks were viewed as problems, projects, or prospective voters for the Republican Party.

However, I can't say that we've ever been genuinely loved by Evangelicals. Granted, we may have been the objects of individual acts of mercy. But while that is a component of love, it's not the total package. From my conversations and interactions over the past twenty-five years, it appears that in general Evangelicals are content to ignore the Black community. When they do address us, it's often to scold us for not taking personal responsibility for our own problems and communities.

Perhaps an example from my marriage might be helpful on this point. Loving my wife means that I'm called to show her acts of kindness. It also means that at times I have to offer loving advice or correction. But if all I did was show an occasional act of kindness and give frequent correction, then my love would fall short. Loving her means listening to her when she needs to express herself about something that's bothering her. It means praying about the concerns she identifies that affect her life. It means caring about the issues and things she cares about and not dismissing them just because they're not necessarily my cup of tea. It certainly means I look to meet her spiritual, emotional, social, psychological, and physical needs.

I'm not saying that Evangelicals must love the African American community to the full extent that husbands must love their wives. Yet we must be aware that indifference is not love. Among other things, biblical love is active. It's proactive. It takes initiative, displays patience, and is willing to sacrifice.

One last reason to embrace a redemptive mindset concerning race and ethnicity is that the pursuit of redemptive ethnic unity is deeply biblical. Though I've hinted at this earlier, I'd like to now give a few examples of the richness of this scriptural teaching.

Genesis 12 records God's covenantal call to the patriarch Abraham. That call included a number of promises, one of which was God's commitment to secure a permanent people for himself through faith in our Lord Jesus Christ. Genesis 12:3 says, "*I will bless those who bless you, and him who dishonors you I will curse, and in you all the families of the earth shall be blessed.*" This aspect of the promise is repeated to Abraham's son and grandson (see Gen. 26:4; 28:14). In Galatians 3:8, the Apostle Paul confirms that this was the message of the Gospel given to our forefather Abraham. It's a message that directly impacts the tangible unity across ethnic lines to which our Lord would call those who are granted the blessing of Abraham to display for his glory and as a witness to the fidelity of God's promise.

How can we know that God intends for those family groups (or people and ethnic groups) in Christ to pursue, demonstrate, and display an actual and visible unity? In Ephesians 2, the Apostle Paul beautifully reveals and describes the various layers of the church's unity. He does so by using illustrations that convey different kinds of connections (race, citizen, family member, and temple stone). While each of these objects can be seen as distinct and individual, all of them are designed to function in a vital connection to the others. This builds upon Paul's earlier declaration in Ephesians 1 that we're all members of one body. While we can distinguish the individual parts of our physical bodies, we'd also consider it absurd to contemplate any of these parts acting independently from the rest of our body.

Consequently, to hold to the conviction that all we need is a kind of "spiritual" unity across ethnic lines that never manifests itself in real live relationships is simply not biblically sound or correct. It's similar to me professing my great, great love for God's people in Bolivia, Ghana, Spain, and

Canada, all the while knowing that my professed love will rarely if ever be put to the test on real, live, breathing people.

If that weren't enough, Paul drives this theme home in the opening paragraphs of Ephesians 3. There he claims that this mystery of actual ethnic unity in Christ is what God is doing through the Gospel (Eph. 3:6–7). Why did the living God choose to bring about this unity through the Gospel? Ephesians 3:10 reveals that God did this to display his multifaceted wisdom to all creation. In Christ, the living God has created a new spiritual race of people that consists of souls from all of the family groups of the world and brought them together in one living, united, vitally and visibly connected church.

And that's why all this is important. That's why it matters. That's why the Evangelical church can no longer shrug off the pursuit of redemptive ethnic unity as if it were some nice option to have a multiethnic church but not a true Gospel necessity.

Now to him who is able to do far more abundantly than all that we ask or think, according to the power at work within us, to him be glory in the church and in Christ Jesus throughout all generations, forever and ever. Amen. (Eph. 3: 20–21)

Chapter 2

Amazing Grace, How Sweet the Sound

Rev. Howard Brown

Howard Brown, a native of Charleston, South Carolina, is Senior Pastor of Christ Central PCA in Charlotte, North Carolina. He planted the church, a multiethnic work in the arts district, in 2003. Howard has degrees from Clemson University (BA) and Covenant Theological Seminary (MDiv). He and his wife, Kellie, have two boys.

I was born and raised in the African Methodist Episcopal Church in Charleston, South Carolina. Our church, Mt. Zion AME, is the daughter church of Emanuel AME church, where tragedy struck June 17, 2015. Our churches both call the historical downtown Charleston peninsula home. Since the churches are less than two miles away from each other, we share families, acquaintances, and much of the same story.

In fact, it is safe to say that all African American churches started before the twentieth century share the same story and historical DNA of slavery, oppression, discrimination, and perseverance. To reflect this perseverance through a tumultuous history, the African Methodist Church took as its symbol the blacksmith's anvil and the motto: Strong as a blacksmith's anvil.

Like the anvil and its function, African American Christianity as a whole was shaped through a faith that survived the fire and pounding of racism, classism, and violence. But the African Methodist Church, along with other African American denominations and churches, believed the anvil was where and how God worked to shape them and their faith like metal under a hammer wielded in the loving, sovereign hands of God. They believed that though the fire and the pain was dealt out by a harsh and sinful world, the Lord alone could shape and make beautiful and resilient what mankind and Satan meant to be ugly and destructive.

This beautiful, persevering orthodox faith was seen in the tragedy that took place in Charleston in 2015 at Emanuel AME Church. At about 9 p.m. during a Bible study led by Rev. Clementa C. Pinckney, twenty-one-year-old Dylann Roof was welcomed to the group by the regular attenders. He then stood up and unloaded not only racially charged and inflammatory statements but also bullets, shooting and killing nine of the Bible study members.

Killed that night were: Cynthia Marie Graham Hurd, 54; Susie Jackson, 87; Ethel Lee Lance, 70; Depayne Middleton-Doctor, 49; Rev. Clementa C. Pinckney, 41; Tywanza Sanders, 26; Daniel Simmons, 74; Sharonda Coleman-Singleton, 45; and Myra Thompson, 59.

Then, only two days later, the Christianity of the African American church shocked the world. At Roof's bond hearing, with the opportunity to speak to the man who had taken their loved ones in a racist, hateful, deadly spray of bullets, the families of the victims returned fire with forgiveness. Their words and actions teach us something about Gospel-driven forgiveness, the providential shaping of hearts through a history of suffering, and the triumph of God's justice.

A Gospel of forgiveness

While we may assume that forgiveness is central to the Gospel, it was the powerful words of forgiveness that made the Gospel walk and breathe with incarnational Jesus power in the courtroom that day. What did we witness? Dylann Roof, the killer, was offered repentance and salvation through Jesus. Here are some words spoken in the courtroom to Dylann Roof that day, recorded by the *Washington Post*.[1] These words are the sound of amazing grace.

Nadine Collier, daughter of victim Ethel Lance, said:

> I forgive you. You took something very precious away from me. I will never get to talk to her ever again. I will never be able to hold her again, but I forgive you, and have mercy on your soul.... You hurt me. You hurt a lot of people. If God forgives you, I forgive you.

1 Elahe Izadi. "The powerful words of forgiveness delivered to Dylann Roof by victims' relatives." *The Washington Post*. June 9, 2015. Accessed October 2015.

A relative of Myra Thompson said:

> I would just like him to know that, to say the same thing that was just said: I forgive him and my family forgives him. But we would like him to take this opportunity to repent. Repent. Confess. Give your life to the one who matters most: Christ. So that he can change him and change your ways, so no matter what happens to you, you'll be okay.

Felicia Sanders, mother of Tywanza Sanders, said:

> We welcomed you Wednesday night in our Bible study with welcome arms. You have killed some of the most beautiful people that I know. Every fiber in my body hurts and I'll, I'll never be the same. Tywanza Sanders was my son. But Tywanza Sanders was my hero. Tywanza was my hero.… May God have mercy on you.

Wanda Simmons, granddaughter of Daniel Simmons, said:

> Although my grandfather and the other victims died at the hands of hate, this is proof, everyone's plea for your soul, is proof that they lived in love and their legacies will live in love. So hate won't win. And I just want to thank the court for making sure that hate doesn't win.

The sister of DePayne Middleton-Doctor said:

> That was my sister, and I'd like to thank you on behalf of my family for not allowing hate to win. For me, I'm a work in progress. And I acknowledge that I am very angry. But one thing that DePayne always enjoined in our family … is she taught me that we are the family that love built. We have no room for hating, so we have to forgive. I pray God on your soul.

Jesus taught such forgiveness in his Sermon on the Mount:

> *You have heard that it was said to those of old, "You shall not murder; and whoever murders will be liable to judgment." But I say to you that everyone who is angry with his brother will be liable to judgment; whoever insults his brother will be liable to the council; and whoever says, "You fool!" will be liable to the hell of fire. So if you are offering your gift at the altar and there remember that your brother has something against you, leave your gift there*

before the altar and go. First be reconciled to your brother, and then come and offer your gift. Come to terms quickly with your accuser while you are going with him to court, lest your accuser hand you over to the judge, and the judge to the guard, and you be put in prison. Truly, I say to you, you will never get out until you have paid the last penny. (Matt. 5:21–26)

At first glance, it appears that Jesus is simply teaching that we should clear our consciences and moral and other debts with others before we come to the Lord with our offerings for forgiveness and thanksgiving. However, if we pay close attention to the brother who is in danger of hell for murder and hatred, we will see that Jesus is calling those of us who are bringing thanksgiving to God to offer reconciliation to those who are angry and hateful to us. If they do, they can be reconciled to each other and possibly God and escape hell. This kind of forgiveness and reconciliation requires the presence of a Savior who has first come to those who have hated God and one another. Jesus, by his sacrifice, has reconciled haters and murderers to God.

The victims' families embraced Jesus's teaching. In their thankfulness for what God had done for them, they went to Dylann Roof, who not only physically killed their family members, but also murdered their God-given image and likeness with his racist beliefs. Racism is murder and Dylann Roof murdered his victims before he pulled the trigger. This behavior is indicative of one who, in his treatment of others, is most likely in the deepest danger Jesus talked about in Matthew, of hell's judgment and fire.

By going to Dylann Roof with messages of reconciliation, the victims' families were giving him a chance and offer to escape hell's fire by preaching the Gospel of reconciliation to him at the expense of their personal pain. The victims' families, like the Matthew passage calls for, had to leave their offering of sorrow and pain and thanksgiving at the altar in going back to Dylann Roof. That kind of forgiveness is hopeful that Roof too will, in coming to Jesus, be able to repent to and for those he terrorized.

In the Sermon on the Mount, it is the unreconciled relationship between people that stands in the way of being right with God. It is a principle we see throughout the Scriptures.

The victims' families did something incredible in presenting the Gospel that day. By going to seek reconciliation with the one who hated them, they were declaring, "We are not holding hatred or debt against you, or requirement that would forbid you from being free to bring your sacrifice of repentance and reconciliation to God." The families were letting Roof know that they were not standing between God and his mercy, not only because they can't, but they won't. Because Jesus their Savior not only stood in the way as the offended Lord between us and God, but actually became the way to reconciliation with God. The families in their forgiveness and expressed gratefulness to God's grace refused to stand in the way, and instead showed the way to reconciliation for Dylann Roof. Their sufferings, like Jesus's own sufferings, became an incarnational means by which a bridge of forgiveness, with the possibility of eternal life, was opened.

Forgiven much, forgive much

The cultural and historical details and ingredients that went into what happened that day are important to understanding the unique means by which God has manifested the Gospel and forgiveness in the African American church. At the memorial service for the nine people killed in the Charleston Massacre, President Barack Obama concluded his eulogy in leading the whole assembly that day in singing "Amazing Grace." Two choruses especially struck a chord of forgiveness that day:

> Amazing grace! How sweet the sound that saved a wretch like me!
> I once was lost, but now am found; Was blind, but now I see.
> Through many dangers, toils, and snares, I have already come;
> 'Tis grace hath brought me safe thus far, and grace will lead me home.

In Luke 7, Jesus comes across a socially oppressed woman who was forgiven by him for her numerous sins. In a fit of passionate thanks, she kisses and anoints Jesus's feet in the presence of so-called holy and righteous people. They are offended by her awkward, tactless, inappropriate show of affection for Jesus. Jesus responded:

> *And Jesus answering said to him, "Simon, I have something to say to you." And he answered, "Say it, Teacher."*

> *"A certain moneylender had two debtors. One owed five hundred denarii, and the other fifty. When they could not pay, he cancelled the debt of both. Now*

which of them will love him more?" Simon answered, "The one, I suppose, for whom he cancelled the larger debt." And he said to him, "You have judged rightly...."

Therefore I tell you, her sins, which are many, are forgiven—for she loved much. But he who is forgiven little, loves little." And he said to her, "Your sins are forgiven." Then those who were at table with him began to say among themselves, "Who is this, who even forgives sins?" And he said to the woman, "Your faith has saved you; go in peace." (Luke 7:40–43, 47–50)

The African American historical and cultural experience in this country is one wrought and wracked with oppression. Like the woman in the Gospel, African Americans have been misused and abused by people and systems in this country since they were stolen from their homeland and brought to America to be sold into a life filled with degradation and oppression.

The Emanuel AME believers who stood in that courtroom with an incredible and, to some, inappropriate message of forgiveness, did so as those who knew and experienced in the history of their faith God's amazing grace. These African American believers, like many others in this country, knew what it was to be treated as "a wretch" and to have come through "many dangers, toils, and snares." They had known wretched treatment in their sufferings of being Black in this country, and yet in Jesus they found comfort and relief. What does this have to do with the offer of forgiveness to a racist? Everything.

On one side of the coin, you have a sinner, and on the other side the sinned against. On one side you have a wretch, and on the other side one who has been wretchedly treated. The African American church has been given, through suffering and oppression, by the work of Jesus, a redeemed coin of grace. By being treated like wretches and thrown into the toils and dangers and snares of evil, hateful people, and this world, they have known what it is like to need grace to make it through.

African Americans historically know what it is like to need favor and grace to be freed and given opportunity to be human. Somehow, based on their offer of forgiveness to Dylann Roof, they long for and recognize the need for Jesus to freely come and offer peace to both victim and victimized. The victims' families offered a grace wrought through historical suffering that kept them from going to hatred and bitterness. There is no good reason for African Americans to be forgiving apart from the fact that Jesus has brought them peace, love, and hope in the midst of a toilsome and dangerous world. These Black brothers and sisters proved that day in court that Jesus was worthy of praise and consideration as Savior. Out of oppression, sin, and hatred came forgiveness, amazing grace, and peace.

I believe the world wondered what their words and actions meant that day, just as did the hearers of Jesus during the Sermon on the Mount. Where did those words of forgiveness come from? They came from an orthodox, holy, and rightly applied understanding and experience of the Gospel. Historically—as a people refused and thus without much entitlement—Black Christians have relied on being forgiven and given grace. It makes spiritual sense that they would be a people who would give much forgiveness and grace.

Forgiveness does not mean no justice

It would be an easy mistake to assume that the words of forgiveness offered that day were an attempt to do away with or disagree with the necessary work and call of the court to bring justice for their loved ones. After the words of forgiveness were uttered, some wrongly began to think and even write that they were amazed that they didn't want Dylann Roof to face a harsh judgment. Anti-death penalty groups took hold of the words as proof that even those hurt by the most terrible crimes did not long for the highest extent of the law against Dylann Roof.

If we take the no-justice-because-of-forgiveness route, we not only insult the blood and God-image of those lost, we insult and lessen the power of forgiveness that day. Remember, from the passage in Matthew 5 that the person accused of murder is accused not just because he physically took the person's life, but worse, he took from them what only God could give—human dignity and the right to live in justice and equality. The hatred Jesus talks about here would include racism.

Jesus wants his listeners to know that he was sent to redeem the image of people broken and destroyed by sin and hatred. That truth must be upheld, especially by those involved in the broken relationship—the victim and the perpetrator. In this passage, Jesus never teaches that the judge would be wrong in bringing judgment on the perpetrator. As a matter of fact, he tells his listeners:

> *Come to terms quickly with your accuser while you are going with him to court, lest your accuser hand you over to the judge, and the judge to the guard, and you be put in prison. Truly, I say to you, you will never get out until you have paid the last penny.* (Matt. 5:25–26)

Jesus agrees with judgment, though this is an analogy about being spiritually judged by God. In the Charleston case, the accusers and family members want Dylann Roof to be made right with God and forgiven for a sin that could send him to hell and leave him not reconciled to God. Their forgiveness was before the trial started, so that he could quickly find forgiveness from God before a possible sentence that could end his life for the murders or before a lifetime jail sentence could harden his heart.

Their forgiveness is powerful because they value human life enough, the lives of their family members enough, to react like Dylann Roof's greatest issue will be facing a God who also values and upholds the justice of human life. They value life so much that hell is a just punishment for hating another human being, much less killing or doing violence toward one. They are not forgiving him because it wasn't that big of deal that people died, but because it is a big deal that people died.

By calling Dylann Roof to repentance through their forgiveness, they acknowledged Roof's humanity instead of denying it. They treated him as if God cared about his soul, even though he was the accused murderer. In this way, their forgiveness recognizes God's call for justice for oppressing, demeaning, and destroying human life and Roof's need as a human to hopefully recognize that quickly. The families in their offer of forgiveness do what it takes for Dylann Roof to know God's justice behind the victims and his own human dignity at the same time. The victims, as their Lord Jesus instructs, are calling Roof spiritually to repent before he experiences earthly justice through the punitive hand of God that works through government.

So the families of those killed patiently wait for justice for their family members through the courts, but with one amazing caveat. If God's call to forgiveness is a call to recognize his justice for human life, then even if justice fails them, as it often has in the past for African Americans, they have put the matter in God's hands. In the passage in Matthew 5, the person, once reconciled, is free to bring the offering to God. That offering is an offering that celebrates God's shalom, God's peace. That peace means that they are not only at peace with Dylan Roof in their forgiveness, but at peace with God's decision concerning him.

This doesn't mean justice on earth for the death of their loved ones is not something to be prayed for and rightly longed. But they have put Dylann Roof and what happened in the hands of God, who will carry them through and give comfort in any subsequent and future disappointments they face. The mourning, the anger, the rage, the desire for swift and heavy judgment in what happened is right and even holy, but they walk, live, and will be kept by the peace of a sovereign God, who has reconciled them and their world through Jesus.

> Through many dangers, toils and snares, I have already come;
> 'Tis grace hath brought me safe thus far, And grace will lead me home.

Chapter 3

"Unintentional" Racism

Dr. Alexander Jun

Alexander Jun is a professor in the Department of Higher Education at Azusa Pacific University, where he teaches courses in advanced qualitative research methods, international comparative education, and diversity and social justice. He has degrees from the University of Southern California (BA, PhD) and California State University (MS). He is also a ruling elder and attends New Life Mission Church in Fullerton, California (Korean Southwest Orange County Presbytery). He serves on the permanent Committee for Mission to the World. Alexander and his wife, Jeany, have three children.

I was speaking recently at a Christian conference. At the end of my talk and throughout the conference, I received compliments, as well as some interesting questions and comments. I heard:

> "Your English is so good. When did you come to the States?"
> "Where are you from? . . . No, where are you really from?"
> "Do you eat dog?"

Microaggressions

These are just a few of the types of questions I get on a regular basis, and depending on my mood at the time, my responses range from gracious to sarcastic. These questions are quite familiar to me; I have been dealing with them my whole life. These are examples of what scholars refer to as racial microaggressions. Racial microaggressions can be defined as brief and commonplace daily verbal, behavioral, or environmental indignities, whether intentional or unintentional, that communicate hostile, derogatory, or negative racial slights and insults toward people of a nondominant group.[1]

Asian American Christians like myself, even if they are second-, third-, and fourth-generation American citizens, continue to experience racial microaggressions like the examples above. Asian Americans are often perceived as perpetual aliens, foreigners, and outsiders by White Americans in the United States. This is also true within our churches. Most of these types of questions have come from my White brothers and sisters. When I get them, I am reminded that I do not fit into their paradigm and implicit definition of an American. Even if I was born in the United States, which I was, and even if I speak English fluently, which I do, and have written numerous articles as a professor, I am reminded time and again, that my existence is both foreign and exotic to an Anglo gaze. I have heard similar experiences from my friends of other ethnicities.

An African American colleague of mine teaches graduate students at a predominantly White Christian institution. He is regularly complimented by Caucasian colleagues about how articulate he is. It is as if people are surprised that someone who looks like him could speak like them; no ghetto vernacular, no street slang, no Ebonics accent. When people say "you are so articulate" as a compliment, it merely reveals that their expectations of him as a Black male are to speak incoherently or perhaps to rap his way through conversations. People also have complimented him on how passionately he sings praises in chapel and how much his Black church culture could help breathe life into their campus chapel services. However, he does not attend a Black church. In fact he has been a member of a predominantly White church and was confused as to what church culture his colleagues were referring. These are microaggressions.

A Korean American pastor friend of mine shared a story of a microaggression. It happened shortly after he was ordained. He met with some older White pastors who were going to help him discern his call and explore opportunities from churches looking for pastors. They told him they were unaware of any Asian ministries around the country. The problem, of course, is

---

1 Derald Wing Sue, Jennifer Bucceri, Annie I. Lin, Kevin L. Nadal, and Gina C. Torino. "Racial Microaggressions and the Asian American Experience," *Cultural Diversity and Ethnic Minority Psychology.* 13:1 (2007): 72–81.

that he never said he was looking to pursue Asian American ministry. Why would these men assume he would only be looking for Asian ministries? Microaggressions.

My own story is not too different. As a child of parents from South Korea who were not fluent in English, I understand why people often remarked so positively on my English-speaking abilities. I did not often find these comments particularly offensive growing up. But the cumulative effect of comments like these, through high school, college, graduate school, and now as a professor were multiplied over time. These multiplied comments were impacted by dynamics of power by senior administrators, and in time, these seemingly minor slights and insults build up and become overwhelming.

At other times, malicious and intentional microaggressions would immediately cut deep into my soul and leave me feeling vulnerable, unworthy, and unwelcomed. Whenever fellow Christians remark upon my good English-speaking skills, I wonder why my eloquence with the language still comes as such a surprise. Should people who look like me not speak like them, or not speak better than them?

Not long ago, I had an opportunity to share the Gospel with a White couple who turned out to already be Christians and were looking for a local church. Delighted at the news that they were fellow believers, I told them I was an elder of a church in the area and invited them to join us for Sunday worship. Their first question was whether the church I attended was an Asian church. I answered that it was, and they responded by saying that while they appreciated my outreach and invitation to them, they were going to look for "just a regular church."

A regular church. This was not only a microaggression, but a statement that reveals a deep-seated assumption about what people in dominant groups consider normal. Scholars have referred to this as "White normativity."[2] White normativity is the idea that "Whiteness" is assumed to be the racial and cultural standard in mainstream American society by which all other ethnic group values and actions ought to be measured.[3] People of other racial or ethnic groups are

---

2 Ruth Frankenberg. *White Women, Race Matters: The Social Construction of Whiteness* (Minneapolis: University of Minnesota Press, 1993).

3 Paul Kivel. *Uprooting Racism: How White People Can Work for Racial Justice* (British Columbia: New Society Publishers, 2002).

therefore understood and seen as "other than" or "less than" the norms of a dominant culture.

Sadly, my story and the countless stories of other Christians of color are not unique. Indeed, among pastors, elders, deacons, and church members of color, our life histories are filled with examples of microaggressive comments and actions that have made us feel like second-class citizens, perpetually playing the roles of exotic foreigner and existing as outsiders, even within our own churches and denominations.

Simply stated, these types of comments are racist. They are subtle—and often born more out of obliviousness than malice—but they are still racist. They reveal a blindness to and unawareness of implicit racial prejudices of undoubtedly well-intentioned people of a dominant group, who are often unconscious of the hidden messages being communicated every single day.

As a result, individuals and families of color do not always feel welcome in our predominantly White churches, Christian colleges, and denominations. Racial microaggressions, from the front of the pulpit and throughout the pews, often serve to amplify feelings of isolation and alienation for minorities. This is because racial microaggressions are tied to White normativity and focus on cultural differences in ways that put the recipient's nonconformity at the center.

When a fellow congregation member remarks on the English fluency of a person of color, the remark inadvertently leads that minority person to question his or her sense of belonging in that community. It also highlights a cultural and ethnic difference in a way that is inhospitable. After the first time happens, it can be overlooked. After the second time it happens, one can explain it away. After the hundredth time, one can only imagine how it starts to become annoying. What happens after several hundred to several thousand racial microaggressions? The cumulative effect can cause minority people to feel insecure, unwanted, and unwelcome.

Intent vs. impact

"I didn't mean it like that."
"That's not who I am."
"I never meant any harm."
"You're just being sensitive. Suck it up!"

These are some typical responses I get when I try to correct someone's comment or question. While I acknowledge that these microaggressions do not necessarily reflect malicious intent, folks from dominant Anglo ethnic groups unintentionally hurt brothers and sisters of color more often than they realize.

Imagine you are traveling on an airplane. You take your aisle seat and settle in. A fellow passenger, while attempting to load her carry-on luggage in the overhead bin, drops her suitcase on your head. Your head is throbbing, your glasses are broken, and you notice that you are bleeding slightly above your ear as a result of what has just occurred. You are hurt. You are confused. Indignant. No words have been exchanged yet. Her response? "Oh, I didn't mean to hurt you! That was not my intent. I was simply trying to load my luggage in the overhead bin." She offers no apology, just her rationale that defends her intent.

What if she replied by accusing you, "Well, your face got in the way of my suitcase, so you are partly to blame for this misfortune." Or worse, she claims that you put too many items in the overhead bin first, taking up all the space and leaving no room for her little bag to fit. You were inconsiderate, and therefore should be held responsible for your own misfortune.

You would be incredulous, right? She could have simply acknowledged that the impact of her action hurt you, even if it was unintentional. Instead, you are left to confess the sins you want to commit against her in thought, word, and deed!

So, I wonder why are we surprised when microaggressions—or worse, outright macroaggressions of violence toward people of color in the United States—are met with a defensive posture that merely talks about intent? I have heard good people far too often defend their oppressive language and actions by shifting the focus to their intent. For me this reveals a position of privilege that continues to make this all about the offender.

I wonder what it will take to move away from intent and begin to focus on impact. After all, how much does intent really matter if the impact continues to perpetuate feelings of marginalization or oppression for minority brothers and sisters in our churches?

In my marriage, if I do or say something that hurts my wife, it doesn't really matter whether I intended to hurt her—the reality is that my wife was hurt. I need to listen to how my actions impacted her. I need to acknowledge the pain my words have caused. I need to apologize for what I did, rather than defend what I intended. Hopefully I can begin to understand the consequences of my actions and strive not to offend again. I can listen. I can repent and change. I can start to see things from her perspective and not just my own.

When we consider how the actions of one group bring about the marginalization of another, the issue becomes one of justice, equity, and reconciliation. We need to listen. We need to acknowledge the impact of church and denominational policies, corporate sins, and historical acts of racism on people of color. If we continue to focus on intent rather than impact, we continue to perpetuate the privilege of the dominant group. Putting intent at the center of the conversation keeps the focus on the offender rather than the offended. This continues the invalidation of the victim's experiences and keeps his or her pain from being discussed.

Selfless love and hospitality

Defensive comments such as "I am not a racist" and "I am not a bad person" still focus on character traits (the intent of an individual), rather than on one's actions (the impact). I'd rather hear someone say he didn't realize what he said was offensive and then say he was sorry, because then we can talk about it. That would be a tremendous conversation! Then we can talk about why it hurt, and I can forgive.

It takes a certain amount of humility and self-awareness to admit that one is racist. A racist person can grow up in a racist system and not realize it. But can a person who is really not a racist still do and say racist things? Yes. Can people of color be racist, too? I would say yes and no. I would argue that while everyone has some level of prejudice—against people who are different from them—racism refers specifically to privilege and power within a system of dominance. Racism is prejudice multiplied by power.

Moving forward, we need to focus on our actions, even our unintentional actions, and their consequences, and do whatever we can to make things right. This is an act of reconciliation, selfless love, and hospitality that we need to covenantally practice. We must be ever mindful of people who are different from us and embrace them. We must confront our biases. We must recognize the impact of our unintentional actions toward others. We must begin to heal.

Chapter 4

Protesting Pastors

Rev. Dr. Mike Higgins

Mike Higgins serves as Dean of Students of Covenant Theological Seminary and Senior Pastor of South City Church (PCA). He previously served as a church planter, Army chaplain, and pastor. He is co-founder of the St. Louis Pastoral Fellowship, which provides training in leader development, social justice, and conflict resolution. Mike has degrees from the University of Missouri–St. Louis (BA) and Covenant Seminary (MDiv, DMin). He and his wife, Renee, have two daughters and two grandchildren.

On August 10, 2015, I participated in civil disobedience with the St. Louis Metropolitan Clergy Coalition. We marched from Christ Church Cathedral downtown to the Tom Eagleton Federal Building. The purpose of this action was to show unity and solidarity, to pray, and to sing hymns. On the steps of the Federal Building, we demanded that the US Attorney for Eastern Missouri move forward on changes to ensure that all who are sworn to serve and protect would be better equipped.

The night before, at our First Friday Prayer meeting, we had heard that federal marshals and the St. Louis Police Department had threatened to use chemical agents if a crowd gathered. Some of us decided then that we would be dragged, tazed, or cuffed as a way to slow down such dispersal tactics, hoping to prevent many (including children) from being harmed. Though we knew we might be arrested, we hoped the authorities would choose to engage in dialogue instead.

I believe we were heard that day in some small way, but I believe we must keep speaking, keep confronting. I would do it again under similar circumstances because I am not just doing it for myself. I was out there for my family and for everyone else. I hope that something I do keeps the next generation from being raised to become racist without even knowing it.

Brothers and sisters, this world is broken. Justice in America—and so many places on earth—is not blind. If she were blind, she would not need to be blindfolded. The truth is, she can see very clearly. She can see which ethnic group you belong to, how old or young you are, which side of the tracks you live on.

Justice, without the blindfold, can be manipulated by those who claim to ensure it. The blindfold was pulled off in this country when, not that long ago, White men constructed a phenomenon called race to make sure that people of color would never be considered equal, based solely on skin tone. Justice needs someone to help her with her blindfold. We marched that Monday to demand that she retie it.

The Constitution says that US citizens are innocent until proven guilty, but as a Black man I am treated as if I am guilty and have to prove my innocence. This is often how the church operates as well. We are a community called to love and trust one another, yet we remain suspicious, cynical, and judgmental of people who do not fit into the categories we have deemed proper. Let's be the first to admit this hypocrisy and turn from it. Let's run to testify to our communities, and let's demand that the authorities search themselves for this hypocrisy as well.

Brothers and sisters, I know that many of you are tired of hearing about Ferguson and Baltimore and Charleston. I am, too. I get so tired of talking about ethnic division, marching about it, meeting about it, sitting on stages in forums about it, but what else can I do when it seems that so many US citizens don't know—or often forget—the history of this country? Many still do not grasp or agree in any way how our cities evolved into their present state.

I grew up in North St. Louis and saw how it became the 'hood. In the 1960s and 1970s, a large tract of North St. Louis (The Ville, Fountain Park, and a few other neighborhoods) were racially diverse, with a large percentage of middle-class households. Then the White folks left the city. Many White churches left, especially White Evangelical churches. It was a westward expansion to St. Louis County. Black people didn't leave. They couldn't afford to.

As a result, St. Louis became a hypersegregated city in a country that seems to be happy with "separate and unequal" standards of social justice for the black and brown underclass. No wonder my actions seem like foolishness to so many. It would seem like foolishness to me, too, if I didn't know what I know about racism—or if I didn't believe my foolish acts could help change things in this country.

Some see me as their pastor, and it is an honor for me to serve them and the Lord in that capacity. However, I would ask all of you to also see me as your friend. As we sit together on Sunday mornings or in other church meetings, we could be tearing down the historical segregation of the American church and working toward true unity.

But we cannot stop there. We must pursue the elimination of racism in all its forms, together. Let's sit together in each other's homes. Sit with me during a traffic stop. Sit with me at the Rib Shack in North City. Sit with me when people think it's weird that Whites have a Black pastor. Sit with me when people think it's weird that so many of the people I serve are White.

I love our country, and I know we can do better—God help the USA. But I love the church more, and I know we will do better, because the Spirit has shown us the end of our story. That's how I know that we cannot give up, no matter how tired or uncomfortable it gets. We march on, pray on, sing on— because we know the God of righteousness and justice, true justice.

This justice is neither blind nor blindfolded; it need not be. While justice in America is blindfolded to ensure some artificial security from bias, true justice sees all our differences, discerns all distinctions, and judges fairly still. This is our future: we will all see, and finally see rightly.

Chapter 5

We've Come This Far by Faith

Rev. Stan Long

*Stan Long has served as Co-Pastor at Faith Christian Fellowship (PCA) in
Baltimore, Maryland, since 2000. He previously served as pastor of another church for
nine years and on staff with InterVarsity Fellowship for eleven years. Stan has degrees
from Frostburg State (BA) and Trinity Evangelical Divinity School (MDiv). He
and his wife, Terri, have five adult children.*

> We've come this far by faith. Leaning on the Lord.
> Trusting in His holy word. He has never failed me yet.
> Oh, Oh, Oh….We can't turn around
> We have come this far by faith.[1]

That song rings in my ears. It summarizes the church experience of my
younger years. As a Black pastor in a predominantly White denomination (the
Presbyterian Church in America) who never hears that great song in our
churches, I wonder: Where are we heading in terms of our relationship with the
people of the Black communities and monoethnic Black churches of our land?

These are stressful times in America. During the last few years, we have seen
the escalation of police brutality and tragic killings of Black youth in very

---

1 "We've Come This Far by Faith." http://www.hymnary.org/hymn/PsH/567. Accessed December
3, 2015. Albert A. Goodson (1963) wrote both text and tune in 1956 for the Radio Choir of the
Fellowship Baptist Church in Chicago, Illinois, where he served as minister of music. The hymn was
published as a Gospel anthem by Manna Music III, 1963. Goodson served Baptist churches in the
Los Angeles area as well as the Fellowship Baptist Church in Chicago. As organist and pianist, he
toured with Mahalia Jackson and has been a prominent figure in the development of African
American Gospel music.

questionable circumstances. In April 2015, we saw demonstrations and riots in the streets of my town, Baltimore. The eyes of the entire world were fixed here as the Sandtown community erupted following the tragic, suspicious death of twenty-five-year-old Freddy Gray. This young man's fatal injuries occurred while in the custody of local police. When he died in the hospital one week later, people demanded answers.

The frustration boiled over so much that in the hours following his funeral April 27, there were scenes of violence and vandalism that had not been seen since the riots of 1968 after the death of Dr. Martin Luther King Jr. The day after Freddy Gray's funeral, I walked the streets with members of our congregation to participate in a "let's go clean up Sandtown" endeavor that was well orchestrated by young people through social media. The Sandtown community is not far from our church.

Two months later, I attended my denomination's annual meeting and marveled as I heard pastors and elders expressing the need to come to grips with our history in such a way that God could do a transformative work of grace in and through us. As an African American, I left with a great sense of hope. Only five days later, another event took place that I thought must surely make clear to even the most unconvinced citizens of our nation that racial prejudice is very much alive and well in America.

In the gut

Late Wednesday, June 17, 2015, while driving home, I was stunned to hear of the tragic shooting of nine believers at the Emmanuel AME Church in Charleston, South Carolina, at their weekly Bible study and prayer meeting. Christians had been murdered for their skin color and beliefs.

Persecution of Christians in South Carolina? We had been hearing about heavy persecution of believers around the world. With radical movements such as ISIS and Boko Haram actively killing believers, Christians across America seemed to be holding their breath, praying and hoping to not hear of the next tragedy for the church somewhere around the world.

But Charleston? South Carolina? In the Bible Belt? In our day and age? We had been hearing that things in the South were starting to revert back to pre-Civil Rights Era days and that White supremacy groups had been on the rise as a clear backlash against the increasing diversity of America. In some ways, this was very hard to understand because I had been so hopeful only five days before. I had cautiously wondered whether we were about to witness a new generation of openness in our denomination and ultimately in our nation. But then came Charleston. . . .

For several years, there has been a debate about who is to blame for the high-profile deaths of Black males. We know that Black-on-Black crime has been destroying our communities. But there have been far too many high-profile incidents of White violence toward Black youth as well.[2]

However, no matter what someone might think of previous incidents, the one in Charleston was different. It "hit me in the gut." There was no ambiguity. There was no debating what had happened. A very troubled young man, Dylan Roof, was graciously welcomed as a visitor, supposedly with a heart that was open to God. He sat through the weekly Bible study and prayer meeting. This is not surprising. Any Black church that I know of would welcome a new face regardless of the visitor's ethnicity. But then when the meeting came to an end, the welcomed sheep put on his wolf's clothing and murdered the nine members, including Rev. Clemente Pinkney,the politically active, well-connected pastor of the congregation.

How tragic. How senseless. How hateful. How Satanic. The next morning after hearing more details, my mind went back to an experience that will forever stay etched in my memory.

---

2 Two articles from the *Washington Post* and the *Atlantic Monthly* magazine for the fall of 2015 can be cited as examples of this ongoing debate. Both were accessed December 3, 2015.

"Should Black Lives Matter Focus on 'Black-on-Black' Murders?" *Atlantic Monthly* article by Conor Friedersdorf interviewing John McWhorter, linguistics scholar at Columbia University and Glenn Loury, Brown University economist at http://www.theatlantic.com/politics/archive/2015/10/black-lives-matter-loury-mcwhorter/409117.

"Black Lives Matter should also take on 'black-on-black crime'" by John McWhorter at https://www.washingtonpost.com/posteverything/wp/2015/10/22/black-lives-matter-should-also-take-on-black-on-black-crime.

Reconciliation instincts

It was a Sunday morning, September 15, 1963. I was nine years old. My mom and dad did what they did every Sunday morning: They packed me and my sisters, ages twelve, eleven, and seven, into the family car to make the twenty-minute drive from our apartment in Anacostia, across the Potomac River, past the US Capitol, around the corner of the White House where President Kennedy resided, up to Northwest DC to attend Sunday School. Our family attended Meridian Hill Baptist Church, which was led by Rev. Dr. Roosevelt MacIntyre, the man who planted and pastored the church for more than fifty years.

My mother and father were both raised in segregated southern Virginia towns—Danville and Big Stone Gap. They both migrated north to Virginia State College, the historically Black institution in Petersburg, just south of Richmond. Their lives intersected, they fell in love, they married, they started a family. They migrated to DC in the early 1950s and eventually raised four girls and one son.

On this particular Sunday morning on the way to church, we heard over the radio the tragic news that a church in Birmingham, Alabama, had been bombed and that four little Black girls—Addie Mae Collins, Cynthia Wesley, Carole Robertson, and Carol Denise McNair—had died. To no one's surprise, the murderers were connected to the Ku Klux Klan.[3] This occurred in the context of great racial tension in the land. There had actually been a period of measured optimism due to the successful August 28 March on Washington. My dad attended that march, despite warnings given to federal government workers, which he was, that they should not attend. Now only two-and-a-half weeks after the great visionary speech by Dr. Martin Luther King Jr. came this harsh reminder that America still had a serious deadly disease that would be fatal to the body politic unless it was addressed.

Four little girls were simply doing what we and many Black kids around the nation did on any given Sunday. They were going to Sunday School to learn about Jesus. They went to sing "Jesus loves me; this I know; for the Bible tells me so. Little ones to him belong; they are weak, but he is strong." They went to

---

3 The history website of the cable network A&E has helpful data summarizing this tragic event. Accessed December 3, 2015. http://www.history.com/topics/black-history/birmingham-church-bombing.

sing "Jesus loves the little children; all the children of the world. Red and yellow, black and white, they're all precious in his sight. Jesus loves the little children of the world."

The dilemma for us as little Black kids was, "If these words in the song are true, then why were we hearing what we were hearing over the radio?" I remember a portion of the discussion that day as we arrived at church and entered the church building: "Mommy, why would those Whites do such a thing like this to innocent little girls going into church? Do any Whites believe in God? If they do, didn't Jesus say we are to love one another, even our enemies? Are there any White people that are Christians for real?"

These were the kinds of crisis-of-faith questions that we as seven-, nine-, eleven-, and twelve-year-olds expressed as we sought to process this tragedy. I most vividly recall my mom's caution to us: "Don't hate all White people. Jesus calls us to love even our enemies." She reminded us that in the world there are some good-hearted White people and some bad-hearted Black people. This was my mother who taught kindergarten to my two older sisters and me before choosing to stay at home. But she never stopped being a teacher as she discipled us skillfully and as she taught her adult Sunday school class for many years.

Both of my parents had very strong Baptist roots and used their teaching gifts in the church. My dad eventually became a deacon and taught the Bible class each week. My mom's Baptist roots didn't just move her to appreciate the ministry of Dr. King. She also appreciated the ministry of his good friend and fellow Baptist preacher, Rev. Dr. Billy Graham.[4] Listening to Billy Graham's thirty-minute Hour of Decision radio broadcast was a weekly routine for her. She had what I call "reconciliation instincts," which spilled over into her daily discipleship and training of us.

---

4 Billy Graham. *Just As I Am: The Autobiography of Billy Graham* (San Francisco: HarperCollins/ Zondervan, 1997), 74. The relationship between Dr. King and Dr. Graham is well documented. These two Baptist preachers from the South had a healthy respect for one another and saw themselves working on the same side with their different strategies. Graham wrote, "Early on Dr. King and I spoke about his method of using nonviolent demonstrations to bring an end to racial segregation. He urged me to keep on doing what I was doing—preaching the Gospel to integrated audiences and supporting his goals by example—and not join him in the streets. 'You stay in the stadiums, Billy,' he said, 'because you will have far more impact on the White establishment there than you would if you marched in the streets. Besides that, you have a constituency that will listen to you, especially among White people, who may not listen so much to me. But if a leader gets too far out in front of his people, they will lose sight of him and not follow him any longer.' I followed his advice."

The idea that only Black people could be good people was what our limited experience of the world had taught us. We often overheard the frustrated discussions of Black adults as they sought to understand how to survive in a racist society. We saw our parents go to church, engage in worship, and depart believing that a better day was coming, even though sometimes it seemed utterly foolish to keep having hope.

They sang songs like, "We've Come This Far by Faith" and kept pushing forward. Despite my mom's great counsel, as children our limited worldview had taught us to be suspicious of every White person we saw. Incidents like Birmingham just proved the point to us: They are all guilty until proven innocent. But her wisdom for that morning was essentially, "Don't let this event cause you to start hating all White people. Let's just go into this church to process this event among God's people, and then let's worship the God who loves all people and especially offers hope to those who mourn."

Forgiving the oppressors

The Charleston tragedy in June 2015 took me back to that morning in 1963 and to the conversations that followed it. Two days later, I watched the news in amazement as the family members of the nine Emanuel AME church victims spoke words of forgiveness to Dylan Roof, the man who had senselessly killed their loved ones.

They said their faith in Jesus Christ compelled them to do so. "I am very angry, but I must forgive. God have mercy on your soul," was their general message. Afterward, the usually cynical reporters were beside themselves as they discussed the responses of the family and sought to understand how anyone in their right mind could respond with words of love and forgiveness in this situation. I was also spellbound. When it was over, I just shook my head in wonder, awe, tears, and praise.

What had I just witnessed? These relatives with total honesty and raw emotion had understood and articulated before the world the simple, biblical facts their Lord and Savior Jesus Christ had said, *"But if you do not forgive others their trespasses, neither will your Father forgive your trespasses"* (Matt. 6:15).

As I sat there and listened, I thought about several things. First, there is the obvious, amazing power of the Gospel of Jesus, the Son of God who is indeed a

Mighty Savior and King. Then I pondered the difficult but effective ministry of Rev. Pinkney, who was able to disciple his congregation to have family members react in such a godly manner. I then thought about my mom's ancestors who were pastors and church planters after the Civil War and into the twentieth century. But most of all, I marveled again as I thought about the historic African American church.

The existence of the African American church is a miracle. Think about it: Europeans brought Africans to the shores of America through the horrific Middle Passage across the Atlantic. We were oppressed through the institution of chattel slavery, while the oppressors encouraged us to embrace some notion of their God. How asinine. How ridiculous. But how incredible the sovereign plan of God! As Joseph stated to his brothers, *"As for you, you meant evil against me, but God meant it for good, to bring it about that many people should be kept alive, as they are today"* (Gen. 50:20). My ancestors had to forgive their oppressors, the very oppressors who had taught them a distorted, unbiblical view of Jesus. Yet somehow we learned enough to declare, *"Father, forgive them, for they know not what they do"* (Luke 23:34).

Because of racism, the evils of slavery, and legal separation, the unique cultural phenomena of the African American church was birthed. Biblical Christian theology meshed with deeply rooted African spiritual instincts to produce a unique brand of religion that has stood the test of time. For decades, yea generations, African American people have exercised simple faith in Jesus.

Like many African Americans, in our formative years my sisters and I were nurtured into the Christian faith through home and church environments that were unashamedly Black. All of us—my parents, sisters, grandparents, cousins—were products of the monoethnic, Black Baptist church. We didn't do the Methodist thing, we didn't do the Pentecostal thing, we didn't do the Catholic thing, and we never even heard of the Presbyterian thing! We were Baptists, and that worked for us. So, seeing Emanuel AME and reflecting on the theology and cultural richness of the Black church community, it became yet another opportunity for me to repent of how foolish I had been as a young, naïve Evangelical Black kid. I had spent my young adult years seeing my early church experience through the narrow lens of American Evangelicalism, despite the fact that:

Before I understood the term "covenant family," I was part of one because of the Black church.

Before I knew about the wheat and the tares living together in the invisible church until the close of the age, I experienced it because of the Black church.

Before I understood that the place to go for answers in a crazy world is to be among God's people, my parents made sure that I did this every single week because of the Black church.

Before I understood that indeed God loves and cares for all people made in his image, even the most flawed image-bearers like me, and that this Gospel and the church is for all people, I felt it and responded to it in faith because of the Black church.

You see, my sisters and I were skillfully discipled in a context where these things were not always clearly taught but were certainly caught. We caught these things not just from the church but from parents who were the best covenant parents any kid could have!

Appreciating both orthodoxy and orthopraxy

My adult life began in the rural western Maryland college town of Frostburg. There I experienced a heavy dose of American Evangelicalism as I participated in the InterVarsity Christian Fellowship chapter at Frostburg State. Those four years were great times of solid, missional activity as we were part of the "Jesus Movement" of the 1970s. After graduation, I was recruited to Baltimore to do campus work with InterVarsity. For the next eleven years while on full-time IV staff, I grew up in many ways. By God's grace, I met and married my wife. We started a family several years later.

During those years, my sense of call to the pastoral ministry was confirmed, so I "came under care" of the local presbytery and slowly began formal theological education. However, I was still trying to understand my Black church background. Unfortunately, I was still evaluating my past with a set of American Evangelical eyes and coming to incorrect conclusions. But God began to challenge my thinking and broke me of my proud, judgmental spirit toward the Black church. During those years, I was a member, then elder, then candidate for ministry in a church in Baltimore—Forest Park Presbyterian. People there strongly encouraged me to go to seminary, provided an internship when I finished, and then in 1991 called me to be their next pastor. Pastor Walter Menges, the White pastor who had faithfully shepherded the church through difficult ethnic and denominational transitions in his twenty-eight years there, had decided to move on. I was humbled that they pursued me.

So after eleven years of serving God in the multicultural context of campus ministry and then seminary training, this kid from Anacostia had the kind of call that seemed too good to be true. You see, I had simply wanted to pastor Black folk who were Evangelical like me. Though the Forest Park members were theologically and self-consciously Evangelicals, when I removed the label, they were just like my parents: They loved Jesus, loved the word of God, wanted to nurture godly children, and wanted to reach their community for Christ. Yes, a PCA church, but with Black folk. My wife Terri and I were thrilled.

Soon our family grew from two kids to five when, to our surprise, Terri gave birth to triplets. We envisioned serving Forest Park long-term just as Pastor Menges had and just as Dr. MacIntyre had. That kind of stability, for both the congregation and the pastor's family, is what I had seen and what we anticipated.

By then I had come to truly appreciate and embrace the many good and helpful aspects of both the PCA and the traditional Black church. I had gone through the normal emotional pattern of many Black Evangelicals. First I felt like the Black church experience was totally a waste. Then I repented and came to grips with the fact that there were some important things God did through those early Black church community experiences. Then I realized that many aspects of Black church community life are actually more biblical than much of the contemporary Evangelical world's expression of church life.

Dr. Carl Ellis is a longtime friend and a great theologian. He mentored me when I started with InterVarsity in the late 1970s. He served as associate pastor at Forest Park in the mid-eighties. In many ways, humanly speaking, he helped develop my theology and worldview.

Dr. Ellis once stated that for the White Christian community, creedal orthodoxy is supreme. It is the primary evaluative tool. However, for the Black Christian community, ethical orthopraxy is supreme. We determine the authenticity of one's confession through ethics, not creed.[5] As usual, Dr. Ellis was spot-on correct.

While many of the mainline Black churches, such as the National Baptists of my youth or the Charleston AME church, do not fully ascribe to the Westminster Confession of Faith, they wholeheartedly adhere to the simple reality of following Jesus, the carpenter of Nazareth, the one who got up from out of the grave on a Sunday morning to reign as King of Kings, and to live a life that glorifies God in this present age by faith. Isn't this really what it is all about?!

So I served at Forest Park as the solo pastor in the '90s. But deep inside I knew I couldn't be satisfied serving long-term in a monocultural church context, even in the Black church.

Longing for a more inclusive church

In the nineties, God gave me vision-expanding experiences at some Promise Keepers gatherings. Also, I kept seeing articles and hearing people discuss "the browning of America" and the need for multiethnic congregations. I had a growing sense that I was only to be a transitional pastor for Forest Park and not the answer they needed long-term. All these factors began to weigh heavily on me. I believed that God was preparing me for a position at a church that was committed to and experiencing Christianity in a multicultural, multiethnic environment.

This movement in me was ironic in light of how I had finally come to understand and appreciate my own Black church roots. With this newfound appreciation for the Black church, I was being equipped to do what God had all my life been preparing me to do—minister to Blacks in a multiethnic church context. So in 2000, the congregation of Faith Christian Fellowship in Baltimore called me to serve as the co-pastor alongside the church's founding

---

5 Carl F. Ellis. *Free At Last: The Gospel in the African American Experience* (Downers Grove, IL: InterVarsity Press, 1996), 83. I have heard Dr. Ellis say this often. Dr. Ellis explains, "The mainline Bible-believing community generally misunderstood the significance of Dr. King—the fundamentalists and Evangelicals primarily because of their defective theological positions and Reformed Christians primarily because of their defective cultural position. Western theology. . . was much more concerned with epistemological issues (what we should know about God) than with ethical issues (how we should obey God)."

pastor, Craig Garriott, who calls himself "a White boy from the rural regions of Baltimore County." But he is much more than that! In 1980, he and his wife Maria planted themselves in Baltimore to carry out God's vision for a different kind of church—a church that would say an emphatic NO to the division of churches into monocultural pockets.[6]

Armed with the John Perkins community ministry philosophy, the Garriotts relocated into the heart of the city to raise a family and build a church that would cross the barriers of race, class, and culture. They went into an area of need, one block from an area of great wealth. My friendship with Craig actually began when I was with InterVarsity, staffing a student summer project. Craig was an optimistic, driven church planter who was seeking to do in 1981 what many are now realizing needs to be done. We knew that God had used him to build a great church because he had dared to look at the American church scene, to look at Scripture, and then to declare that despite what we see, God has a better vision for his people. Craig took at face value the high priestly prayer in John 17, where Jesus pleaded to God that his followers be unified, not just theologically, but in terms of local worshipping communities. So in 2000, Craig and I came together to serve the church and the city uniquely as a full-time, Black-White pastoral team.

God has placed our church in a unique spot in the world. Our congregation sits in the middle of a triangle of diverse universities. There is Johns Hopkins University, where intellectuals from around the world gather to study and do world-changing research. There is Morgan State University, a historic Black college. Then there is Loyola College, a Jesuit school where many nominal, millennial Catholics from the mid-Atlantic region gather to pursue a liberal arts education. In many ways, our congregation, located in the Pen Lucy community, reflects the diverse cultures represented by those three institutions.

The fact that my denomination also is pursuing becoming more inclusive is both fantastic and long overdue. But when we talk about African Americans or

---

6 Maria Garriott. *A Thousand Resurrections: An Urban Spiritual Journey* (Washington, DC: CitySongs, 2006). The Faith Christian Fellowship story has been documented by Maria Garriott. The book is a must-read for any who relocate into so-called "at-risk communities" seeking to be the presence of Christ alongside those already serving him there.

Latinos or Asian believers becoming part of predominantly White denominations, we should never think in terms of what they can learn from us. We need to understand that there is so much we can learn from our "other ethnic" brothers and sisters. There will be huge implications for how we worship, do community, and do church business, which will be challenging. No culture perfectly reflects the heart of God. But God is in the business of creating a cross-cultural body that will be faithful to the Gospel. He is creating a people, who by being his body on earth, will reflect the incredible diversity of heaven.

Yes, I have a great love for Black people and for the Black church of my youth. However, I cannot get beyond the vision of every nation, tribe, and tongue worshipping the Lamb of God (Rev. 7). That glorious future demands that we do all we can to maintain the unity of the Spirit in the church of God (Eph. 4: 3). Paul's vision was that Jew and Gentile together would *"with one voice glorify the God and Father of our Lord Jesus Christ"* (Rom. 15:5–13). In the Lord's Prayer, we plead, *"On earth as it is in heaven"* (Matt. 6:10). As difficult as that task is, we must not do less than what God has called us to do.

We've come this far by faith. Leaning on the Lord.

Trusting in His holy word. He has never failed me yet.

Oh, Oh, Oh….We can't turn around we have come this far by faith.

Notice how that simple song has so much theology in it:

- "We have come this far"—The plural pronoun speaks to a corporate community of believers as opposed to merely an individualistic community of believers (1 Cor. 12:12–13).
- "By faith"—The Gospel that justifies sinners is from faith to faith. Sola fide! (Rom. 1:16–17).
- "Leaning on the Lord"—The one who encourages us to abide in him says that apart from leaning on him we can do nothing (John 15:5).
- "Trusting in His holy word"—He has given us a final, definitive, perfect word to save us and transform our lives. Sola Scriptura! (2 Tim. 3:14–17).
- "He's never failed me yet"—Despite our frailty and weakness, great is his faithfulness (Lam. 3:23–24).
- "We can't turn around"—He will preserve us and complete his work in us, demonstrated by the perseverance of the saints (Phil. 1:6). We shall be glorified by his grace (Rom. 8:28–29).

I didn't learn the foundations of Reformed theology through reading Luther, Knox, Edwards, or Calvin. Instead, it was in the context of a Black family and a Black congregation. As Christians, we need to understand and appreciate the contributions of other cultures to our understanding of God's designs for his church. Then, we must seek to create new twenty-first-century models of the church and invite people of all colors to participate as equal members of his glorious body. We need to learn from each other.

May God give us the humility and courage to embrace all those who our heavenly Father embraces as his own. I continue to hope that there can and will be true appreciation within the church at large for the diverse body of Christ. As I continue to look back on my journey from Meridian Hill Baptist Church, to InterVarsity, to Forest Park Reformed Presbyterian Church, to Faith Christian Fellowship, I marvel at how God has helped me stay the course, as he did for many others who came before me.

Awakening to Privilege

Chapter 6

A New Lens for Race, Media, and the Gospel

Rev. Dr. Timothy R. LeCroy

Timothy R. LeCroy is the pastor of Christ Our King Church (PCA) in Columbia, Missouri, and an adjunct instructor of Church History at Covenant Theological Seminary. Timothy has degrees from North Carolina State University (BS), Covenant Theological Seminary (MDiv), and Saint Louis University (PhD). Tim serves on the Board of Directors of the Presbyterian Church in America. Tim is co-editor and co-translator of Volume XVII *of the* Works of St. Bonaventure: Commentary on the Sentences: Sacraments. *He and his wife, Rachel, have two children.*

I'm a White man. Born and raised in the rural South. Not the aristocratic well-to-do South of old money, plantations, and gentility, but the poor, working-class South of small farms, factories, and textile mills in the Appalachian foothills of northwestern South Carolina. And though I did not live in poverty, the memory of it was strong in my family and feared above all else. The remedy for poverty was education. Therefore education was highly valued in my family. Education was the way out of the poor White South.[1]

---

1 Stephen A. West details the distinct difference of the Piedmont region of northwest South Carolina in his 2005 article, "Minute Men, Yeomen, and the Mobilization for Secession in the South Carolina Upcountry." *The Journal of Southern History*, 71: 1 (February, 2005), 80–81. There he demonstrates how in the mountainous regions of this area slave owning was rare and support for secession was tepid at best. In the 1850s movements for secession in South Carolina, the county I grew up in soundly rejected the measure.

A culture of racism

Racism was prevalent where I grew up. Confederate flags abounded. I remember seeing a graffito scrawled onto an overpass that read, "Stonewall Jackson lives! The South will rise again!" The KKK had a presence in our town. There were at least two horrible lynchings in our past. Video footage of a parade in 1968 reveals marchers bearing Confederate flags. This was during the height of the Civil Rights Era.[2]

I wasn't raised to hate Black people, but I wasn't raised to particularly appreciate them either. The truth is that I didn't really know any Black people. In my sophomore class yearbook, there were 180 students pictured. Two were African Americans; one was Hispanic; 177 were White. My church was 100 percent White. My neighborhood was 100 percent White. Race was not something I ever had to deal with or even think much about.

Because I didn't know any Black people, I didn't know much about Black people. I basically "knew" three things about Black people. I knew they were poor. There was one public housing complex in my town, and that's where the Black people lived. I also "knew" they weren't very smart. They were always struggling in school, and I was in the "gifted and talented" classes. The third thing I knew about Black people was that they were good at sports. In fact, both of the African Americans pictured in my sophomore class yearbook were varsity athletes.

You see, I didn't hate Black people, but I was still a racist. I was a racist because I looked down on African Americans. I stereotyped them. I didn't seek to know them or understand them. I may have never called them names or raised a Confederate flag or done anything overtly racist, but I was racist nonetheless—racist in ways that I am only now coming to understand.

---

2 Poor White areas like the one I grew up in became radicalized during Reconstruction by movements like Benjamin Tillman's Red Shirts, who used terror to promote White supremacy and keep equal rights from coming to fruition in South Carolina. This paved the way for Jim Crow laws. See Ben Robertson, *Red Hills and Cotton: An Upcountry Memory* (New York: A. A. Knopf, 1942); Stephen David Kantrowitz, *Ben Tillman and the Reconstruction of White Supremacy* (Chapel Hill: University of North Carolina Press, 2000); Stephen A. West, *From Yeoman to Redneck in the South Carolina Upcountry, 1850–1915* (Charlottesville: University of Virginia Press, 2008). Also see endnote 3 below for Martin Luther King Jr.'s astute observation of this development.

In the Rev. Dr. Martin Luther King Jr.'s 1965 speech at the conclusion of the march from Selma to Montgomery, he remarked on the poor White South and Jim Crow:

> If it may be said of the slavery era that the White man took the world and gave the Negro Jesus, then it may be said of the Reconstruction era that the Southern aristocracy took the world and gave the poor White man Jim Crow. (Yes, sir.) He gave him Jim Crow. (Uh huh.) And when his wrinkled stomach cried out for the food that his empty pockets could not provide, (Yes, sir.) he ate Jim Crow, a psychological bird that told him that no matter how bad off he was, at least he was a White man, better than the Black man. (Right sir.) And he ate Jim Crow. (Uh huh.) And when his undernourished children cried out for the necessities that his low wages could not provide, he showed them the Jim Crow signs on the buses and in the stores, on the streets and in the public buildings. (Yes, sir.) And his children, too, learned to feed upon Jim Crow, (Speak) their last outpost of psychological oblivion. (Yes, sir.)[3]

I was born thirteen years after that speech. And though segregation had ended, its effects were still prevalent. I may not have been the child of Jim Crow, but I was the grandchild of Jim Crow and deeply affected by the segregation that was not even a generation in the past.

When I left my small town of four thousand people for college and seminary, I lived in much larger cities with a substantially larger population of African Americans. It was there that I learned something new about Black people. I learned to fear them. I "learned" that Black people were criminals, were addicted to drugs and alcohol, and would attack, rob, and kill. Certainly I didn't believe this about all African Americans, especially those who were educated, but still I believed it. So in certain parts of town, I learned to fear the Black man.

---

3 Martin Luther King Jr., "Address Delivered at the Steps of the State Capitol at the Conclusion of the Selma to Montgomery March," (speech, Montgomery, AL, March 25, 1965), https://kinginstitute.stanford.edu/king-papers/documents/address-delivered-steps-state-capitol-conclusion-selma-montgomery-march.

Race and politics

Another aspect from Dr. King's speech that was true of my story was the marriage of politics, religion, and White supremacy at the expense of minorities. My grandparents' generation were Southern Democrats, a coalition between powerful rich Whites and the poor Whites forged on the tenets of White supremacy.

> Toward the end of the Reconstruction era, something very significant happened. (Listen to him.) That is what was known as the Populist Movement. (Speak, sir.) The leaders of this movement began awakening the poor White masses (Yes, sir.) and the former Negro slaves to the fact that they were being fleeced by the emerging Bourbon interests. Not only that, but they began uniting the Negro and White masses (Yeah.) into a voting bloc that threatened to drive the Bourbon interests from the command posts of political power in the South.
>
> To meet this threat, the Southern aristocracy began immediately to engineer this development of a segregated society. (Right.) I want you to follow me through here because this is very important to see the roots of racism and the denial of the right to vote. Through their control of mass media, they revised the doctrine of White supremacy. They saturated the thinking of the poor White masses with it, (Yes.) thus clouding their minds to the real issue involved in the Populist Movement. They then directed the placement on the books of the South of laws that made it a crime for Negroes and Whites to come together as equals at any level. (Yes, sir.) And that did it. That crippled and eventually destroyed the Populist Movement of the nineteenth century.[4]

I, however, was not raised as a Southern Democrat. I was raised as a Reagan Republican. My parents were a part of the Reagan revolution, when the old Southern Democrats moved to the Christian Right, a marriage between Evangelicals and the Republican Party. The core tenets of our political ideology were fiscal conservatism (no new taxes), social conservatism (enforcement of Christian morality through legislation), personal liberty (less government), and personal responsibility (God helps those who help themselves). Over time this political coalition was wed with the conservative media, which took advantage of

---

4 Ibid.

new avenues available in cable television, AM radio, and the burgeoning Internet.

As a young adult, I bought into this political movement wholesale. I nursed at the teat of the conservative media machine. I loved political debate and would often yell at the television if I disagreed with the "liberal" media. I supported Republican policies vigorously without much thought. I could not see how a Democrat could be a real Christian and vice versa. I took my marching orders from the likes of Rush Limbaugh and Sean Hannity. I have voted in every presidential election since I turned 18: Dole, Bush, Bush, McCain, Romney. When George W. Bush won for the first time I was elated because an Evangelical had won the presidency. When Barack Obama won in 2008, I was despondent, not because he was an African American, but because he was an ultra-liberal. I was as typical as typical gets: White, male, Christian, Republican, and angry.

In many ways I still resonate with those core political ideals (less government, fiscal responsibility), but I am coming to see the connections between the racist policies of the Southern Democrats and the conservative policies of the Reagan Republicans. I also have come to see how manipulative and slanderous the conservative media can be when championing a cause.

Summer 2015

I don't know exactly when my attitudes regarding African Americans began to change, but I do think there was a period of rapid change the summer of 2015. The events around our annual denominational meeting the second week in June and the Charleston Massacre the third week of June were significant.

I know that my awakening had not yet occurred in 2014, because when I heard of the shooting of Michael Brown that August, I instinctively went to the rationale and talking points of the Right. I had lived in St. Louis for nine years before moving two hours west to take a pastorate in Columbia, Missouri. I distrusted African American voices and defaulted to the position that if the police shot him, he must have done something to deserve it.

However, as fall 2014 rolled on I began to soften my position. African American leaders in my denomination were speaking up and educating me and others on the issues behind the shooting. For the first time, I began to hear voices that were close to me, voices I respected, who were challenging my default position, the Reagan Republican, Christian Conservative position fed by the conservative media machine.[5] Through reading and listening to what these brothers and sisters were saying and recommending, I began to see the systemic side of why things were the way they were. I began to see the existence of systemic racism. I began to ask the question, "Why are people poor? Why are they in trouble with the law?" And the answer no longer was simply, "Because they are lazy" or "Because they are immoral." My answer was increasingly becoming, "Maybe there are systems of oppression that contribute to the situation of minorities and the poor in our country."

My wife and I watched The *Pruitt-Igoe Myth*, a documentary on the infamous St. Louis housing project, and we learned about how hardworking Black people were generationally oppressed by corrupt housing policies. I read about racist housing covenants and local laws that forced Blacks into certain areas, restricting the opportunities available to them. I read about oppressive policing and how various municipalities function and gain their revenue at the expense of the poor and people of color. I began to believe in the existence of entrapment and racial profiling. I began to believe that there was more than just personal responsibility in our American story of race and poverty. The cold exterior that Jim Crow and its after-effects had put on me was melting. I was beginning to see race through the eyes of people of color for the first time.

The result of this was that when Tamir Rice, Freddie Gray, and Sandra Bland died at the hands of police in late 2014 and early 2015, I responded differently than I did to the killing of Michael Brown. I had changed. My default position was no longer to blame the person of color. It had shifted to believe in the innocence of those people and question why they had to die. I began to distrust the police in these instances, not all police in all instances, but to definitely see that the position of police should not always be trusted. Because of this change, I also began to distrust more the conservative media. They did not see things the way I now saw them.

---

5 Many of the voices I was listening to are authors in this volume.

All of this was in the air as our denomination convened for its annual meeting—General Assembly—in June 2015.[6] Thus, when two pastors proposed a resolution for our denomination to repent of our sins during the Civil Rights Era,[7] it was not a shock. Though formal action on the resolution was postponed, the Holy Spirit moved and brought us all to our knees. I was raised Pentecostal, but I have never felt a move of the Spirit like I felt in that room, late on a Thursday, in Chattanooga, Tennessee.

As one of the founders of the denomination passionately confessed and repented of not speaking up and helping his African American brothers and sisters during the Civil Rights Era, many in the room began to weep. It was as if a great weight were lifted. We were finally beginning to be honest about our denominational past and confess our sins so that healing could come. When the moderator opened the floor to a season of prayer, men began flooding to the microphones to confess their sins of involvement in and complicity with racial injustice. This period of prayer lasted for about an hour as men continued to confess their sins and pray for healing.

Charleston

After General Assembly, I planned to address my congregation on Sunday, June 21, on the subject of race. Before I had the chance, mid-week on June 17, a White man walked into a Bible study at Mother Emanuel AME in Charleston, South Carolina, and gunned down nine of my brothers and sisters in the name of White supremacy. Nine dear saints were martyred as they prayed. They welcomed the assassin into their midst. He said later that he almost didn't go through with it because they were so hospitable to him.

That man is a White supremacist, a neo-Confederate terrorist born and raised in my home state, nursed on the same hate I was. In his writings, he said he intended for the shooting to start a race war. The Charleston Massacre hit home to me like none of the other shootings did. It was in my home state. A

---

6 The 43rd General Assembly of the Presbyterian Church in America took place in Chattanooga, TN, June 8–12, 2015.

7 The full text of this resolution may be found at: http://byfaithonline.com/personal-resolution-on-civil-rights-remembrance.

fellow South Carolinian committing a horrible act of hate on other fellow South Carolinians.

I think another reason the Charleston Massacre hit home to me was that it confronted me with the reality of overt racial hate and injustice and my need to do something about it. Ringing still in my ears was our denomination's founding member confessing that he did nothing to help his Black brethren during the Civil Right Era. The reality hit home that I not only needed to be active in my denomination with regard to these issues, I also needed to be active in my local context. That next Sunday I stood in the pulpit and confessed to my congregation that although I had been listening to African Americans discussing the need for reconciliation in my denomination, I did not even know one Black pastor in my own town. That's wrong, I said, and that's going to change.

That very week I worked my sermon into an op-ed for the local paper, confessing this sin before the community.[8] Then I went out and made contact with another local African American pastor in my town and met him for lunch. We've since become friends, welcoming each other in worship and inviting each other to preach at our churches. I've also met other African American pastors and have greatly enjoyed their fellowship and learning from their wisdom.

One of my deepest desires now is for the unity of the church. Our Lord, on the night he was betrayed, in his anguish sweating great drops of blood, prayed that the church would be one (John 17:21). That unity, we are shown in the Revelation of John, includes every tongue, tribe, and nation (Rev. 7:9).

Mizzou

Later in the summer of 2015, winds of protest began to blow in my city of Columbia on the campus of the University of Missouri. This began late summer when the university administration abruptly canceled stipends that helped to cover graduate student's health insurance, despite the fact that these graduate students had signed contracts guaranteeing that benefit. Over the course of the first week of classes, graduate students began to protest, joined by some faculty.

---

8 Timothy R. LeCroy, "Lip-service Not Enough to Bridge Race Gap: Get Busy, Do Something Real," *Columbia Missourian*, June 24, 2015. The piece can also be found at: http://www.columbiamissourian.com/opinion/guest_commentaries/guest-commentary-listen-learn-and-live-the-faith-after-charleston/article_908f9f2c-19dc-11e5-a6d0-cbf2e7d83ca5.html.

They held rallies and planned a classroom walkout.[9] In the face of this, the university administration gave into the demands of the graduate students and temporarily restored their stipends. This event, though not overtly having to do with issues of race, showed the students that they had power to effect change on campus. One of the students who led these graduate student protests was Jonathan Butler, the young man who would go on a hunger strike later that fall.

After the graduate student protests died down, there were several racially motivated events that sparked a separate set of protests.[10] These events, a swastika painted with human feces, as well as several verbal attacks on African Americans in which racial and homophobic slurs were used, were not hoaxes.[11] They were all well documented in the local press and backed up with incident reports from local police. In the wake of these events, the university administration, the same who had callously canceled the graduate student insurance stipends, was seen to be slow to respond and insensitive to the events. This was especially so of University of Missouri System President Tim Wolfe, who got into several shouting matches with protesters in which he stated that he did not believe in systemic racism.

As tensions mounted, several African American student leaders decided to protest for racial justice and unity on campus. That's when Jonathan Butler began a hunger strike, refusing to eat until the demands of his group were met. The protests grew and became the main story of our town. Eventually several football players joined the protesters, vowing they would not participate in any football-related events until demands were met and the strike ended. Then, on Sunday, November 8, head football coach Gary Pinkel sent out a Tweet showing the solidarity of the entire football team with their teammates, joining the boycott of football-related activities. This was the point when the national media descended upon Columbia.

---

9 Many graduate students teach classes at the university as adjunct instructors. The university, like so many around our nation, could not continue without graduate students filling this vital role.

10 This article in our local paper, the *Columbia Missourian* details the timeline of events that fall: http://www.columbiamissourian.com/news/higher_education/racial-climate-at-mu-a-timeline-of-incidents-this-fall/article_0c96f986-84c6-11e5-a38f-2bd0aab0bf74.html.

11 Some conservative media outlets alleged that these events were hoaxes in an attempt to minimize the protests.

The next morning I was driving to St. Louis to teach a class at Covenant Theological Seminary. On the way, Ruth Serven, one of my church members, sent me a message asking me to pray for Mizzou. She was a student reporter covering the events for our local paper, the *Columbia Missourian*. She told me the national media was present, and protests were reaching a fever pitch. Before I had even arrived in St. Louis, word was getting out that Wolfe was going to resign. By 10:00 a.m. Monday, November 9, he had done so in person to the Board of Curators. Later that day, Chancellor R. Bowen Loftin also stepped down. In response, Jonathan Butler ended his hunger strike. The demonstrations ended that day, and the national media began to disperse. But the conversations and the events were not over.

The next day several threats were reported on campus. Some of them were credible. Others were not. One man made death threats via social media and was later arrested.[12] Later that week, the sign at the on-campus Black Culture Center was vandalized.[13] The result of all this was that students felt unsafe on campus that Wednesday and many stayed home. Many professors canceled class. Campus was eerily empty and silent that day, a drastic change from the great upheaval from a couple of days before.

In response to the threats and the retreat from campus, I sent a few emails and organized a prayer time on campus. Our group met every day at 5:30 p.m. and prayed for peace and justice on campus and in our city. Our prayers continued for a week and a half until campus broke for Thanksgiving. Over the course of those prayer meetings, thirty to forty different people joined us. Some were a part of our congregation; others were not. All desired God's justice and peace to come. All desired unity and wholeness on the campus and in our city.

Some of the most significant things that occurred in the wake of the protests at Mizzou did not take place in our town. They took place on the Internet. Conservative media of all types were mobilized to address the events at Mizzou. The difference for me was that this time I was on the ground for the event. I saw what really happened. And I was getting my information from

---

12 Reports on the threats made that week may be found at: http://www.columbiamissourian.com/news/local/threats-and-fear-nearly-bring-mu-campus-to-a-standstill/article_ed76ff3c-88d1-11e5-8a55-ef7d7f0623cd.html.

13 Reports on the vandalism may be found in the MU student paper at: http://www.themaneater.com/stories/2015/11/12/black-culture-center-sign-vandalized/.

quality local reporters, not just national pundits. Thus I was dismayed not only to see how national conservative media distorted the events on the ground in order to promote their message, I also was disheartened to see how conservative White Christians bought the message of the national conservative media wholesale, sharing posts on social media and voicing their opposition to the protests. The national conservative media painted the Mizzou protests as political correctness run amok. They condescendingly chided the student protestors as childish crybabies. At every turn, they delegitimized the cause of the protestors, discounted their reports of racism, denied the presence of any systemic injustice, and minimized the suffering of those who had spoken out. *Ad hominem* attacks were used to discredit Jonathan Butler and other leaders. There was almost no wrestling with the real issues. It was all cast in terms of national politics.

These were many of the same media voices I had listened to for years, on which I had based my political and social opinions. And yet because I was on the ground where it happened, not just for a weekend, but for the weeks and months and years leading up to these events, and because I was getting my information from trusted local sources, I saw what the national media was selling. The message they were sending, especially conservative media, was not accurate and was designed to create outrage, divisiveness, and keep the conservative talking points moving along until the next scandal happened and the same talking points and the same outrage and discontent could move along to the next item in the news cycle. It was as if a veil was lifted, and I saw for the first time that not only were the "liberal" media biased and agenda-driven as I had been told all along, but the conservative media were just as deeply so, maybe even more so.

I lost faith in conservative media after the events of last fall. Yet I see that so many White Evangelicals still depend on those voices to develop their opinions on politics, society, culture—even religion. This is eerily similar to what Dr. King described fifty years ago in his speech in Montgomery that I mentioned above:

Through their control of mass media, they revised the doctrine of White supremacy. They saturated the thinking of the poor White masses with it, (Yes.) thus clouding their minds to the real issue involved in the Populist Movement.[14]

Is the national conservative media trying again to revise the doctrine of White supremacy? I don't think so. But is it manipulating us into certain kinds of thinking that serve the rich and powerful? Yes. And should we who depend on such media to form our opinions on nearly every issue of life now look at those sources with eyes of wisdom and discernment? Absolutely.

Awareness of my privilege and responsibility

That six-month stretch from June to December 2015 was momentous in my life. In reviewing that time, I can see how a change that was slowly occurring in my heart and mind was put into fast-forward. My attitudes about race, American society, and the White conservative church have changed. I no longer discount minority voices when they speak, but seek to listen and understand. I no longer believe that personal responsibility is the end of the story with race and poverty, but now acknowledge the existence of systemic oppression. I no longer see racially related incidents as isolated, but as a part of larger systems and contexts. After a long history of being discerning when listening to the "liberal" media, I now seek to be just as discerning with "conservative" media. Remember, I was as conservative and Republican as anyone could get. Now, while I've not become a liberal, I'm changed. I see the flaws in all sides. I'm looking for a savior that's not of this world.

Before, even though I didn't hate African Americans or actively oppress them, I also did not seek to engage and understand—to love. I avoided discussing or thinking critically about issues of race. I viewed anyone who spoke on a more macro, systemic level as a liberal or a communist. I viewed African American leaders with suspicion, judging their motives, discrediting their lives.

Now I am appalled and ashamed by my racism. I now see that I have benefited from the same systems and structures that have oppressed people of

---

14 Martin Luther King Jr., "Address Delivered at the Steps of the State Capitol at the Conclusion of the Selma to Montgomery March," (speech, Montgomery, AL, March 25, 1965), https:// kinginstitute.stanford.edu/king-papers/documents/address-delivered-steps-state-capitol-conclusion-selma-montgomery-march.

color in this country. My dad's father had the opportunity to earn a high school diploma and land a good paying job that provided for his large family. My father, based on that provision, had the opportunity to attend college and earn bachelor's and master's degrees so that he could get a stable, good paying job with benefits and retirement. Though my mom's father was legally blind and not able to work, my mom's mother was able to get a factory job and make enough to get the family by, though they were very poor. And even though my mother came from poverty, she had the opportunity to work hard in school and go to college, earning bachelor's and master's degrees, gaining the same level of employment as my father: a good paying job with benefits and retirement. The result of all that opportunity and hard work was that I was well provided for and had a great education in the best schools in the nation and never had a day of want in my life. I had the luxury of not depending on the government and touting personal responsibility because others had paved the way.

But still, it took two or three generations to escape the poverty in my family's past. It took two or three generations of hard work and achievement to escape poverty. And yet, somehow, the Reagan Republicans and the Christian Right of the '80s and '90s could, with a straight face, look at the poor Black man and blame him for his own poverty and situation in life.

Segregation was legal until 1965. It was not fully eradicated until some time later. The fathers and grandfathers and great-grandfathers of the African Americans I went to school with did not have the same opportunities as mine. They did not have access to the same high schools, even if they did work hard. They did not have access to the same colleges, even if they did work hard. They did not have access to the same jobs with the same benefits, even if they did work very hard. They were systemically oppressed and beat down.

The ink on the laws forbidding segregation was barely dry before White Christians were imploring Blacks to be responsible and heal themselves, when it took the very same people two or three generations to escape the same poverty while not being actively oppressed while they were trying to do so. "How long," we hear many say, "How long will we have to keep repenting? For how long do we owe restitution?" We owe it while the beaten man is still recovering from his beating. We owe as much as it takes for the beaten man to be fully restored to health and wholeness. We owe it for as long as it takes.

I am privileged because I'm White. I have had opportunity because I am White. I have the luxury of ignoring issues of race and poverty and their systemic causes because I am White. I have benefited from racism and segregation and hate. I have callously ignored the beaten man, lying in the ditch, and thought to myself, "Why don't you heal yourself?"

I am grateful for the voices of my dear brothers and sisters of color who have spoken up. I am thankful for their courage. I am thankful that they continue to have hope. I am thankful that they didn't give up on us majority-culture folks, but continue to persevere, hopeful that things can change. I am so grateful for you. You have helped me to see so many things I've needed to see. I hope I continue to see more.

And also let me say, "I'm sorry." Please forgive us for the ways we are callous or dismissive. Please forgive us for not truly listening to you or seeing you. Please forgive us for marginalizing you, discrediting you, and ignoring you. Please forgive us for hoping that this whole race thing would blow over soon. Please forgive us for always having to be in control. Please forgive us for not recognizing our own race and our own culture and our own privilege.

Please forgive us. Please continue to help us. Please do not give up on that dream, that prayer of Christ in the Garden of Gethsemane. Please continue to believe and hope and pray and work to make the church be what it mystically is, what it will be on the last day, beautifully comprised of every race, tongue, tribe, and nation: One.

Lord, heal us.

Chapter 7

Race, Reconciliation, and the American Church

Dr. Otis W. Pickett

Otis W. Pickett serves as Assistant Professor of History, Director of Social Studies Education Programs at Mississippi College, and the President of the Mississippi Council for the Social Studies. He is also co-founder of the Prison to College Pipeline Program, which provides for-credit college courses to incarcerated learners in Mississippi state penitentiaries. Otis has degrees from Clemson University (BA), Covenant Seminary (MATS), College of Charleston (MA), and University of Mississippi (PhD). He and his wife, Julie, have four children.

My name is Otis Pickett. From my name, you might think my parents were either huge Motown fans or fans of the 1978 film Animal House. You might also assume, as do most people before they see me, that I am an African American male.[1]

I am actually a White Southern male and the fourth-generation of Otis Picketts. My dad, his dad, and my great grandfather were all Otis Picketts from Charleston, South Carolina. My son is the fifth Otis and will, Lord willing, carry on the "Otis" legacy.

---

1 This essay initially appeared as a larger, seven-part article series on Race and the American Church for *Reformation 21*. *Reformation 21* and its editorial staff have given permission for portions of this content to be reprinted for the purposes of this volume. The article series in its entirety may be found at http://www.reformation21.org/otis-w-pickett.

I say all this to point out that when we think about race in America we often think in terms of stereotypes and prejudge based on our own assumptions. My personal story is complicated and mixed with inequality, equality, hate, love, sin, and everything in between. My hope is that White Christians will read this perspective from another White Christian and thus attempt to understand the frustrations of their African American brothers and sisters with a bit more grace and love. My hope is that my African American brothers and sisters will continue to extend grace, even as they call White Christians to wake up to our blindness in this area.

I love being from the South and have come to realize that my privilege or position in society as a White male is not sinful in and of itself. However, how I choose to use that privilege can be. I can therefore shed anything resembling "White guilt." I can go to the cross with my guilt and shame. I can freely accept Jesus's great gift of forgiveness and mercy, while I can also embrace the other gifts our heavenly Father has bestowed on me.[2] However, these gifts are not only for me, my family, or my brothers and sisters in Christ. They are to be used for all.

When we talk about suffering in United States history, we have to talk about race. It has taken time and grace from many African American brothers and sisters who have taught me, pastored me, befriended me, and listened to me. They have been kind enough not to leave me in my ignorance. I thank God for them!

Many White Christians want to know and do more, but don't know how to begin. We need friends to lovingly teach us, and we need the Holy Spirit to soften our hearts. We also tend to get defensive because our ancestors might have been a part of that history, and we are fearful of what this could mean for their legacies and for us today.

Many White people also feel castigated for something they did not participate in. Forgive us for this. This is yet another characteristic of privilege. We want all the positive benefits of what was passed down to us (our faith, land, wealth, education, honor, a "good" name) without also accepting and owning the consequences for the negative aspects of our ancestors (racism, greed,

---

2 Anthony Bradley has spoken widely about this idea of Whites embracing their privilege, and I am borrowing heavily from his ideas here in a talk he gave at Mt. Helm Baptist Church on February 22, 2013, during the Bradley Rhodes Conversation event in Jackson, Mississippi.

segregation, and cowardice). By cowardice, I mean the failure of our forefathers to speak the biblical truth of the imago dei into a society that believed one race was superior to all others and codified this belief into law.[3] This cultural captivity driven by economic greed on the profits made from slaveholding kept Christians from speaking into this injustice.

I have come to learn that if I accept the benefits of privilege that have been passed down to me, I also have to accept and own the sins of my fathers, repent of them, and work hard to undo them. I am comfortable with the fact that I will be working my entire life and my children and their children will be working their entire lives to undo the mess made by our forefathers. To me, this is what it looks like to bear the sins of the fathers to the third and fourth generation (Exod. 20:5).

I have spent much of the past thirty-five years seeing, reading, visiting, studying, listening, writing, and processing race in America. But even after getting a PhD in US history, teaching US history the past five years, and attending a multiethnic PCA church, I am only now starting to "get it." Decades of privilege have blunted my senses.

My grandfather

God has been pulling me into places of racial interaction ever since I was young. It is only because God has lifted a few of the scales from my eyes that I am beginning to see.

My journey started with an Otis. This was Dr. Otis M. Pickett Jr., a small-town family medical practitioner in Mt. Pleasant, South Carolina, and my grandfather. Papa "Beach," as I called him, was the most gentle, loving man I have ever known. I watched my grandfather interact with patients at his doctor's office, treating each one with dignity, honor, and respect.

Many of my grandfather's patients were African Americans. They were the proud descendants of the Gullah, a people whose ancestry can be directly linked to ancient civilizations in West Africa. Amidst the tremendous stresses of the institution of slavery, they kept alive their language, cooking, weaving, and blacksmithing traditions. Many of these folks knew and loved my grandfather

---

3 I am borrowing these ideas heavily from the thoughts of Carl Ellis whom I have heard present on these ideas at General Assembly and at Reformed Theological Seminary-Jackson.

dearly. I had the blessing of going with my grandfather on house calls many times. We were treated like family in the homes of these friends.

When I was six or seven, my grandfather and I would go on walks on the beaches of Sullivan's Island, where our family home was, and he would tell me about the ships coming in and out of Charleston harbor. One evening, a young African American boy and his mother walked by us in the opposite direction. For some reason, the boy and I exchanged looks of disdain. We both attempted to throw sand and seashells at the other. I will never forget what my grandfather did. He jerked me around (this from a man who never laid a hand on me), got down on his knee, looked at me with teary-eyed resoluteness, and said, "You must never hurt anyone like this. Go tell that boy you are sorry." I went over and apologized to the boy. His mother and my grandfather exchanged smiles.

Somehow, growing up as a young White boy in the South, there was already disdain for someone of another color. How did that happen? Part of it was the sin in my own heart. Part of it was my context. I grew up in a society that believed that White people were superior to African Americans. This was codified into law for three centuries, and there were thousands of other less formal ways this belief was communicated to White children. I grew up in this world and context, was a product of it, and still see manifestations of it in my heart from time to time.

But the experience on the beach changed me forever.

My mother

My mother, Martha "Marty" Westbrook Pickett, was from Fairfield County, South Carolina, and was sent to boarding school in Charleston in the 1970s. She grew up with many African Americans and appreciated them as friends, companions, and people deserving dignity and respect. She brought this mentality with her to Charleston. Throughout her life, she has modeled this in raising me. To this day, my mother feels more comfortable and "at home" around African Americans than she does with White people.

One summer when I was eight or nine, she insisted I watch the entire black-and-white movie version of *To Kill a Mockingbird*. I ended up loving it and watched the VHS version over and over. I memorized many of Jem and Scout's lines, and I think she took great pleasure in hearing me recite them around the house. But much of the plot was lost on me at the time. It has only been in my adult years and with my own children that I realized why she made me do this.

In the 1990s, there was severe racial tension in Charleston for a variety of reasons. My mother and her best friend decided to go to a meeting in downtown Charleston of "concerned citizens" to discuss the racial tension and to pray. My mother took me with her to the meeting. I didn't pay much attention to what was happening, but a kind man named Herman Robinson took an interest in me and my mom. I think he was struck by a White lady bringing her son to a meeting on racial tension. He invited us to his church, Trinity Baptist.

My mom and I started going to the Rev. Herman Robinson's church, and we were pretty much the only White people who attended. I loved it. I loved everything about it. I loved the music, I loved the genuine community. I loved how welcomed we were and how we were so cared for. Until that point, all I had known was our Episcopalian church with its kneelers and Book of Common Prayer. Old stern ladies in big hats were what church meant to me.

Most of all, I fell in love with Jesus and God's word as it was presented to me by the faithful preaching of the Rev. Herman Robinson. Herman discipled me and told my mom that I was going to be a teacher of God's word. He told her that God had marked me out and set me apart for great things that the Lord would do. I strive every day to live up to his encouragements.

College years

I went to Clemson University and joined a fraternity so I could share Christ with people there. While there were good aspects to the fraternity, it also was filled with only White males, and there was resistance to admitting African Americans for membership. The exclusion was not formally in our by-laws, but it was communicated by conversations and in symbols of the Confederacy that hung in brothers' rooms. The general feeling was that "African Americans have their fraternities and sororities. We have ours."

I largely just adopted this systemic self-segregation as normative. Despite my grandfather's example, my mother's teachings, and my pastor's modeling, I lacked the tools, language, and ultimately the strength to challenge such an institution. I was already basically an outcast to my fellow brothers because I didn't participate in many of the normal "activities" of the fraternity because of my faith. To attempt to challenge them on racial inclusion would have made things worse. Also, I was scared and a coward. It is only recently that I can admit this.

While I was in college, there was discussion of taking down the Confederate flag from the State House of South Carolina. Many of my fraternity brothers took this as a personal challenge and decided to fly Confederate flags in their rooms and out their windows in defiance. I myself, a history major who was proud of being a descendent (albeit indirectly) of General George Pickett, had a (more genteel and less abrasive) First National Flag of the Confederacy as well as a portrait of Pickett on my wall.

Soon, as was his yearly habit, Herman made a trip to Clemson to visit me, minister to me, pray over my room, and take me to lunch. I remember seeing his face when he saw my living quarters for the first time. It was a combination of sadness, deep pain, and disappointment. I had seen that face before on a beach in Sullivan's Island. For the first time, I think I felt a bit of the pain that our African American brothers and sisters might feel upon seeing these symbols.

For my White readers, you have to understand that these images are powerful, and to many African Americans flying a Confederate flag is like saying, "I'd like to go back to a time when African Americans were enslaved." It can be deeply painful to see these images, especially in the homes and residences of people you thought knew better.

I did know better. To my White readers, please learn from this and don't get defensive. Removing these images from your homes is not "giving up the Lost Cause." It is caring for your brothers and sisters and lovingly laying down your own preferences in light of Paul's charge in First Corinthians 10 to not cause pain to brothers and sister in Christ, but to build up the body. I would call this a laying down of pride and preference to better love, serve, and care for our brothers and sisters.

Rev. Robinson (or Herman, as I now call him) continued to care for me, come alongside me, pray for me, and minister to me. He did not leave me in my state. When I was leaving for Covenant Seminary in the summer of 2003, Herman and his wife came to our wedding and presented me with one of my most prized possessions, a picture of Martin Luther King Jr. and Ralph Abernathy kneeling in prayer on the streets of Birmingham. It hung proudly in his office for as long as I had known him. He handed it to me as if to say, "Let images like this decorate your new home." It is now the first thing visitors to our home see when they enter.

I do not hide my ancestry, nor am I ashamed of it, but I wish it to be redemptive rather than destructive. I think, if my Confederate ancestors are in heaven right now, this is what they would want. They would not want to be lifted up and their "cause" perpetuated. They would want Christ to be lifted up and would want their lives to be used to unite people rather than separate them.

Covenant Seminary

In 2003, I enrolled at Covenant Theological Seminary in St. Louis, Missouri. I had traveled a fair amount but had never lived anywhere outside of South Carolina and had always lived in majority-White, middle-class suburbs. Covenant placed my wife and I in a seminary-owned apartment in a working-class African American neighborhood just six miles south of Ferguson. I learned more about what it is like to be an African American in the US in those three years than I have learned in my entire life.

However, friends who visited from South Carolina found our new home somewhat startling. Ninety percent of our neighbors were hardworking African American families. The apartments were not the fanciest living spaces, and many of our neighbors were single parents with latchkey kids. In the summer, the kids were there all day, from nine to five, just hanging around the neighborhood with nothing to do and few adults there to make them lunch, help them plan activities, or engage with them. Many times we had kids come to our door asking for a glass of water just to be able to come into our home and sit in the air conditioning. This absence of parents led to all kinds of activities within our neighborhood such as unwise decision-making, teenage pregnancies, poor diets, and interactions with the police. As seminary students, many of us organized activities, lunches, Bible studies, and field trips for the children and got them involved in local churches with vibrant youth ministries.

In many ways, our neighborhood was similar to Ferguson, and when the events in Ferguson took place, I watched them unfold with empathy and concern. Some of the frustrations the people of Ferguson have with regard to targeted policing and justice are very real. I often saw similar scenarios of unbalanced policing with African American youths, compared to youths in White, middle-class, suburban sections of St. Louis.

I remember one day the boys in the neighborhood were playing football in the yard between the apartments. There was a tussle, some pushing and shoving, because someone was playing dirty or throwing elbows. A police officer came by in a cruiser, got out of his car, and walked up to the boys. These boys were no more than thirteen, and the youngest of them was probably nine or ten. He questioned them about where they lived, what their names were, and said he was getting complaints from neighbors about fighting and brawling in the yard. No one was arrested, but information was written down. These young men were now on the "radar" of a patrolling officer in the area. What struck me were the hundreds upon hundreds of times that my friends and I played what we used to call "highly emotional" basketball and football. We got into arguments, furious shouting matches, brawling fights, but eventually we would get back to the game. In my neighborhood growing up, the cops never came, we were never asked questions about who we were or where we lived, neighbors never called the police on us, and we were far more violent toward one another than these young boys had been.

I realized that simply because of where I lived growing up, my parents' income and my race, I was protected by a sphere of White privilege that served as a buffer to targeted policing and other potential issues. If the police would have questioned us on a regular basis because we were playing football and tussling, my mother would have been on the phone in a heartbeat with an attorney and would have made the proper inquiries toward the police department about harassment. She and my father would have called people with influence who would look into the matter as a personal favor to them and our family. This access to power afforded by enhanced educational opportunities and having friendship and kinship networks in spheres of influence limited the effects of a targeted over-policing of our neighborhood.

I am not at all anti-police. However, it doesn't mean the police are not fallible and not part of a larger system of systemic racism that cannot be questioned. We also have seen far too many young African American men shot by the police in our country to any longer consider it a coincidence. We must begin to ask questions and demand better for communities where over-policing or targeted policing toward African Americans is taking place. As Whites, we must lose our complacency and self-interest and be willing to declare with our African American brothers and sisters that African American lives matter and then do something to display that. It might be as easy as looking through our contact list, picking up the phone, and advocating for a particular community.

Covenant taught me a great deal. The student body was fairly multiethnic, with a sizeable international population and a growing African American population. Professor Jerram Barrs taught me much about the importance of repentance over our national, regional, and denominational sins of racism, recognizing past sins, admitting them publicly, and seeking forgiveness from our African American brothers and sisters.

I remember him saying something like, "It doesn't even matter that I am British. I'm White. Therefore, when I go and preach in African American churches, I always acknowledge these sins, repent, and ask for forgiveness over these sins. Many of the congregants weep openly over this and come to me afterward saying it's the first time they have ever heard a White man saying these things."[4]

How could I not, as a White Southerner from the US, go and do likewise?

In my time at Covenant, the seminary hired the first full-time, tenure-track African American professor in the school's history. His name is Dr. Anthony Bradley. Bradley has since moved on from Covenant, published numerous books, and has been involved in pushing forward the conversation on race in his denomination for the last several years.

I will never forget the day that Dr. Bradley showed the class a pro-Confederate/Reformed theology website that, at the time, was put together by people within Reformed Presbyterian circles who were also very proud of their Confederate heritage. On the website was an article about Covenant Seminary hiring him, and there was a comments section below. Dr. Bradley did the painful work of reading each comment out loud to the class.

The comments on this website contained some of the most racist, offensive, and hateful language I had ever heard. Many of the seventy-plus students that day wept over the sin and hate contained in this website. We lamented over the pain this must have caused Dr. Bradley who should have been celebrating

---

4 I am paraphrasing a well-known story that Jerram Barrs tells in one of his lectures at Covenant Theological Seminary during his Apologetics class.

finishing his PhD and receiving a coveted tenure-track teaching job. Instead, he found himself being attacked by Christians in his own theological tradition who were posting hateful language about him simply because of his race. I asked Dr. Bradley if we could go to lunch, and he began walking me through some of the difficult history of race in America and in the church.[5]

In the two years that followed, I learned a great deal about Presbyterian history from Dr. Sean Lucas and Wayne Sparkman, and I found myself far more interested in pursuing a PhD in history and teaching than I did in becoming a full-time vocational pastor. As Dr. Lucas's student, I learned how important it is to present history in all its complexity and nuance, to write the truth and let the chips fall where they may. He also taught me the importance of balance in history, that history is not simply about angels and demons, but about fallen men who sometimes make good decisions by God's grace and sometimes are incredibly blind. It doesn't mean that we erase these men from memory or cease to think upon their biblical examples. However, we also must not fail to speak about their failures.

After completing my degree at Covenant, I was accepted to the College of Charleston and found out that I had received a graduate assistantship at the Avery Center for African American History and Culture. In May of 2006, my family packed our things and moved back down South.

Back in the South

Not only would I learn more about my own research, but I would learn, or re-learn, the history of Charleston, through the lens of the African American experience. As part of my assistantship, I helped process archival collections, and I gave tours to visitors who came to Charleston from all across the US. You must understand, many of these groups were reunion groups, church tours, and families (most of whom were African American). The director of the center placed me at the front desk, so the first thing these folks saw when they walked in "THE" Center for African American History and Culture in Charleston was a bow-tie clad White man named Otis. It usually took people the better part of an hour to process this.

---

5 This website has since been taken down, and one of the chief authors of the website has contacted Anthony Bradley to apologize.

The Avery Center does an amazing job of examining slavery, segregation, and the Civil Rights Movement as well as African American culture and education in the Lowcountry of South Carolina. As I was learning this history in graduate classes, my eyes began to open about the town I called home. For instance, I had never been taught extensively about the millions of Africans who came through the port of Charleston and sold as human property. I had no idea that my hometown (Sullivan's Island) was the "Ellis Island of the South" and served as a quarantining station for enslaved Africans.

What I learned the most in that experience was that truth-telling and walking through the difficult and disturbing parts of our history openly and honestly is necessary, cathartic, and can be an incredible way to break down racial barriers. We also need to speak historical truth along with our African American brothers and sisters so that they are not the only ones saying it. We need to support African American history along with the learning of the histories of all ethnic groups in America. We need to support African American History Month, but we also need to do better at weaving African American history into the overall narrative of American history. By the end of the tours, most folks saw that I was speaking truth, no matter how difficult it was to say, and together, as Whites and African Americans, we processed, lamented, struggled, sometimes cried, and experienced the pain of this history together.

I then moved with my family to the University of Mississippi to work on my PhD. Not only would I continue my graduate studies and research on these topics, but I would meet people who had been working on race relations and racial reconciliation for more than fifty years. Many might say Mississippi is an unlikely place to study race relations, but it actually is home to a number of churches, centers, and organizations focused on racial reconciliation.

Learning more about how the racial climate in America affected the church, too, made me even more aware of the need to work for reconciliation. A brief survey of that history might help my White brothers and sisters more fully understand how our African American brothers and sisters have been mistreated by those in the church as well and why there is still much hurt that needs to be healed.

History of race and the church

In my studies, I have seen how race was socially constructed through particularizing an ethnicity of people (Africans) as somehow inferior and thus worthy of enslavement. This eventually led to systematic, profit-driven, man-stealing. It was unbiblical and un-Christian. Do not let any person try to convince you that African-based slavery beginning in the seventeenth century was biblical. It was not. It was race-based, for-profit, man-stealing with no hope of freedom for those who were enslaved. Men, women, and children were ripped away from their families, and millions would die in the horrific Middle Passage. The Christians who lived in these societies are culpable and connected with this sin because they lived comfortably off the fruits of this trade system and largely did not speak into this traffic of human beings until the late eighteenth century.[6]

This collective choice to categorize Africans as somehow degraded and the practice of selling them into lifelong forced labor was present when the first colonists came to Jamestown, Virginia. Soon after the colonists' arrival, a Dutch ship on August 20, 1619, carried twenty enslaved Africans to be sold as property there. In the very earliest days of our colonial society, slavery was woven into the fabric of our history. African people occupied a separate position as property specifically because of their race.

We therefore cannot say that race does not matter. We can trace the economic, political, cultural, and social patterns of the beginning of our country back to the subjugation of one race by another. It is a part of our American DNA. The sooner we realize this and begin to understand it, the sooner we will begin to unite and reconcile. We will also better see the reason why some of our brothers and sisters are insistent that we talk about race. It is not just a phenomenon of the Civil Rights Movement or Jim Crow. It has been with us from our very inception as a nation, has deeply affected African Americans (indeed, all of us) in the US, and will continue to be with us as long as we do not take steps to undo the effects of it over time.

---

6 If you are interested in the Middle Passage, read the works of E. Franklin Frazier, Melville J. Herskovitz, Marcus Rediker, Hugh Thomas, and David Eltis. Other historians on slavery and human bondage such as Winthrop Jordan, John Hope Franklin, Adam Rothman, and Anthony E. Kaye are also good. I would especially recommend David Brion Davis's *Inhuman Bondage: The Rise and Fall of Slavery in the New World.*

When slavery made an agrarian economy profitable, the church, largely in the South, began its pro-slavery position. Fledgling congregations and their young pastors would not have a strong position on the Southern landscape until they were able to woo the older, landed, male planter elites to their churches.[7]

In 1793, Eli Whitney's cotton gin had made slavery extremely lucrative. After Whitney's invention was commonplace on plantations across the South, the harvest of raw cotton doubled every decade moving into the mid-nineteenth century. After this, few church pulpits, both North and South, were bold in preaching the abolition of slavery. The Southern economy was making incredible profits on cotton yields, and the Northern economy was earning tremendous revenue on by-products of cotton in the textile industry and in trade with Europe. In the span of a decade, the value of enslaved Africans, as chattel property, nearly doubled. The system benefited the North as well as the South.

Indeed, much of the wealth of the US South was not in cotton fields or rice crops—it was in the commodification of enslaved human bodies. The price of enslaved Africans would also go up after 1807 because Congress ended the international slave trade. This was less an act of altruism and more a way for Southern slaveholders to make larger profits on an increasingly limited "commodity." They could make more profits from hiring out the labor of their slaves and selling their enslaved Africans' offspring.

Once an enslaved African became a member of a church, his or her ecclesiastical status and relationship to White members as co-members of the church should have given both ecclesiastical equality under the church as well as eventual bodily freedom and liberation. However, Southern Christians were captivated by the potency of the peculiar institution and chose instead to keep enslaved Africans in perpetual bondage while attempting to meet their spiritual needs. This is false and inconsistent with orthodox Christianity. We have also failed to fully understand the experiences of African American Christians and

---

7 If you are interested in church history, Southern religious history, and the church's switch from an antislavery position to one that adopted the cultural and economic status quo, then I would recommend reading the works of historians Rhys Isaac, Christine Heyrman, Anne C. Loveland, Janet Cornelius, Beth Barton Schweiger, Don Matthews, John Boles, Samuel Hill, and Eugene Genovese.

the role of African Americans in helping to shape Christian theology in America and the South.[8]

Also, I have heard many brothers and sisters in Christ from the South say the Civil War was about states' rights and was not about slavery. This is somewhat true in that the right that every single state in the South was concerned about was slavery. All one needs to do is read the ordinance of secession for each Southern state to see that the Confederacy was fighting a war largely to preserve the right of each state to promote and continue the institution of slavery.

Christians, by and large, became captive to the culture. If the culture said that making money from enslaved labor produced through man-stealing was good, then the overwhelming Christian response was to affirm this status quo rather than challenge it. Consider, if your entire station (and everyone else you knew), status, and livelihood were based on the institution of slave labor, how willing, able, and effective would you be in challenging it? If you challenged the system as unbiblical, then you were basically saying the entire system of labor on which the South (and the entire nation via the South's materials) made the majority of its income needed to be overturned. To say the least, this would not to be a popular or well-received position. You might even be hated or ostracized for taking it.

Plus, if you were a Baptist or Presbyterian minister in the nineteenth century and your congregation, session, or diaconate was made up of wealthy slaveholders (and many were), and you attempted to challenge the institution of slavery, then you were either going to be out of a job, or worse, perceived as an outside agitator and "dealt with." The slavocracy system had become so corrosive and controlling that a pastor would not have even been able to question, from the pulpit or publicly, whether the institution was consistent with the spirit of

---

8 Read Carl Ellis *Free At Last? The Gospel in the African American Experience*, Thabiti M. Anyabwile *The Faithful Preacher: Recapturing the Vision of Three Pioneering African-American Pastors*, and Carter G. Woodson *History of the Negro Church*. Woodson's work can be found at http://docsouth.unc.edu/church/woodson/woodson.html.

Christianity. This is how captive the church became to the culture on this issue.[9] This is a great lesson for modern-day discussions. If we are not, as Christians, able to raise a critique or question on something that grips the church and are fearful of being removed from a community because it is questioned, then it is probably a good sign that we have become culturally captive to the issue in question.

A new slavery

Indeed, many Americans over the next eighty years worked hard to remove opportunities for African Americans to participate as first-class citizens. They worked to remove the right to vote, hold office, receive due process, and sit on juries. They worked to segregate public spaces and to continue to degrade the lives of African Americans through violent mob rule, lynching, and a eugenics movement driven by a racially oriented social Darwinism. This work occurred both above and below the Mason-Dixon Line. In order to secure the Presidential election of Republican candidate Rutherford B. Hayes, the Compromise of 1877 essentially ended Reconstruction by removing the federal government's protective presence throughout the South.

Many churches adopted a position that the church was only a spiritual entity and should only work for its spirituality and holiness, not in activity toward justice or civil rights issues. While many still recognize that the church, in its systems and courts, should not engage in political or social matters, the larger doctrine had the effect of causing individual Christians (mostly in White denominations) not to speak or act with regard to injustice or civil rights.[10]

Southern landholders (largely ex-slaveholders) worked to prevent African Americans from achieving advantageous economic opportunities and maintained a deceptive sharecropping and tenant farming system, which perpetuated cycles

---

9 Read Mitchell Snay *Gospel of Disunion*, Don Mathews *Religion in the Old South*, John Boles *Masters and Slaves in the House of the Lord*, H. Shelton Smith's *In His Image But,… Racism in Southern Religion 1790–1910*, Eugene Genovese *A Consuming Fire*, Sean Michael Lucas *Robert Lewis Dabney*, John Patrick Daly's *When Slavery Was Called Freedom: Evangelicalism, Proslavery and the Causes of the Civil War*, and Jim Farmer's *The Metaphysical Confederacy: James Henley Thornwell and the Synthesis of Southern Value.*

10 Read Stephen R. Haynes, Pete Daniel, Paul Harvey, and Carolyn Renee Dupont.

of debt and largely kept African Americans in successions of poverty by having to pay unfair dividends from crop profits and high interest rates at plantation commissaries for the goods needed for farming. Therefore, African American farmers were not able to gain much of an economic toehold over the next century.[11]

Further, the "separate but equal" educational institutions in the South were indeed separate, but far from equal. African Americans typically attended underfunded schools for only a few months out of the year in substandard buildings using outdated textbooks. This made it highly unlikely they would be able to enter top universities and receive salaried jobs. This was all carefully crafted by Southerners in power, which included Christians living in the South, who were both a part of sharecropping and making sure that White people received a better education than African Americans.[12]

One of the saddest things about this structure is that it was allowed to invade and take hold of Christ's bride: the church. However, some historians have looked to the church as a leader in segregation and in buttressing a Lost Cause ideology that had a deep impact among Southern Christians. Sometimes the distinctions between Christianity and the Lost Cause were hard to define. Southern Presbyterians helped defend the Lost Cause by celebrating its acolytes rather than challenging the racism inherent in their theology. To be sure, rather than being captive to the culture, in 1874 the Presbyterian Church (PCUS) or the Southern branch of American Presbyterianism voted during its annual meeting for "organic separation" of the church along racial lines. This was twenty years prior to Jim Crow segregation in the South. The churches set the tone. Some churches that had enjoyed a multiethnic community from 1865 to 1874 were forced by the church courts to segregate. Rather than being "culturally

---

11 David Oshinsky addresses this issue at length in the chapter "Mississippi Plan" in *Worse Than Slavery: Parchman Farm and the Ordeal of Jim Crow Justice* (New York: Free Press, 1997), 31–54.

12 Bobby Griffith delivered a paper that covered the entire history of race and the church in America during the Bradley Rhodes Conversation in Jackson, Mississippi, in February 2013. His work at that conference and his continued encouragement has been a source of inspiration to me and many others in the Jackson area. Much of this section is borrowing from his thoughts and ideas. His paper may be found at https://bradleyrhodesconversation.wordpress.com/2012/11/27/2013-bradleyrhodes-conversation-featuring-the-rev-bobby-griffith-jr-and-rev-cj-rhodes/)

captive," the Southern Presbyterians created a model for what the Southern landscape would come to resemble after Plessy vs. Ferguson in 1896. The church, in many ways, helped define what segregation would look like and how it would be done.[13]

Truth-telling

I believe that in order to have true reconciliation we must openly and honestly walk through our shared history and "truth tell." I also believe that only in Christ can true reconciliation happen. Only Christ can redeem something as dark as two centuries of the institution of slavery, plantation brutality, legalized Jim Crow segregation, lynching without due process, violence against peaceful protesters, the murder of innocent leaders, as well as continued violence against Black males and our current situation of mass incarceration.

Further, it is only through Christ that our African American brothers and sisters will have the grace necessary to forgive us and love us. As Ligon Duncan, Chancellor of Reformed Theological Seminary, has said before (and I am paraphrasing), it is not us who ask for forgiveness who are the heroes, it is the ones who grant it who are the heroes. Our role is to listen, love, serve, repent, and humble ourselves. We need to pursue relationships with these brothers and sisters and use the benefits of our privileged status to be advocates in the best way we can.

I am thankful for the experiences God gave me through my grandfather, mother, seminary, the history classroom, and many other stops and people along the way. I pray and trust that God will continue to make me aware of my blind spots and of ways he would have me use the blessings he has given me to bless others.

---

13 You can read more about this in an article I have written on John Lafayette Girardeau at http://www.palmettohistory.org/scha/proceedings/proceedings2010.pdf and in an article by the Rev. Dr. C. N. Willborn at http://www.pcahistory.org/HCLibrary/periodicals/spr/bios/girardeau.html.

Chapter 8

Overcoming Made in America Racism

Rev. Sam Wheatley

Sam Wheatley is the pastor of New Song Presbyterian Church (PCA) in Salt Lake City, Utah. He is a founding board member of the Reformed Communion, a fellowship of pastors and congregations dedicated to cultivating unity and mission in the church. Sam has degrees from Clemson University (BS) and Westminster Theological Seminary (MDiv). He and his wife, Kate, have three children.

"Let others do it. Who am I to say anything? I'm a mid-career, Anglo pastor of a not-large Presbyterian church in a place of limited racial diversity. Who am I to say anything helpful about the thorny issue of race? I should just let others contribute—people who have more experience, individuals from more diverse neighborhoods, leaders with more credentials."

This is the inner dialogue of many of us who struggle with our conscience and comfort level on the issue of race in America. However, race and our common struggle with it touches everyone, regardless of location, age, or background. We all must testify to our experience, struggles, and failures to begin to see the dimensions of the issue.

Regarding race, I held all the proper views inherited from my place as a middle-class educated clergyman. My views didn't come from genuine reflection as much as they were attitudes I'd adopted like a style of clothing.

Race was a topic I didn't much think about. I was busy with pastoring a church and raising a family. All the attendant personal and corporate challenges of those callings conveniently kept me busy. For the past twenty-five years, I have been preoccupied by church and home. The issue of race was relegated to a small area at the periphery of my thoughts. This, I see now, is one of the insidious masking powers of racism among a White majority—we can be oblivious to something that for so many others is a daily, unrelenting wound.

Only occasionally would a news story ping my awareness. Recently, that pinging became more frequent. "Stop-and-Frisk." "Trayvon." "Ferguson."

Finally, it was "Charleston" that broke the dam and ended the comfortable illusion that we live in a post-racial society. When a White gunman who had been shown hospitality in a Black church, brutally murdered those who had welcomed him, when the clear motivation for those attacks was his hatred of their race, the narrative I'd used to explain the world no longer fit reality. Racial bias, hatred, and bigotry were not part of the past, but active and violent players in the present world in which I lived.

Previous to this revelation when I'd noticed obvious issues of race (such as the overwhelmingly White complexion of my denomination), I would look to the presence of the few Latino, Native American, Asian American, and African American pastors as welcome signs of imminent and inevitable changes on the horizon. Those few pastors gave me all the encouragement I needed to think we were on the right track.

However, I now see that there are deep structural and economic forces that actively fence out certain people and actively preference certain others. I now see that I have to be involved. I now see that I need to acknowledge where we really are instead of making up my own narrative.

As a White man, I was able to soften my Southern accent, improve my grammar, get an education, and increase my status. At the time, I never saw this as a racial story. Rather, I saw it in terms of self-effort and hard work. I now see that I was able to profit from racial stereotypes to improve my own standing while others struggled to overcome ingrained racial biases stacked against them.

Confronting the evil of racism

In the past few months, I've been blessed to have mentors guide me into new ways of viewing the continuing relevance of race. One of the most powerful insights was from the brilliant mind of W. E. B. Du Bois in *The Souls of Black Folk:*

Between me and the other world there is ever an unasked question: unasked by some through feeling of delicacy; by others through the difficulty of framing it. All, nevertheless, flutter round it. They approach me in a half-hesitant sort of way, eye me curiously or compassionately and then, instead of saying directly, How does it feel to be a problem? they say, I know an excellent colored man in my town; or, I fought at Mechanicsville; or Do not these Southern outrages make your blood boil? At these I smile, or am interested, or reduce the boiling to a simmer, or as the occasion may require. To the real question, How does it feel to be a problem? I answer seldom a word.[1]

I have never felt that I was a problem. I have always felt that I was a solver of problems. As Du Bois's words sank deeper, I began to perceive that for a human being to be perceived primarily as a problem is a curse worse than the most censored language. To move toward another human being as essentially a problem is to deny his or her fundamental nature as a uniquely blessed being, made in the image of God. It is this "problem-ification" of people that leads to unwarranted suspicion, to derogatory language, to willful ignorance of the plight of others, to the quiet segregation of society, to White people getting easily offended by the simple honesty or anger of those who have been daily offended by real blows, to a divided church unable to repent or change, to fluttering round the division that is killing us. There is a problem, a deep open wound in our history, that all the blaming, circumnavigating and pretending won't change. The problem is not a person. The problem is evil itself.

We like to think of evil as some future Armageddon. But the evil we are called to oppose is the one we can see and name and face in our own lives. That evil is our peculiar form of Made in America racism.

Along with me, you may recoil and say, "All I can do is hole up, hide, and avoid saying anything that's going to cause offense. Let someone else talk. I don't want to." But avoidance is a false hope. It's empty, because this is not a fight we can simply opt out of.

---

1 W. E. B. Du Bois, *The Souls of Black Folk* (Chicago: A. C. McClurg and Co., 1903).

The way of the Cross

There is a way through this that many of us in the Protestant tradition know and preach regularly, even if we've somehow failed to apply its power to the evil of racism. It is the way of the Cross. It's the path where those in power willingly lay it down on behalf of others and where those without power are given honor, respect, and a privileged place at the table.

Yet while easy to state, it is hard to implement. The first step for those like me, comfortable with the status quo, is to listen to voices outside of our closed circles, to those who have had an experience far different from ours. Read, listen to the stories of others, look into the history of American slavery, Jim Crow, and racism. Seek truth and embrace the calling of humility.

Next, pray with new urgency and understanding. Take what you've learned and sit with God in quiet. Let the stories from books or others' mouths shape into groans too deep for words to express. Confess your avoidance, pride, arrogance, and legion of other sins that have been fed by your comfort-loving heart.

Then, receive what we have in Christ: forgiveness. We have a forgiveness that forges our wills to move away from the past and toward people in love. Genuine grace from God will empower us to not shy away from difficulty. It is a grace that is OK with discomfort, because it knows that in that space new habits and attitudes are being formed. Understand where we have been entrusted with power and creatively plot how to share, loan, or give that power to others we would have previously considered problems.

Last, hope. Hope comes not from immediate success, but from confidence that this call to reconciliation and peace is from the one true God who bends the course of the universe toward justice and love. To oppose God's ambitions is to side with evil and to suffer its destiny. To stand with God is to confidently face setbacks, defeat, and even death with resurrection hope.

Chapter 9

Black Friends

Rev. Dennis Hermerding

Dennis Hermerding is the founding pastor of King's Cross Church, Cypress, Texas. He previously served as the Reformed University Fellowship campus minister at the University of Arizona and in congregations in Madison, Mississippi; Tucson, Arizona; and Spring, Texas. He has degrees from University of Memphis (BA), Trinity International University (MA), and Reformed Theological Seminary (MDiv). Dennis and his wife, Jane, have three children.

I was born in Selma, Alabama, in 1966. I entered into the world at University Hospital, the same hospital where most of the African Americans who had been beaten on the march from Selma to Montgomery were taken for treatment. As I grew up in the city of Memphis with part of my family being from the Midwest and part of it being from the Deep South, I found myself wrestling with issues involving people with whom I was related and people with whom I interacted on the playground and in the classroom.

Perhaps you grew up like me, having family members tell you things like, "Black people are fine, but further down the evolutionary chain than we are" or "Black people are to be cared for, but they are under the curse of Cain and Canaan." Some family members would tell me it was fine to have Black friends but not to drink after them or use the commode after them.

My parents divorced when I was three years old, and as a White boy with a single mom, we were frequently looked at with pity or scorn when we entered various Evangelical churches. It was within the Black community that I often found acceptance and encouragement as a boy because their mamas never told them, "Don't play with that boy because you know the kind of person his mama is." By the time I was in high school, I had several friends who were African American. In my rebellion during those years, I prided myself on being more enlightened and a better person because I had them as my friends. I didn't think of myself as a bigot or prejudiced or a racist because I had Black friends. However, my college experience showed me how wrong I was.

Learning to listen

My first roommate in college was an African American student who was a senior. Looking back, I see how kind he was in putting up with my stupid freshman antics. I remember one time when he was making a point about something I had said, I was about to interrupt him and he said, "Please don't tell me again about how you have Black friends." His words stung and angered me.

The next semester, after I made a comment in a class where we were discussing the Civil Rights Movement, an African American classmate said, "You stupid White boy. You need to learn the difference between overt and covert oppression." Again I felt the sting of being told I didn't understand. I was faced again with the glaring reality that I didn't really understand what had been done to African Americans over the last four hundred years.

God was beginning to expose my sinful use of my Black friends. He was beginning to awaken me to an understanding of privilege. A number of years later, in 1994 when I entered seminary at Trinity Divinity School, I joined a group called American Believers for Black America. As we began to discuss issues especially related to serving the Black community in the city of Chicago, I was confronted again with the reality that I was very happy having Black friends and helping Black friends, but not in really listening to Black friends.

In one meeting, a Korean American student and an African American student discussed how a particular text related to issues of justice in our society. When several White students questioned whether these students had a valid right to give a different interpretation, someone asked when theologians from other ethnicities ever would get an equal voice at the table. Initially I thought, "What is the big deal who says it if it is the truth?" Then it occurred to me that's how privilege works. White people can easily not see how our backgrounds, cultural circumstances, and the issues of the day shape how we read, interpret, and apply Scripture. The issue wasn't whether Calvin was right or wrong, but rather were we going to allow for a "Calvin" or "Luther" to arise from other ethnicities, too, to enrich, expand, and correct our understanding of God in his fullness.

I began to think about how I had not given enough thought to how my culture, my family, and my own heart had done damage to ethnic minorities, not only by the things that had been done but also by the things that had not been done. I thought of the many ways the dominant culture had not allowed them to have a voice.

Being a good neighbor

Partway through seminary, I transferred to Reformed Theological Seminary in Jackson, Mississippi. After graduation, I became a campus minister with Reformed University Fellowship and began a new work at the University of Arizona. In Arizona, the issue of ethnic equality moved from a discussion of my Black friends to interacting with students of Hispanic backgrounds. I began thinking through issues relating to worship style, preaching style, praying style, and cultural impact on the interpretation and application of Scripture.

Again I was forced to face the realities of privilege. Many of the pastors I interacted with were amazing Christians, but their access to theological resources and training was limited due to language barriers, economic barriers, and location barriers. I also had to deal again with how much my views were shaped by my culture.

I now am planting a church in Cypress, Texas, a suburb of Houston, one of the most ethnically diverse cities in the United States. While our church reflects the demographics of our community, my daughter as a senior in high school recently lamented the racism she sees daily in her school. She hears statements about her Black friends like, "Well I didn't know which one he was. I can't really tell them apart. They really all look alike." She was in a relationship with an African American young man, and one of her classmates asked her, "Don't you know what people will think about you and your children if you marry him? Besides the Bible tells us not to marry people from other races." Do you hear these kinds of statements in your communities?

As a family, we discuss and pray about such injustices, as well as events that seem to keep happening in our country—Ferguson, Cleveland, Jackson, New York. We discuss privilege, God's view of righteousness and justice, love of neighbor, and caring for the least of these. Recently, I have been wrestling with how to be a good friend. How would I want people to care for me and my family and friends if they were being targeted? What if we hadn't been and still weren't being listened to? What if I had to tell my son how to avoid a dangerous situation when (not if) he is pulled over by the police for no apparent reason?

Where can we go from here

I have been wrestling with the Scriptures as well as the confession and catechism that my denomination—the Presbyterian Church in America—use to help understand and explain the Scriptures. I am seeking to apply these words to our present context.

In the *Westminster Larger Catechism*[1] we read the following:

Question 75: What is sanctification?

Answer: Sanctification is a work of God's grace, whereby they whom God has, before the foundation of the world, chosen to be holy, are in time, through the powerful operation of his Spirit applying the death and resurrection of Christ unto them, renewed in their whole man after the image of God; having the seeds of repentance unto life, and all other saving graces, put into their hearts, and those graces so stirred up, increased, and strengthened, as that they more and more die unto sin, and rise unto newness of life.

Question 78: Whence arises the imperfection of sanctification in believers?

Answer: The imperfection of sanctification in believers arises from the remnants of sin abiding in every part of them, and the perpetual lustings of the flesh against the spirit; whereby they are often foiled with temptations, and fall into many sins, are hindered in all their spiritual services, and their best works are imperfect and defiled in the sight of God.

---

1 *The Westminster Confession of Faith*, Center for Reformed Theology and Apologetics, 1996–2006. Accessed January 3, 2016. http://www.reformed.org/documents/wcf_with_proofs/index.html.

The *Westminster Confession of Faith* says:

> As every man is bound to make private confession of his sins to God, praying for the pardon thereof; upon which, and the forsaking of them, he shall find mercy; so he that scandelizeth his brother, or the Church of Christ, ought to be willing, by a private or public confession and sorrow for his sin, to declare his repentance to those that are offended; who are thereupon to be reconciled to him, and in love to receive him.[2]

As I consider these words, it seems to me that if an individual is bound to publicly repent, how much more should a church or Christian organization? In addition, if sanctification is an ongoing work in which the Spirit of God is bringing awareness of sin both individually and corporately to the mind of his people, then we should not be surprised when the church through that conviction both individually and corporately should be called to make public its awareness of this sin and seek to root it out of its people and its organization. It is an act of love and desire to see the visible witness of the church increased and enhanced as well as the desire to love our neighbors as ourselves that compels us to act.

I am praying for the church; I am praying for my nation; and I am praying for our world. How we deal with these issues will impact generations to come. Jesus has come to break down the barriers and walls of separation that alienated us from one another (Eph. 2:13–19). Jesus has come to set the captives free from all manner of bondage whether it is spiritual, emotional, physical, or mental (Is. 42:5–7; Is. 61:1, Luke 4:17–21). The Holy Spirit is doing his work of convicting us and the world of our sins (John 16:7–8). How will we respond? Will we listen and be good neighbors and friends?

---

2 *The Westminster Larger Catechism*, Center for Reformed Theology and Apologetics, 1996–2006. Accessed January 3, 2016. http://www.reformed.org/documents/wlc_w_proofs/index.html.

Chapter 10

Privileged to Serve

Rev. Mark Peach

Mark Peach is pastor of City Presbyterian Church, a downtown Salt Lake City, Utah, church that he began in 2012. He has degrees from the University of Nebraska (BA) and Covenant Theological Seminary (MDiv). He and his wife, Melissa, have three children.

As an undergraduate student at Weber State University in Utah, I bumped into Dionne, a Black Christian friend I had gotten to know through a campus ministry. I will never forget her words.

"Mark, you need to come back," she said. "You need to come back to taking Jesus's work in your life seriously."

I was caught off guard. How did she know I was struggling with a half-hearted devotion to Christ? At a time in my life when the quest to be accepted turned into an allegiance to many other things besides Jesus Christ, Dionne spoke into my life. Her prophetic voice changed everything as the Holy Spirit began to work to convince me of my great need for Jesus.

That conversation also shaped how I think about race relations. I look to it as an example of a time I would have missed the blessing of God if I had viewed someone with suspicion because of her skin color.

White privilege

In July 2015 when I saw the video of Sandra Bland, a Black woman, being forced from her car by a White police officer during a routine traffic stop, I was shaken. I was further disturbed to know that she died in a Texas jail cell three days after the arrest. I wondered who Sandra had influenced in her life. I wondered who she would never have the chance to influence.

In a system where White culture is at the center and all other cultures are pushed to the periphery, being a White male has allowed me to isolate myself from racial injustice that is a part of American culture and of many people's experience. As a White person, I am much more prone to embrace the false reality that I have what I have because I worked hard for it. I also am prone to believe that, in general, those in authority treat people equally across the board. This is simply not true.

I think part of the reason the Sandra Bland incident gripped me so powerfully was because I thought: What if that were my friend Dionne? As a White person, I have found that having real relationships with those who are ethnic minorities significantly changes the way I perceive events in the news. In that framework, I see how Bland, a twenty-eight-year-old Black woman, was unjustly victimized by a system of White dominance.

I am increasingly troubled by the oppression and violence against ethnic minorities in our country and around the world. However, like many, I am at a loss as to what to do. While so much racial injustice happens far from my life context, I cannot close my ears to the penetrating words of Martin Luther King Jr., "Injustice anywhere is a threat to justice everywhere."[1] I also hear the call from the Bible to do justice. In the words of the prophet Amos, *"Let justice roll down like waters"* (Amos 5:24).

For too long the voices of minorities in Christian churches have been minimized and silenced. This may not have occurred as overt, violent force, but rather as a deadly silence, with the unwillingness of White people to give up privilege and power. Or it may be seen as the unwillingness of White people to use their privilege for the common good.

---

1 Martin Luther King Jr. *Letter from a Birmingham Jail.* Accessed April 12, 2016. http://web.cn.edu/kwheeler/documents/Letter_Birmingham_Jail.pdf.

In the United States, White privilege has historically reinforced and perpetuated systemic racism. Many White people see no need for that to change. For many who are White, it is tempting to write off racial injustice, blame shift, or simply respond with, "It isn't my problem." Or we may congratulate ourselves on the few African Americans, or Asian Americans, or Hispanic Americans in our church and tell ourselves we are doing a great job toward racial solidarity.

In *The Next Evangelicalism: Freeing the Church from Western Cultural Captivity*, Soong-Chan Rah says Western culture has been dominated by White people throughout its history, and American Evangelicalism has been held captive by the culture rather than by that which is biblical. He also says, "While the demographics of Christianity are changing both globally and locally, the leadership of American Evangelicalism continues to be dominated by White Americans."[2]

What is the reason for this? Rah says the "White captivity of the church" in the United States has been influenced by our culture of individualism, consumerism, materialism, and racism. As we look to the future of the American church, there is a tendency to believe that those who have wealth, power, and privilege will be the ones who will serve and lead those who do not have wealth, power, and privilege. Power and privilege entitle certain groups to exercise an authority over those who are without power and privilege. Rah then asks:

> Is it possible we are so ensconced in the Western, White captivity of the church and its corresponding value of success and power that we are unable to see the dignity and worth of the marginalized and the very least of these?[3]

White privilege also has theological implications. The White cultural captivity of the American church has led to the perpetuation of a theology of celebration over and against a theology of suffering. It has led to an emphasis only on the blessings that come through a relationship with Jesus Christ at the

---

2 Soong-Chan Rah, *The Next Evangelicalism: Releasing the Church from Western Cultural Captivity* (Downers Grove, IL: InterVarsity Press, 2009), 18.

3 Ibid., 145.

expense of an emphasis on the reality of suffering or a clear understanding of the place of struggle in our relationship with Jesus Christ.

However, if we are to really understand the biblical idea of peace and unity, of shalom, we must hold to a theology of both celebration and suffering. But having privilege leads to a disconnect from those without privilege, from those who struggle particularly from oppression. This is problematic. Basically, to have privilege is to be one of the "haves" in a society of "haves" and "have-nots." As a person with privilege, having includes having social mobility and power that does not seek unity, peace, or shalom. Rah states:

> The power to choose mobility is real power. As individuals have an opportunity to move up, they often are moving away. As highly mobile individuals, therefore, there is limited opportunity to connect with those who are held in place by a system of survival and suffering.... Disconnection caused by mobility leads to a negative perception of those who dwell in a theology of suffering by those who dwell in a theology of celebration. The assumption of power and privilege means that those in our society who have the power of mobility assume a superior position over those who do not.[4]

To embrace a Christianity that leads to shalom, there must be an embrace of both a theology of celebration and a theology of suffering. Jesus Christ was not only resurrected from the dead, but in his incarnation, was willing to suffer and die on a cross. To serve God means to humbly step down, to give up social mobility for the sake of listening to, learning from, and being led by those without social mobility and power.

Listening to, learning from, and being led by

To move forward in peace and unity, we must have a robust understanding of the Gospel and the trajectory of the story the Bible tells. In *Aliens in the Promised Land*, the editor, Dr. Anthony Bradley states:

> The challenge with this book is to get readers to listen to someone outside their tribe.... I am afraid that if we do not, we will not see our blind spots, will repeat the same mistakes, will waste time and resources

---

4 Ibid., 149–151.

reinventing the wheel, and will not make much progress. In fact, in the discussion of race, for those of us born after the Civil Rights Movement, the discussion is focused, not so much on reconciling past oppression, pain, tensions, and grievances, as on moving forward—putting on display before a watching world how the Gospel creates the platform for racial solidarity (Gal. 3:28).[5]

Bradley acknowledges the progress made by those who have promoted racial reconciliation and those who have desired to see a new era of unity and peace after the Civil Rights Movement, but he says the dreams of those who have sought racial reconciliation have not been fulfilled. He offers a way forward that is rooted in the biblical concept that all people are created in the image of God. He says:

> But I am convinced that the church will be able to lead society on race only if it moves beyond racial reconciliation and pursues racial solidarity, which means embracing our common human dignity (Gen. 1:26–28), as a human family in ways that celebrate and respect differences between ethnic communities for the common good. If we look to the story that the Bible tells, we see a story unfold in which racial diversity and racial unity are valued by God because all are made in the image of God.[6]

How might change begin to happen, and how might we move forward in race relations? While it is right for White Christians to ask, "What is my role in seeking justice for all?" there is a temptation to believe there is an easy fix. History reveals there is no simple solution to an embedded racial problem. Instead, we must be willing to humble ourselves before those for whom injustice is an everyday reality.

To honor God is not disconnected from honoring the beauty of God's image found in a range of cultural expressions and in the whole spectrum of human races. This certainly includes the marginalized! We must seek a seat for all ethnicities at the table. To achieve this, White Christians must be willing to take a backseat by listening to, learning from, and being led by minority leaders.

---

5 Anthony B. Bradley, *Aliens in the Promised Land: Why Minority Leadership Is Overlooked in White Christian Churches and Institutions* (Phillipsburg, NJ: P&R Publishing, 2013), 151.

6 Ibid., 152.

Until this happens at a significant level, we will continue to have disunity in the very institution that God has called to be one under the Lord Jesus Christ.

A few years after meeting Dionne, I left Weber State and went to the University of Nebraska, where I had more friends who were ethnic minorities. At Nebraska, I struggled academically, with homesickness, and with depression. In the midst of feeling alone, like an outsider, I began to observe, from afar, how groups of people were isolated or simply interacting among their own ethnic group. I read African American authors in my sociology classes, including *The Souls of Black Folk* by W.E.B. Du Bois. This statement caught my attention:

> It is a peculiar sensation, this double-consciousness, this sense of always looking at one's self through the eyes of others, of measuring one's soul by the tape of a world that looks on in amused contempt and pity. One ever feels his twoness—an American, a Negro; two souls, two thoughts, two unreconciled strivings; two warring ideals in one dark body, whose dogged strength alone keeps it from being torn asunder.[7]

If my sense of being on the outside was painful, as a person with privilege, how unbearable the pain for a person who has been consistently marginalized in our society?

I began to gravitate toward ethnic minorities, especially African American students. While I read about double-consciousness, I also witnessed it. I began to see glimpses of the pain and anxiety of the African American experience brought down through history and exhibited as I heard about incidents of racial profiling that friends described to me. This raised the question that I continue to ask more than twenty years later: What is the role of White people in the quest for racial justice?

The more I have wrestled with this question, the more I have arrived at the conclusion that nothing less than seeking to submit to the leadership of minorities will do. So I began seeking to place myself under Black leaders. I sought to become a member of a church that was led by a Black pastor. As I looked to his leadership, I found myself being challenged to think about God and his world from a new perspective. Most of all, as I was pastored by a man who had gone through and was experiencing significant challenges that I have

---

7 W. E. B. Du Bois, *The Souls of Black Folk* (New York: New American Library, 1969 [1903]), 45.

never experienced as a White man, I saw real genuine faith in Christ expressed by him in a way that I had not seen faith expressed before.

For the first time, I was experiencing not simply a theology of celebration and resurrection, but a theology of suffering that led to an even greater experience of Jesus's resurrection. Through it all, I saw a man of tremendous faith in Jesus, a man who gave a reason for the hope that he had, and I knew that his hope was found in Christ alone. Perhaps it is the weariness that comes from experiencing racial injustice that God used in his life to lead him to find and experience such joy and hope in Christ. I wanted to experience that kind of joy and hope, too.

During graduate school I sought an internship where I could be mentored by someone who was a racial minority. As an intern, I grew in my love for God as I experienced unconditional love through my supervisor who was Black and had experienced discrimination to which he had every reason to be skeptical and cynical toward White people.

God has used Black leaders in my life in significant ways. I see God differently, not because of my White privilege, but because of the privilege of being led by someone who knows more of what Jesus knew about being forced to the margins. As Christians, we are called to give up our privilege, to lay down our rights, to give up seeking meaning and significance in our own power, and to follow after the Man of Sorrows, the one marginalized and crucified outside of Jerusalem.

As I pastor a church that is mostly White, I regularly ask: What is my role as a White person in seeking racial justice in America? Recently I have had opportunities to participate in decisions that affect the future of my city, such as serving on the advisory team for the city's downtown, twenty-five year master plan. I look around at such meetings, and in a city where 35 percent of the population is non-White, I see almost zero non-White people in positions to make decisions that affect the future. This must change! But how?

For one, I can speak up and say, "I think we need to have ethnic minorities at this table." For another, I could honestly consider whether God is asking me to give up any of my positions of influence—including as pastor—to an equally capable person of color so he or she can have a prominent voice.

What are other ways those with privilege and power could humbly take steps toward listening to, learning from, and being led by those who society has relegated to the margins? What might God be asking you to do?

Sins of Omission and Commission

Chapter 11

On Earth As It Is in Heaven

Samuel N. Graham

Samuel Graham is a native Memphian, CEO of Diversified Trust Company, and an elder at Independent Presbyterian Church in Memphis. He has degrees from the University of Tennessee (BS) and the University of Memphis (MBA). Samuel is a member of the Board of Trustees of Covenant Theological Seminary, Chair of the Board of Trustees of Memphis University School, a member of the President's Council for the University of Tennessee, and a founding board member for Teach for America's Memphis regional Advisory Board.

> *"You shall love the Lord your God with all your heart and with all your soul and with all your strength and with all your mind, and love your neighbor as yourself." And he [Jesus] said to him, "You have answered correctly; do this, and you will live." But he, desiring to justify himself, said to Jesus, "And who is my neighbor?"* (Luke 10:25–29)

A Memphis native son

It has been said there are no maverick molecules randomly floating around the universe. I agree. Similarly, we are not randomly situated in life. Where we are born and where we live are not coincidental circumstances, and they have a profound impact on how we see things and how we live. I was born, raised, and continue to live in Memphis. I love this city—warts and all. Wherever I travel globally, complete strangers smile when I tell them I am from Memphis. They usually ask, "Did you know Elvis?" Memphis is known for her incredibly innovative, world-renowned personalities and entrepreneurial leaders. Their number is significantly disproportionate to her size. She is also known for her moments of epic tragedy. Earlier this year, a high school classmate described so well Memphis's most notable tragedy by calling it "that seismic event that still shapes the city's sense of itself, the flash point by which any understanding of Memphis must be gauged: the MLK assassination."[1]

Memphis is where the mojo of the Mississippi Delta meets the rockabilly and country vibe of rural White east Arkansas, the Missouri bootheel, and west Tennessee. In addition, our city has more churches than gas stations. Memphis has a powerful, combustible mixture of elements prone to ignite either amazingly creative genius or fire and destruction. I've witnessed both.

My Gospel story has a lot to do with Memphis and her cultural challenges and opportunities. I could never explain who I am today without describing the place where God decided I would be born and raised. Two blocks from the maternity ward where I was born in 1962 is a park where the Confederate General Nathan Bedford Forrest is buried. Above his grave, a prominent life-sized statue of the wizard in the saddle looks southward at a street ironically called Union Avenue. Adjacent to Forrest Park you can walk across the street into Sun Studios where in 1954 Sam Phillips recorded the first rock-and-roll song, "That's All Right, Mama," by Elvis. And if you dispute the historicity of that claim, Phillips also recorded "Rocket 88" by Ike Turner, which others claim to be the first rock-and-roll record. Sun Records later recorded debut singles for Johnny Cash, Jerry Lee Lewis, Roy Orbison, and Carl Perkins—all twentieth-century icons.

One mile west on Union Avenue is the Peabody Hotel—the South's grand hotel, about which historian David Cohn wrote in 1935, "The Mississippi Delta begins in the lobby of The Peabody Hotel and ends on Catfish Row in Vicksburg."[2] Jefferson Davis once lived in The Peabody as he began his post-Confederacy life. When you walk out the front door of The Peabody on a Friday night, you are drawn by an irresistible smoky, savory smell coming from an alley that leads to a stairwell which takes you to a basement where you enter the iconic culinary world capital of BBQ, The Rendezvous. Over the last few years,

---

1 Hampton Sides, "City Portrait: Memphis, Tennessee," *Garden & Gun*, April/May, 2015, http://gardenandgun.com/article/city-portrait-memphis-tennessee.

2 David L. Cohn, *God Shakes Creation* (New York: Harper & Brothers, 1935), Chapter 2, first sentence.

the Prince of Wales and his brother, the Prime Minister of Japan, a sitting US President, along with thousands of others have made the pilgrimage to enjoy its world-famous dry ribs.

Another 150 yards west on Union Avenue, you can find WDIA radio station which was launched in the 1940s and soon became the first radio station in America programmed entirely for African Americans. WDIA pioneered the employment of Black radio personalities, who in turn hired Black musicians early in their careers and played their music to an audience that reached from the bootheel of Missouri through the Mississippi Delta all the way to the Gulf Coast. One block south is Beale Street, where numerous Mississippi Delta bluesmen became world famous—W.C. Handy, B.B. King, Muddy Waters, Furry Lewis, and Howlin' Wolf, just to mention a few.

One block south of Beale Street is Clayborn Temple, a church frequented by Dr. Martin Luther King Jr. during the 1950s and 60s. Up until the mid-1940s, this same church building had been the site of Second Presbyterian Church, an all-White congregation of prominent and influential community leaders. Less than a mile south of Clayborn Temple is the Lorraine Motel, where Dr. King often stayed while in Memphis because it was owned by African Americans whom he wanted to support. During the 1960s, you could also find other prominent African Americans on the Lorraine's guest list—Otis Redding, Wilson Pickett, Aretha Franklin (who was born in 1942 three miles from there), Mavis Staples, and Ray Charles. It was on the balcony outside Room 306 at The Lorraine where Dr. King was assassinated by an out-of-town, deranged zealot of a bigoted cause as the sun set on April 4, 1968.

In 1991, I met Rosa Parks at The Lorraine when it was being dedicated as the National Civil Rights Museum. I will never forget her effortless grace, quiet strength, genuine humility, and indisputable dignity. It was easy to understand how a lady of such qualities could inspire so many.

One might travel a great distance to link so many historically significant places. In my case, they are all within walking distance of the hospital where I was born. Jim Crow was still alive when I was born, though he was on his deathbed. I remember well the marks of those days: separate water fountains, Black people expected to sit at the back of the bus, and "No Coloreds Allowed" signs.

I especially remember the "I Am a Man" signs that were prevalent during the Memphis Sanitation Workers' strike. The fact Black men in their sixties, seventies, and eighties had to proclaim manhood—translation "stop calling me 'Boy'"—is hard to imagine today, but it was very real at the time. That was the world I had known as a child and had never questioned until 1968.

Memphis, 1968

Through the eyes of a six-year-old White boy, I witnessed the sanitation workers strike of 1968, which brought Dr. King to Memphis. I remember mostly because my primary household chore was to take the garbage out to the edge of our property where it (to me) magically disappeared once a week.

The strike began as a protest over the unsafe and uncivil working conditions of the City of Memphis sanitation workers. Earlier in the year, one of the workers had been crushed to death by a garbage truck compactor while picking up the trash on the street where one of my East Memphis friends resided. Dr. King had heard about this tragedy and was moved to come help these workers. All I understood as a young White boy was that our family's garbage was piling up because no one was making it disappear anymore.

My two older brothers told me a "black panther" was going to kidnap me one night when I emptied the garbage. I had seen these angry, militant Black men on TV in their black leather suits. I was terrified of them. One evening my devious brothers dressed up impersonating black panthers and popped up from behind the garbage cans to scare me. I can still recall the powerful feeling of terror I had that day. I didn't know who Dr. King was. I didn't really even know who LBJ was. My parents didn't talk much about politics or social issues. I only vaguely recall overhearing some adults saying Dr. King was nothing but a troublemaker because wherever he went, trouble soon followed.

Dr. King's first visit to Memphis that year had ended in violence on Beale Street during a march: broken windows, looting, police on their horses with billy clubs. The vandals were reported to be a group called The Invaders (the Memphis version of the Black Panthers). A few years ago due to an unusual set of circumstances, I had a one-on-one lunch with a former leader of The Invaders whom I had been so afraid of as a child. He was now in his seventies, well-mannered, and very engaging—not at all what I had imagined. I told him my childhood story, and he laughed and said, "Yeah, we were scared of you White people, too. And frankly we had much more reason to be scared of you than the other way around."

Dr. King's second visit to Memphis ended on that fateful day on April 4, 1968. I was visiting my aunt that day. Without any advance warning and with no reason given, I was told to stay on the floorboard of our 1966 Oldsmobile and not to peek out the window as we drove home with sirens blowing from every direction. The radio said Dr. King had been shot. No one was allowed outside by order of the mayor and the police. Even at age six, I knew something important had happened.

What I did not know at the time was that twenty or so hours before that infamous shot rang out in the Memphis sky, Dr. King had delivered his famously prophetic "I've Been to the Mountaintop" sermon at Mason Temple just south of downtown Memphis. It had lasted forty-three minutes, interspersed with loud thunder claps from an ominous, early spring thunderstorm just outside the church's stained glass windows. I have that sermon on my iPod. It is an oratorical masterpiece and a poignant personal testimony about a lifetime devotion to the Gospel, to nonviolence, to protesting the injustices of those who are among the least of these—and that night for the basic human rights of Memphis garbage men. As a lifelong Memphian, it is particularly moving and convicting. One particular part echoes in my ears, heart, and mind:

> It's all right to talk about streets flowing with milk and honey, but God has commanded us to be concerned about the slums down here, and his children who can't eat three square meals a day. It's all right to talk about the new Jerusalem, but one day, God's preacher must talk about the new New York, the new Atlanta, the new Philadelphia, the new Los Angeles, the new Memphis, Tennessee. This is what we have to do.[3]

The New Memphis. Dr. King's final moments were dedicated to the New Memphis. He literally gave his life for the men who picked up my garbage.

---

3 Martin Luther King Jr., *I've Been to the Mountaintop*, sermon delivered April 3, 1968, minute 21, second 14 to minute 22, second 2, Mason Temple (Church of God In Christ Headquarters), Memphis, Tennessee. Accessed December 14, 2015. http://www.americanrhetoric.com/speeches/mlkivebeentothemountaintop.htm.

I do not wish to deify Dr. King. He was a flawed man just like the rest of us. But no reasonable person can deny the fact that he lived a life of great sacrifice serving the poor and disenfranchised—to the point of losing his life for the rights of garbage men. How in good conscience can I be indifferent about injustice? Though I have been spared almost every form of hardship, as one who believes and loves the Gospel, am I not commanded to seek the shalom of Memphis?

Sins of omission

Have I been part of the Gospel solution or part of the problem? Indifference, passivity, and silence are major parts of the problem. I am guilty of them all. The sins of omission are perhaps the most pernicious and destructive of all.

In 1970, my siblings and I were enrolled in private, Christian schools. Bussing had begun in Memphis, and there was genuine fear in the White community about its impact on children who had been attending their neighborhood public school. Private, Christian schools were popping up all around to provide a safe landing place. Safe from bussing, safe from mandated integration, safe from the great unknown. From third grade forward, my classmates were all White. "White flight," as it was later called, drove the wedge of social and economic separation deeper and deeper, concomitant with an exacerbation of fear and xenophobia between races. My parents did what they considered to be best for us, and I am confident I would have done the same if I would have been a parent in those times. They were scary times for both White people and Black people. The old social order was changing to something new and unknown. The White church for the most part remained on the sidelines. Sadly, segregation had been defended and rationalized by many in the Southern Presbyterian church. To my African American friends today, this remains a stain on our Gospel testimony, which needs to be washed clean by public confession and repentance.

It is difficult to identify when I first began to be convicted about the social injustices experienced by the poor and economically disadvantaged in my hometown, much less anywhere else. At some point it occurred to me I did not have any friends who looked different than me. But that was normal, right?

Birds of a feather...? My grandfather once told me enduring love must be intentional. The same can be said of friendship. According to the 2010 national census, Memphis has the sixth highest percentage of Black citizens for cities of more than 100,000 people. Does Scripture permit me to handpick my neighbors whom I am commanded to love? Is it OK they all look like me, think like me, and live like me? Is that the example of Christ?

In 2007 our church's session passed a unanimous resolution in support of the PCA Pastoral Letter on The Gospel and Race, which had been adopted at the 2004 General Assembly held in Birmingham, Alabama. The PCA's pastoral letter was adopted in full by our session. However, nothing of consequence really changed after that. We passed a resolution. It made us feel better; perhaps soothed our conscience. But so what?

Public confession

In 2010 our session appointed an ad hoc committee to propose actionable steps to be more intentional and proactive about racial reconciliation. This committee's work culminated with a two-week sermon series preached by our senior minister entitled "The Gospel+IPC+Memphis/Gospel and Race." The second sermon took place on Mother's Day—May 13, 2012.[4] Our senior minister, Richie Sessions, acknowledged the noble reasons around the founding of our church in 1965—chief among them being the strict adherence to cardinal doctrines of historic Presbyterianism and the Reformed faith during a period of increasing liberalism and relativism in the Southern Presbyterian church. This part of the story is absolutely true, and we celebrate it. But then he also told a part of the story that had been kept largely silent for decades. Particularly in polite, Southern culture, there is an unspoken rule that some things are better left unsaid. One cardinal rule of a genteel society is never to air your dirty laundry in front of others. Never! However, the unspoken part of our church's story was already known by many—in both the Black community and in the White community. We as a church had never openly acknowledged it, much less addressed it. But on this day, the Holy Spirit grabbed our senior minister and would not let go as he pastored our congregation with a heavy dose of the truth

---

4 This sermon is still available on our church website, and I commend it to you. http://media.indepres.org/sermoncatalog/(May 13, 2012).

—the whole truth—both the honorable and not so honorable aspects of our history as a corporate body.

Some of my friends were less than enthusiastic about resurrecting this painful topic and called this sermon "The Mother's Day Massacre." I agree. It was a massacre. We massacred the deafening silence and faced the whispers about our past. It was uncomfortable, to say the least. But our session decided it had to be done; public confession and repentance of a public sin. At the end of the sermon, I was asked to address our congregation on behalf of our session. It had taken more than five years to go from passing a motion of repentance to facing our congregation with its truths and publicly acknowledging this sin. Our corporate silence toward racism had finally been broken. The following is the text I read to our congregation that day:

It is my privilege and responsibility on behalf of the Session to communicate the following four statements:

1. The congregation of Independent Presbyterian shall be informed of the PCA Pastoral Letter on the Gospel and Race. The Session's adoption and full endorsement of this PCA Pastoral Letter shall be:

   a. Made available on the IPC website
   b. Made available to the congregation through other means

2. Our Session and teaching elders shall ensure our congregation is given a faithful account of IPC's history concerning this subject.

3. There shall be set aside a season of prayer and study of the Scriptures regarding corporate and individual confession of sin—with specific acknowledgement of the sin of racism using the Scripture-based PCA Pastoral Paper as a guide.

   b. Proverbs 28:13—*He who conceals his sins does not prosper, but whoever confesses and renounces them finds mercy.*[5]
   c. Nehemiah 1:5–6—*I confess the sins we Israelites, including myself and my father's house, have committed against you.*

---

5 Scriptures from this message were taken from the New International Version of the Holy Bible. Copyright 2011 by Biblica, Inc. Used by permission. All rights reserved.

   d. 1 John 1:9–10—*If we confess our sins, he is faithful and just and will forgive us our sins and purify us from all unrighteousness. If we claim we have not sinned, we make him out to be a liar and his word has no place in our lives.*

  4. We begin this process with a reminder of the atoning work of Christ as the foundation for all we do. As we address the sin of racism, we do so NOT because it may be considered politically correct, nor out of any pressure from outward society. We do so because it is our desire to live out the whole counsel of God's word.

On behalf of the Session, this public address to you today specifically marks the beginning of a time of corporate confession and repentance by Independent Presbyterian Church (past and present) regarding the sin of racism.

  Just as we celebrate those aspects of our history at Independent Presbyterian Church of which we are proud, we must also acknowledge with sadness and renounce and repudiate those practices in our history that do not reflect biblical standards. We profess, acknowledge, and confess before God, before one another, and before the watching world, that tolerance of forced or institutional segregation based on race, and declarations of the inferiority of certain races, such as once were practiced and supported by our church and many other voices in the Presbyterian tradition, were wrong and cannot and will not be accepted within our church today or ever again. The Lord calls us to repent of the sin of prejudice; to turn from it and to treat all persons with justice, mercy, and love.

  As a church, we will strive to be more intentional and proactive with ministry opportunities for the congregation to serve the city of Memphis as redemptive, Gospel-driven agents seeking the peace and prosperity of ALL of Memphis.

   Jeremiah 29 says, *"Seek the peace and prosperity of the city to which I have carried you into exile. Pray to the LORD for it, because if it prospers, you too will prosper."*

It is known throughout our nation that the city of Memphis has a long and difficult history of racial strife. Our church was born perhaps at the height of the civil rights struggle. Three years later, the world witnessed the tragedy of the assassination of Dr. Martin Luther King Jr., which took place only nine miles from here.

Today IPC has a unique opportunity to demonstrate how God has transformed a church that once held firmly to segregation principles into a church whose heart is broken over the racism in this city and a church that devotes significant time and resources today to serving the inner city's poor and proactively seeks racial reconciliation through the Gospel.

Our congregation, the broader Evangelical church, Memphis, the South, and the world would benefit from hearing about IPC's testimony of God's grace and redemptive work in this area. Consistent with our historical adherence to Scripture, our church shall not allow anything to get in the way of the proclamation of the whole counsel of the Gospel. The doors of this church shall be open to ALL, regardless of race, ethnic differences, or social class.

Now let us go to our God who is the only source of redemptive power and who can help us press forward.

Holy Triune God, we have just heard your inerrant word preached boldly. We thank you for our Senior Minister, your servant Richie, who has been so powerfully anointed by your Spirit. Please protect our church and protect Richie and our other ministers from the arrows of the wicked. May this church always be known as a place where your Word is preached in Grace and Truth.

Father, for over forty-seven years, you have loved the people of this church with unfailing grace and mercy, and you have constantly called us, but we have not loved you above all nor have we consistently listened. You have asked us to love one another and to love our neighbors as ourselves, but all too often we have been wrapped up in our own concerns, and we have been selective about who we choose to call our neighbor. Father, please forgive us.

On this second Sunday of May, 2012, before You and before a watching world, we Lift High the Cross / the Love of Christ Proclaim and as unanimously resolved by the elders of this church we corporately confess the sin of racism both past and present; overt racism and the equally if not more sinister clandestine, covert racism of which I too am guilty.

Father we repent of our pride, we repent of our complacency and our indifference. As a church, we corporately repent of our prolonged silence and complicity regarding the wretched sin of racism that has tormented our city and our nation and divided too many for too long. Forgive our faults and failures, our deceit and disobedience, both of yesterday and also today.

We repent in spirit and in truth, confessing this sin and humbly receiving your forgiveness through Jesus Christ. We pray you will fill us with your Spirit and help us as a church to share the truth of the Gospel adhering both to orthodoxy and to orthopraxy through our deeds (both as individuals and also as a church) as we love ALL of our neighbors with open arms and open hearts. Father, use IPC as a Gospel Witness in this city. May this church be a shining example of your redemptive power as we spur one another on to love and good deeds acting according to the Gospel across all social, racial, and economic boundaries to the Glory of your name.

Thank you for the healing power of confession, repentance, forgiveness, and reconciliation. May we go forward this day in renewed commitment to the whole Gospel. May it be known throughout this city and beyond ... that the doors of this church are open to ALL—to sinners and to saints.

May we be a warm and welcoming congregation reflecting the love and mercy of Christ both inside and outside of this church. May our love be so amazing, so Christ-like, that it will permeate our souls, our lives ... our all. May our words, our attitudes, and our actions, serve only to glorify You as your light shines through this church to brighten this city, this nation, and this world.

In the name of Him ... who alone knows the hearts of all men. Our Savior and Redeemer, Jesus Christ. AMEN.

A healing opportunity

In the spring of 2014, our church was invited by Second Presbyterian Church to participate in a commemoration service for the fiftieth anniversary of the 1964 Kneel-Ins, when Black and White students peacefully kneeled at the entrance of the church in protest of its policy to not allow Black people to worship there. This is the same church my forefathers, whom I loved and still love, had left in the wake of that controversy. Years before, Second Presbyterian Church had made its public statement of repentance regarding its role in institutional racism. Now it was inviting those former kneel-in students and their families who had been barred from its sanctuary in 1964–65 to a service to acknowledge the wrong done to them. When I walked into the sanctuary that morning, I arrived at the same time as an elegant, older African American lady. We walked in together. She had friends and family waiting for her inside, and I saw some ministers from my church and gravitated toward them. The service was a series of speakers (alternating between Black and White) giving testimonies about what had happened and why we must acknowledge it, repent, reconcile, and move forward together. I discovered the lady with whom I had walked into the sanctuary was the sister of Joe Purdy—the first Black man who had been denied entry to the sanctuary in 1964. Carolyn Purdy McGhee told of her brother's gentleness, his godliness, his character, his lifelong quest to honor God, his dedication to the Christian faith. At the end of this service I had the opportunity to meet her. I told her I was the spiritual offspring of the men who had blocked her brother from the sanctuary fifty years before. They were good men in so many ways, but I could not explain or justify their actions toward her brother. I expressed remorse for what had happened. She was incredibly gracious toward me, and we prayed together. I prayed a prayer of repentance. She prayed a prayer of forgiveness. We both wept.

What happened during the kneel-in controversy of 1964–65 is well documented. Those who were in positions of authority at the time are either well advanced in age or no longer with us. I knew many of them. They were kind to me. My forefathers in the church were dedicated to historic orthodoxy. Social changes did not fit into that paradigm. They did not care for change. They preferred things the way they were. The mixing of the races was against how they had been raised and lived their lives. Did they have a significant blind spot concerning the Gospel and race? Yes, they did. Do we have significant blind spots today? Of course we do. I pray God's grace of sanctification will reveal them to us.

Weeks after the kneel-in commemoration service, Carolyn Purdy McGhee invited me to her home. We both knew there was unfinished business. I am not sure whether she was nervous about my visit to her house. I know I was. This was a step of faith by both of us. When I knocked on her front door, she welcomed me into her home and introduced me to her family. They were all hospitable and kind. She asked me some honest, tough questions. What does it mean to be a Bible-believing Christian in a city where White people and Black people still practice cultural segregation—especially in our churches? Doesn't Revelation 7 describe the church as the redeemed from every tribe and nation?

110

How could Christian men act the way they did to her brother in 1964? She held her Bible in her hand and asked, "Is this the same book they had? Did they really believe what it says?"

Her questions were not accusatory. Her tone was not angry, but rather one of great pain with a genuine desire to understand. I sought to explain what I had been told. Our church's forefathers had serious fears of godless Communism running rampant in the Civil Rights Movement. They would die at their posts before allowing the desecration of God's sanctuary by political demonstrators. There had been increasing theological liberalism in the Presbyterian Church, which was openly denying the cardinal doctrines of the faith. Carolyn listened carefully. She simply pointed to a photo of her brother, held her Bible in her hand and gently but firmly said, "My brother Joe was there simply to honor God in the face of godless racism and evil manmade segregation. He was a mild-mannered Christian young man seeking to peacefully enter a Christian church in his hometown."

Carolyn and I have become pen pals via email. We have visited each other's home. We plan to attend church at the other's church. With her permission, I am sharing the following which reflects how God has worked to heal old wounds:

Dear Sam:
Good morning my brother-in-Christ. The Holy Spirit is all over this restoration. My daughter and I were talking about Saturday's commemoration service. She said, "Mama when you were going up to the podium, it was as if you were going to the mountaintop" and when you, Sam, referenced that in your email... both of us were so very taken by it. Thanks for sharing truth, insight, and spiritual sensitivity as God works through the indwelling presence of the Holy Spirit. It's making crooked places straight. I shared the communication with other members of the family, it's bringing about a lot of healing!!! Please continue to pray for us.

Blessings upon you and your family, Carolyn, sister-in-Christ
Dear Carolyn:
I was a little White boy in Memphis when Dr. King told the nation about his dream in August, 1963, and I am so happy I became a small part of the fulfillment of that dream yesterday when you and I joined hands as a sister and brother in Christ and when you and I prayed

together that the crooked places would be made straight. May God be praised! We still have a long way to go to truly live out that dream in Memphis, but yesterday you and your family were a great witness of the Gospel to all of us by your kindness, love, and mercy as we all remembered a painful chapter in our mutual history. You showed us all what it really looks like to honor God.

Dear Sam:
You know before I left coming to your home yesterday, I asked the Holy Spirit to guide my tongue, to lead and guide my spirit, during our time together. And I truly believe that's what happened. His Spirit was working through all of us. It wasn't combative even though we touched upon some very pointed areas. One thing I know for sure, it was God ordained. Each one of us in our own unique way was in real need of our time together. There were racial breakthroughs. It was like Jericho... walls began to fall down... allowing each of us an opportunity to exhale... an opportunity to move forward and express ourselves with/in purity. That I believe is the beginning of a great relationship and my prayer is that we will trust God with the rest being mindful that "obedience" is our part. I am so thankful to God for Him to orchestrate this relationship. Keep me updated on how the national denomination ministers and elders are moving forward.

Blessing and favor to you, Carolyn Purdy McGhee

P.S. Communicating with you always reminds me that my brother Joe's work was not in vain.

Love them as neighbors

This past August, my twenty-five-year-old son asked an important question to Carolyn and her daughter whom we had invited over for lunch in our home. My son is a math teacher at a school where 87 percent of the students are defined as economically disadvantaged and qualify for free and reduced lunch.

His question was, "How do I convince my students I truly care about them and want what is best for their future? They see me as a White guy from a privileged background, and they are not sure they can trust me." Carolyn's answer was profound in its simplicity, "Get to know them and listen to their stories. Value them as individuals made in the image of God. Love them as neighbors as you love yourself."

All have sinned and fallen short of the glory of God. That applies to us in the church today as much as those who came before us. It is convenient and perhaps even self-righteous for me and my contemporaries to point out flaws of church leaders of decades past without first being repentant of our own sins. We must lead by example and acknowledge we still have significant flaws as leaders today, present company included. Though I want to believe otherwise, I have no confidence I would have acted any differently than my forefathers did during the 1960s.

While the unbelieving world is obsessed with political correctness, should not the church be even more obsessed with biblical correctness, which trumps any attempt by the world to out-love and out-care for the poor and disenfranchised? While the world is motivated by the virtues of humanism, should not the church be "all in" when it comes to Matthew 22:37–40, the first and second greatest commandments?

We cannot undo that which has been done. We can, however, be faithful today wherever we see injustice. The magnitude of today's racial strife might cause one to say it will always be this way. Yet I harken back to the wise advice Carolyn Purdy McGhee gave my son. It is possible to have genuine healing and reconciliation between Christians of different races and economic perspectives if we simply … Get to know each other and listen to each other's stories. Value each other as individuals made in the image of God. Love each other as neighbors just as we love ourselves. Pray with each other. If our churches stand up and preach boldly the whole counsel of God in regards to loving our neighbors and sacrificially serving each other regardless of race or economic status, nothing is impossible.

Memphis will be fully redeemed one day. So will your hometown. In the meantime, we must keep busy tending the vineyard that has been entrusted to us. We must be faithful to love one another just as God has loved us. Every nation, tribe, people, and language—abroad, yes, but most assuredly also 24/7 in our own hometowns—we must prepare the bride for the groom.

Thy kingdom come, thy will be done. On earth as it is in heaven.

Chapter 12

Silence Far Too Long

Rev. Jonathan A. Price

Jonathan Price is the pastor of Covenant Community Presbyterian Church in Wexford, Pennsylvania, a suburb of Pittsburgh. He has degrees from Geneva College (BS) and Covenant Theological Seminary (MDiv). Jonathan previously ministered to children and youth in various ministries and churches. He and his wife, Meagan, have three children.

When I recently commented on a Facebook thread about the state of race relations in the United States, I noticed that fellow White people were quick to denounce racism but not to acknowledge how they've benefited from it or admit that the divide is still deep between Whites and Blacks, even in the church. There was direct opposition to the idea that anyone should have to repent or seek reconciliation for something for which he was not personally culpable. It made me wonder whether repentance and reconciliation were needed in this area, or whether we just needed to get over it and move on.

The Apostle Paul in Philippians 3 says:

> *Though I myself have reason for confidence in the flesh also. If anyone else thinks he has reason for confidence in the flesh, I have more: circumcised on the eighth day, of the people of Israel, of the tribe of Benjamin, a Hebrew of Hebrews; as to the law, a Pharisee, as to zeal, a persecutor of the church; as to righteousness under the law, blameless.* (Phil. 3:4–6)

When it comes to race relations, as a White middle-class male, I have all the confidence of Paul. I was raised in a family where I grew up hearing stories of my dad's childhood in the 1950s and his best friend who was an African American. Our family had African American friends who we considered extended family. We were members of a denomination that was anti-slavery even before its emigrants came to the United States and continued to denounce slavery in this country. Many of the churches were even stops on the Underground Railroad. Geneva College, where I completed my undergraduate degree, was founded in 1848 to educate ministers, freed slaves, and women. I had three African American roommates in college on a predominately White campus. As a student, I helped form an organization called One In Christ that worked toward racial reconciliation on campus. The church I currently pastor is, by God's grace, showing signs of becoming a multiethnic church.

In terms of race relations, I, like Paul, can say that I have confidence I am not a racist or bigot and that I have nothing to repent of. Yet when I search my heart, I know there is still much to repent of.

Not the way it is supposed to be

As one who believes in total depravity, I am not surprised there is still a problem with racism. The problem has played out in Ferguson, Baltimore, and various other communities around the United States. The reality is that White Americans enjoy privileges that many of us do not even recognize. After the Great Depression, when many people, both White and Black, were left destitute, government assistance was only available to a small number of Blacks. Most Whites qualified for the assistance and were able to get out of poverty, while many Blacks were left behind. We live within a generation of practices such as Jim Crow segregation, and redlining (a northern practice of keeping minorities, especially Blacks, out of certain neighborhoods). These practices and policies helped create a racialized society where Whites benefit beyond what we can see.

White Americans don't have the same anxieties that minorities, particularly Black people have. As a White male, I've never worried about being treated suspiciously by a police officer. When I was a sophomore in college, I'll never forget coming back from summer break and hearing my Black roommate recount the night that he was roughed up by police, pulled over, and dragged out of his car because "he fit the profile" of a suspect they were looking for. He was shaken by the experience, and I was shaken because I was given a glimpse of a world I didn't believe existed. I'll never know what it's like to be followed around a department store because of my skin color. I'll never know what it's like to be passed over for a job because my name sounds ethnic. Yet many people experience these things regularly. That's not the way it's supposed to be.

As a Christian, I have received the greatest good: the gift of Christ. I have *"redemption through his blood, the forgiveness of our trespasses, according to the riches of his grace, which he lavished upon us"* (Eph. 1:7). In light of that reality, it is time to take seriously the instruction of the Apostle Paul that Jesus himself has broken down the dividing wall of hostility and made us one (Eph. 2:14–16). As Paul says, Jesus reconciles us *"both to God in one body through the cross, thereby killing the hostility"* (Eph. 2:16). Yes, the dividing wall was between Jew and Gentile specifically, but it doesn't stop there. There were, and continue to be, dividing walls.

But Jesus broke down the dividing wall of hostility between all peoples. Jesus is the King and Lord of all peoples, and he calls all his people to be one. This oneness isn't merely or only spiritual. Jesus prays that his people will be one. Yes spiritually, but also physically, so that the world might see and know his love. Spiritual oneness can only be seen by the world if it manifests itself physically. That's what Jesus prays in John 17.

If the Gospel has won our affections and bound our soul fast, then the mystery of the Gospel (which Paul says in Eph. 3:6 is that Gentiles—all people —are fellow heirs made one in Christ—Gal. 3:28) must be displayed to the glory of Christ Jesus. Because this is true, we can't remain silent. We can't remain in our "safe" church bubbles where everyone looks, thinks, and acts the same. We cannot continue to establish churches with those educated like we are and in the same socioeconomic strata. In response to this kind of homogenous thinking, Dr. Edmund Clowney gives a candid challenge:

> American Evangelicals have a tradition of individualism that sees the church as a voluntary club for the converted. Until we have a deep biblical sense of the corporate identity of the new people of God, we will not be able to present the Gospel of peace on the front lines of our culture wars. The true drawing power of the church transcends the cultural enclaves of contemporary society to dissolve the hatreds of a fallen world in the love of Christ.[1]

---

1 Edward Clowney, *The Church: Contours of Christian Theology* (Downers Grove: InterVarsity Press, 1995), 163–164.

Doing this challenge will not be easy. It will take overcoming our presuppositions of what we look for in a "good church" (good programs for me and my kids, music I like, etc.) and will call us to sacrifice what we're comfortable with for the sake of the Gospel, for the sake of Christ's church.

Breaking the silence

I can easily be left wondering what I'm supposed to do. I'm not always certain what I must confess. I'm not confident my confession will be heard or needed.

After all, I wasn't born until 1975! So how could the issues surrounding the Civil Rights Movement be my fault? How could it make any sense for me to confess as sin the past and current racially divided nature of the church, or for that matter the current state of race relations in our country? Are any of these specifically my fault? Am I responsible?

To the best of my knowledge, specifically, no. However, I have personally benefited from this racially broken situation. I often have not seen or considered it and have rarely challenged it. These are sins of omission. And in another sense, these are sins of mine because I'm connected to others who have gone before me. I have been made one in Christ with my brothers and sisters, so covenantally, I have responsibility.

As author Steve Garber once said, "At our best and worst, we are sons of Adam and daughters of Eve."[2] At my best, I am the son of my ancestors who fought for racial equality and freedom. At my worst, I am the son of my ancestors who were racists and used their positions for their own advancement while not seeking justice for those who were left behind. You see, God providentially created me a White male, gave me to a White middle-class family in the United States. So, while I had nothing to do with God's providential will for who I am, that doesn't mean that God doesn't call me to use my position for his glory and the good of others.

If I'm honest, there is a part of my heart that is racist, or at the very least bigoted. It's a part of my sinful nature. The fact that there's still a problem in our nation should be a wake-up call for us. I believe we deceive ourselves if we say there is no problem.

2 Richard Doster, "How Do We Love a Broken World?: Our Conversation with Steven Garber," *By Faith*, September 23, 2014, 34.

It is time for those of us in the majority culture (particularly White males) to break the silence. It's time for us as the church to break the silence. It's time for us publicly, personally, and corporately to repent of our forefathers' sins.

In 2002, my denomination, the Presbyterian Church in America, passed an overture confessing the sins of racism. While it was a needed step in the right direction, it wasn't enough. Years later, in the midst of racial unrest in our country, it reads a bit like a celebrity apology, "If I've offended anyone, I'm sorry." It lacked specificity. Scripture repeatedly calls God's people to specifically repent, not just generally.

We need to specifically repent as churches and as a denominations. This was outlined by my denomination in the 2004 Pastoral Letter on Racism that was adopted by our national governing body, the General Assembly. This well-done document on how to move forward as Christians and as a denomination was sent to the floor of our General Assembly where it was adopted, never to be heard of again. We were content with the silence. Twelve years later, we still see the same issues in our culture and even in our churches; little has changed. Will we continue to remain silent, just hoping the issues of racial divide go away?

At our 2015 annual General Assembly meeting, the tone of confession was very different. The Spirit clearly was at work as a few men initiated a discussion of the need for corporate repentance regarding the lack of concern during the Civil Rights Era on the part of founding churches and leaders in our denomination. As I listened to numerous men publicly confess and repent, I felt compelled to formally document my support for the resolution. As men prayed their hearts, I started typing, incorporating the words of those praying.

I hoped a few of my friends would stand with me, but I had no idea whether they would. I can say that it honestly didn't matter whether I stood alone. If I was the only one, then I was the only one. I knew that the Lord had been preparing me to speak, even in my weakness. He was calling me to not remain silent.

When I walked to the front table to formally file my document in the record, I was going on my own. But as I filled out the paperwork, a brother placed his hand on my shoulder and said, "Thank you for doing this." I turned around and saw a line of men that stretched to the back of the assembly hall, waiting to sign the document. I was deeply moved. We were not remaining silent.

Moved to action

Whether you agree with my understanding of the situation or not, hopefully you are asking yourself, "Now What?!?" While I don't have all the answers, the following are ways that I have personally experienced change, and how others much more qualified than myself have outlined a move to action.

We must teach and preach how the Gospel is for all people from every tribe, tongue, and nation. In our North American context, this means that it's not just the church universal where we should see this diversity, but in our local churches as well. This will require us laying down our desires and having a new vision—God's vision—for his church that reflects the glories of God's multiethnic people.

We need to individually and corporately seek relationships across cultural and ethnic boundaries, believing that the dividing wall of hostility has been broken down. It's time to seek forgiveness, even for sin we didn't personally perpetrate, but that is part of our heritage and inheritance and privilege.

We must pray for God to change our hearts, to change our churches, to give us wisdom and discernment, and to give us hope and courage.

We must not remain silent when our brothers and sisters do or say things that compromise the integrity of the Gospel in reflecting the truly diverse kingdom of God. That is not only true in personal relationships, but at the church, presbytery, denominational, and institutional levels as well. For example, we must not remain silent when a partnering agency names its chair of systematic theology after Morton H. Smith, a man who has published and defended racist beliefs from Scripture. We cannot stand by and allow actions like this to alienate our brothers and sisters in Christ.

We need to pray for and seek to raise up men and women from diverse backgrounds into the leadership roles of the local church. Our churches should seek to call people to ministry from different ethnic backgrounds. We must reconsider how we search for qualified candidates, and how we might engage in that process so that those who are not from our cultural position are not disadvantaged.

I pray that by God's grace the church of God might be known for being faithful to the Scriptures and obedient to the Great Commission of Jesus Christ. I pray we would be a church for all peoples. May the church of Jesus Christ be on earth as it is in heaven!

Chapter 13

All in the Family

Rev. Walter Henegar

Walter Henegar serves as Senior Pastor at Atlanta Westside Presbyterian Church in Atlanta, Georgia. He has degrees from Northwestern University (BA) and Westminster Theological Seminary (MDiv). Walter and his wife, Anne, have two teenage daughters.

I am the White pastor of an in-town Presbyterian church. Our parish, the West Side, straddles the jagged demographic seam between Atlanta's affluent, majority-White north side and its impoverished, majority-Black south side. While half of the faces I see on the street or in the grocery store are Black, 90 percent (at least) of the faces I preach to on Sundays are White. This lamentable contrast has set me on an ongoing quest to unleash the disruptive truths of Scripture on the hearts and minds of my congregation—and myself. I believe God has specially positioned me to help fellow White Christians understand the pervasiveness of this problem, along with the powerful resources of the Gospel to combat it.

To start, we must look at the relationship between Black and White people in America, and its particular expression in the South. Even though Hispanics recently passed Blacks as the largest US minority, the history of our country for the last four hundred years has been most indelibly shaped by the broken economic, social, and psychological relationship between majority-culture White people and minority-culture Black people. Complex emotional issues like race are also inevitably shaped by the personal histories we bring to them, so let me invite you to reflect on your own racial story by telling mine.

White guilt

I grew up middle-class in Chattanooga, Tennessee. A friend of mine once asked my father what race relations were like growing up in the South in the 1940s and '50s, and he said with sadness, "Well, we were racist." I can now look back on my own childhood in the '70s and '80s and say the same thing: To my shame, I was racist. Like many White Southerners, my parents hired a Black woman named Clara Mae to clean our house once a week. We loved Clara Mae like a grandmother, but our lives rarely intersected outside of my home. Half of my education was spent in public school, where I was a minority. My closest friends were Black, White, and Cambodian; my first crush was a Vietnamese girl named Hien. The other half of my education was spent in private school, where I was in the White majority. Our church was 99 percent White.

We knew not to tell "Black jokes" in public, but at home we did and we would imitate the accents of our Black friends. I remember a great-aunt of mine telling me, "They love their fried chicken," and "The blacker they are, the harder they work." Years later, my father-in-law observed that in the South, White people didn't care how close Black people got, as long as they didn't get too successful; and in the North White people didn't care how successful Black people got, as long as they didn't get too close. We were either unequal but together, or equal but separate.

After high school, I lived in Chicago, Nashville, and Philadelphia, where exposure to all kinds of people fed an increasing spiritual hunger to heal the racial wounds of my past. One big influence was my college roommate from Mississippi, who became an expert in Civil Rights Era American history and now teaches at Emory University. A bigger influence was the Bible. Its glorious portrait of God's church stood at odds with my own experience in majority-White churches.

Sometime after moving to Atlanta, I began to better understand what was going on inside me. I had a powerfully warped sense of identity known as White guilt. White guilt fueled a subtle strain of self-hatred in me, while simultaneously reinforcing a desire to justify myself and a superior sense of responsibility to do penance for the sins of my race.

By the time I set out to plant a church in 2007, all of the people in our core group, most of whom were White, shared my longing to become a multiethnic, socioeconomically diverse church. We wanted it and still want it, mainly for theological reasons, but for me at least, White guilt also played a big role. Sometimes I wish I were Black instead of a boring White guy. In many other ways, though, I'm the poster boy for Stuff White People Like. I prefer Wes Anderson's movies over Tyler Perry's, folk music over hip hop, dry humor over jokiness.

Yet I am genuinely drawn to some elements of Black church culture, especially its capacity for emotional expressiveness that seems so much freer than my own. In terms of worship music, I'd be happy if 75 percent of our songs were Black praise and worship, with clapping and swaying and dancing in the aisles. I love to hear Amen! when I preach.

Then there are also some things I associate with Black culture that drive me crazy. All this makes me a tangle of contradictions, longings, and fears.

A family divided

These personal and historical reflections led me to an unlikely text to wrangle with the subject of race, the Old Testament book of Second Chronicles. Here's what you need to know to understand it: After its first three kings, the Hebrew kingdom had divided. The three tribes of Judah, Benjamin, and Simeon lived in the South, which was known as Judah, and the nine other tribes in the North were known as Israel. For centuries, both kingdoms warred with other surrounding nations and sometimes with each other. Chapter 28 describes one of those wars in the eighth century BC, during the reign of Ahaz king of Judah. Ahaz had led Judah into some of the worst idolatry in its history, even sacrificing his own sons to pagan gods. So God disciplined Judah by letting both Syria and Israel defeat them in battle. Here's what happened in the wake of that battle:

> *The men of Israel took captive 200,000 of their relatives, women, sons, and daughters. They also took much spoil from them and brought the spoil to Samaria. But a prophet of the LORD was there, whose name was Oded, and he went out to meet the army that came to Samaria and said to them, "Behold, because the LORD, the God of your fathers, was angry with Judah, he gave them into your hand, but you have killed them in a rage that has reached up to heaven. And now you intend to subjugate the people of Judah and Jerusalem, male and female, as your slaves. Have you not sins of your own against the LORD your God? Now hear me, and send back the captives from your*

relatives whom you have taken, for the fierce wrath of the LORD is upon you. Certain chiefs also of the men of Ephraim, Azariah the son of Johanan, Berechiah the son of Meshillemoth, Jehizkiah the son of Shallum, and Amasa the son of Hadlai, stood up against those who were coming from the war and said to them, "You shall not bring the captives in here, for you propose to bring upon us guilt against the LORD in addition to our present sins and guilt. For our guilt is already great, and there is fierce wrath against Israel." So the armed men left the captives and the spoil before the princes and all the assembly. And the men who have been mentioned by name rose and took the captives, and with the spoil they clothed all who were naked among them. They clothed them, gave them sandals, provided them with food and drink, and anointed them, and carrying all the feeble among them on donkeys, they brought them to their kinsfolk at Jericho, the city of palm trees. Then they returned to Samaria. (2 Chron. 28:8–15)

In her excellent book, *United: Captured by God's Vision for Diversity*, Trillia Newbell interviews a Black, Reformed pastor named Thabiti Anyabwile. He argues that not only does the Bible never talk about race, but the whole concept is a "social and psychological construction" that didn't exist until about 350 years ago, when European scholars tried to categorize humanity into various groups. Anyabwile says we're all the same biological race, so a more accurate term is "ethnicity." Ethnicities are "large kinship and language groups," which are bendable and permeable, changing over time through immigration and intermarriage. So he says whenever we have to select our race on a form, we should all check "Other."[1]

In the classic hymn, "And Can it Be," one verse says Jesus "bled for Adam's helpless race." In other words, there are thousands of ethnicities, but we're all Adam's helpless race, equally glorious in the image of God and equally stained by the rebellion of sin.

The Jews in Second Chronicles 28 may have had different accents, but they all looked the same and spoke the same language. Verse 8 calls them "relatives." What created the animosity and division between them was their history. Two hundred years before, Solomon's son Rehoboam had ruled so oppressively that Jeroboam and the Northern tribes rebelled, quickly synthesizing and corrupting Judaism with pagan religions. That made them religious half-breeds, while their

---

1 Trillia Newbell, *United: Captured by God's Vision for Diversity* (Chicago: Moody, 2014), 146.

relatives in Judah were religiously pure, worshipping at God's one and only temple in Jerusalem.

Racialization

The same kind of dynamics shaped America. Historical events and patterns, combined with skin color, bodily features, language, and culture have influenced the value we assign to people. Sociologists call it racialization. In their eye-opening book, *Divided by Faith*, Michael Emerson and Christian Smith explain, "A racialized society is a society wherein race matters profoundly for differences in life experiences, life opportunities, and social relationships."[2] This is why, on one hand, there's no such thing as "Black culture," because there are many Black cultures in this country. On the other hand, because of racialization, there is a common "Black experience" that every person with Black physical features feels, whether in the 'hood or the White House.

And from what I've learned, it's not just racialized attitudes from non-Black people, but from other Black people as well. Some Black members of our church have been called "bougie" for being bourgeoisie, or financially successful. Or maybe you've heard the old St. Lunatics song, "Boughetto." "Boughetto" lampoons Black people who act "bougie" but are really "ghetto." If you haven't heard either of those terms, you've probably heard "Oreo": Black on the outside, but White on the inside. These offensive terms continue to plague and pigeonhole our Black brothers and sisters today.

A related concept is "code switching," a practice dating from the American slave era when Black people used different vocabularies and speech patterns around White people. Today, Black people who are culturally fluent in majority-White culture often feel the pressure to do the opposite. The biracial comedians Key & Peele have a remarkable sketch where they play strangers talking on their phones next to each other at a crosswalk. Both speak like swaggering gangsters until they separate, when we realize they were both simply intimidated by the other.

If you related to my story of White guilt, try to imagine what it's like to live with an identity warped by racialization in a majority-White society. How do

---

2 Michael O. Emerson and Christian Smith, *Divided By Faith: Evangelical Religion and the Problem of Race in America* (New York: Oxford, 2000), 7.

you think it would feel? Disorienting? Schizophrenic? Most Black people—and many people of other ethnicities—would just call it "everyday life." Recently one of our Black members who attended a wedding for a White couple was asked by three different guests if he was part of the wait staff. If you're non-White, you learn to navigate between minority and majority cultures from childhood. But most White people never have to learn that. One of our White members told me, "Whenever I don't perceive race as an issue, that carefree state in itself reveals my privileged position."

Sins of our own

God disciplined Judah for its particular sins, but in Second Chronicles 28:9 the prophet Oded made it clear that Israel, too, had sins of its own. They added to their existing guilt with violence, greed, and vengefulness by trying to enslave their relatives—and God hated it. He hated these sins just as much when White Europeans and Americans enslaved their African relatives. And he hates these sins today when some Black people do violence to their Black and White relatives. The rampant crime and family breakdown in poor, majority-Black communities is well-known. But ultimately, it's not culture that has divided us. Sin has divided us, and it's sin in all of us that keeps us separate.

In the June 2014 issue of *The Atlantic*, a Black writer named Ta-Nehisi Coates wrote an article called "The Case for Reparations."[3] Coates, who has since won a Pulitzer Prize, chronicled in chilling detail the cruel history of slavery, social discrimination, and what he calls "economic piracy" by Whites against Blacks from 1619 to the present day. It's a depressing, heartbreaking read, but I encourage White Christians especially to read it. We don't have to agree with all of his analysis or prescriptions, but we cannot argue with the facts.

Coates admits that things have gotten better, but our nation is far from healed. Jim Crow laws, school segregation, redlining, anti-miscegenation laws, and Black voting rights were only legally addressed within the lifetime of my parents, and there are still abuses. Even in the last four years, both Bank of America and Wells Fargo settled anti-discrimination lawsuits totaling $530 million for predatory lending practices that some of their own lending officers called "ghetto loans." While Wall Street got bailed out or jumped out in golden

---

3 Ta-Nehisi Coates, "The Case for Reparations," *The Atlantic*, June 2014.

parachutes, Black neighborhoods more than any others crumbled. In a majority-Black neighborhood in our own parish, 30 percent of homes are still vacant.

A Black pastor in New York named Bryan Loritts writes in *Letters to a Birmingham Jail* about a conversation he had with a friend on the subway one day. Every time the train stopped and the doors opened, his friend would close his eyes until everyone was on and it started moving again. When Loritts asked why, his friend said his mother raised him to give up his seat if women were standing, so he figured if he just closed his eyes he wouldn't have to face the choice.[4] Brothers and sisters, we cannot close our eyes to the ongoing problems of race, even if it makes our heads spin! Jesus insists that if we keep our eyes open, his Gospel can bring radical, healing change.

Before we mine those resources, though, we must confront two common errors that tend to undermine our confidence in the Bible's teaching about ethnicity.

Isn't the Bible OK with slavery?

No. The one kind of slavery that we're all most familiar with—kidnapping people and shipping them to other countries—is explicitly condemned in Exodus 21. It was called "man stealing" and was punishable by death.

All other forms of slavery depicted in the Bible were either economic or political, never based on ethnicity. You could become enslaved if your nation was conquered, like Israel was in the time of Daniel, or to pay a debt, or even voluntarily if you had no way to support yourself. Slaves were not considered sub-human but had certain biblical rights; some could own property and even become wealthy and have servants of their own. The Bible never approves of any of these arrangements, but (as with polygamy, war, and other fallen cultural practices) it regulated slavery until the full force of Christ's redemption could eradicate it. And when God rescued Israel from slavery in Egypt, his Law constantly beat the drum of justice for the poor and oppressed by reminding them that they themselves had been slaves!

Ta-Nehisi Coates is a self-described atheist, but he opens that *Atlantic* article with a quote from Deuteronomy 15, which states that Hebrew slaves

---

4 Bryan Loritts, "Why We Can't Wait for Multiethnic Churches." In *Letters to a Birmingham Jail: A Response to the Words and Dreams of Dr. Martin Luther King, Jr.*, ed. Bryan Loritts (Chicago: Moody, 2014), 16.

must not only be released after six years, but "furnished liberally" with everything they need to start a life on their own, which is exactly what the Israelites did with their captives in Second Chronicles 28, and exactly what American slaves never got after the Emancipation Proclamation.[5] What did they get instead? More subtle and devious forms of economic and social oppression. And it was all grossly unbiblical.

What about the "Curse of Ham"?

As recently as 2002, I heard an educated, White Christian raise this question, and I'm sure there are others who still hold it today. It's an interpretation of Genesis 9, where Noah's son Ham dishonored his father, who then cursed his son's descendants, the people of Canaan. For centuries, some Christians have wickedly argued that since Ham's son Cush was associated with Ethiopia, Black people must bear that curse. It is a misinterpretation and an abomination that still warps the way all races perceive Blackness today, and an easy text to refute it is in Numbers 12. There Aaron and Miriam wrongly confront Moses for marrying a Cushite, or Ethiopian, woman. God responds by punishing Miriam, making her skin "leprous and white as snow." Using the same hermeneutic, we could just as easily argue that White people bear the "Curse of Miriam" for demeaning Blackness!

After centuries of European art depicting biblical characters as Caucasian, it's amazing how easy it is to forget that everyone in the Bible was either olive-skinned, brown, or black. The only reason there are any White Christians is because people with darker skin than us obeyed Jesus and took the Gospel to all nations, including to our own ancestors.

If this is sounding like a pity party for poor Black people or a smack-down on wicked White people, remember: We don't just have sins of our own. By God's grace, we all have glories of our own. The fact that many Black people have achieved extraordinary gains, and the fact that many White people have boldly fought the injustices against them, has nothing to do with any intrinsic ethnic nobility on either side. No. It is evidence of the grace of God working through redeemed human beings to restore their equal dignity in the image of God.

---

5 Ta-Nehisi Coates, "The Case for Reparations," *The Atlantic*, June 2014.

So the Bible does not approve of slavery, but it happened in this country. Nor does the Bible approve of discrimination, but it happens in this country. The effects of both sins are still with us today. If you're White like me, chances are good that your present education, wealth, and success have been accumulated in part by generations of advantages unjustly gained on the backs of Black labor. And former White slave owners can't just clothe and feed former slaves and carry them back to Africa. They're all dead; the economic debt is in the trillions; and the social, psychological, and spiritual debt is incalculable. A friend of mine says being Black in America is like joining a game of Monopoly after everyone else has been around the board a few times: No matter how good you are, it's almost impossible to catch up. One of the Black men quoted in Coates's article, Clyde Ross, fought against racist housing practices in late-60s Chicago. He said, "The reason Black people are so far behind now is not because of now. It's because of then."[6]

The hidden wound

That's not to say White people aren't paying a price. A White author named Wendell Berry wrote a book called *The Hidden Wound*, reflecting on his own childhood growing up on a segregated Kentucky farm. He says:

> If the White man has inflicted the wound of racism upon Black men, the cost has been that he would receive the mirror image of that wound into himself. The more deeply he has hidden it within himself, the more painful it has grown.... It is a profound disorder, as great a damage in his mind as it is in his society.[7]

White guilt isn't a strong enough term for that wound, is it? And if you don't believe it's real, can you at least acknowledge that our whole society, which includes all ethnicities, is paying a huge price for its effects? We have the highest rates of incarceration in the Western world, rampant gun violence, infant mortality, inner-city turmoil, and the collapse of the two-parent family. Blackness didn't create those problems; all shades of human sin did. But slavery and subsequent racialization were the meat and potatoes in the stew.

---

6 Ibid.

7 Wendell Berry, *The Hidden Wound* (San Francisco: North Point, 1989), 4.

And that's not even the worst part. The worst part is that the one group of people with the most powerful resources for healing these wounds, the Christian church, has often been one of the worst offenders. The Body of Christ has been dismembered! Have you ever wondered why the term, "Black Presbyterian Church" sounds like an oxymoron, even though there are some? It's because Presbyterianism has a horrible record on racism. As recently as the mid-80s, deacons at a PCA church in Atlanta turned some Black people away at the door of the church. And sadly, that's not an isolated example.

Gospel resources

What resources do we have to turn that tide? If all we had were Second Chronicles 28, here's what would have to happen: White people, terrified by the threat of the fierce wrath of God, would have to repay and restock every former slave and their descendants for four centuries of piracy, oppression, and racialization. And if that makes you despair, it should, because it's impossible.

But thanks be to God, this is not all we have! We must read the Old Testament, but we can never stop there. Because all thirty-nine books are pregnant with longing for a Rescuer, and his name is Jesus. David Powlison says, "Jesus is not just the pointer... he is the one to whom all pointers point."[8] Jesus gave his life on the cross to satisfy the fierce wrath of God for all these sins and countless others, so that those who believe it can embody his just character in his world.

Jesus came as a Jew to the Jews, but one of the most striking features of his ministry and the church he founded was his insistence that reconciliation between God and people both requires and empowers reconciliation between people. Second Corinthians 5:18 says God *"through Christ reconciled us to himself, and gave us [all Christians of every ethnicity] the ministry of reconciliation."* And no matter how many centuries of Christians have forgotten it, it's still true. The Holy Spirit of God will not rest until people of every tribe, language, nation, and ethnicity are fully united in Christ Jesus.

That's the picture of God's consummated kingdom in Revelation 5 and 7. And if that's what heaven will look like, don't you want to experience as much of

---

8 David Powlison, "'I'll Never Get Over It: Help for the Aggrieved," *Journal of Biblical Counseling* 28:1 (2014), 13.

it as possible now? It's not part of a liberal agenda to conform the church to a secular vision of multiculturalism; it's not even just Martin Luther King Jr.'s dream of the Beloved Community; it's God's agenda to re-form the church to its glorious beauty as the spotless bride of Christ. And he's already doing it. Even non-Christian scholars will admit that the Civil Rights Movement could not have succeeded without unleashing the prophetic force of the Christian Scriptures on majority-White America.

Changes afoot

White Reformed Christians have been some of the slowest to change, but we're beginning to. When my denomination, the Presbyterian Church in America, was formed in 1973, its leaders were offered a seven-figure donation if we would commit to an explicit segregationist policy. To their credit, they turned it down. In 2004, we passed a resolution repenting for decades of complicity, cowardice, and perpetrations of racism, calling for aggressive efforts at reconciliation and other "deeds in keeping with repentance." In 2014, two PCA churches in Memphis publicly repented of blocking Black Christians from worship fifty years before by inviting those who were still alive to worship with them in a special service (you can read about that in Sam Graham's chapter in this book). In a 2014 panel on race in the PCA, Ligon Duncan, the Chancellor and CEO of Reformed Theological Seminary, summed up the PCA's history this way: "There is much to be ashamed of and much to be forgiven for. When people say to me, 'Isn't it time to move on?' I say to my African American brothers and sisters, 'You tell me when it's time to move on.'" In 2015, PCA pastors and elders, at the annual denominational meeting, began to repent of the denomination's lack of solidarity with Black brothers and sisters during the Civil Rights Movement.

I've deliberately focused most of this chapter on the reality of what's wrong, because I don't think most White Christians understand the depth of the problem. But I want to close with a positive vision for what healing could look like for churches like mine. And I want to speak directly to White Christians, to Black Christians, and to all of God's family.

To my White brothers and sisters

We are the cultural majority in this country, if only for a few more decades. And the cross of Jesus didn't just save us; it showed us how to live. As Paul put it in Philippians 2:6–7, Jesus *"did not consider equality with God a thing to be grasped, but emptied himself, taking the form of a servant."* That means we must voluntarily embrace cultural marginalization and endure the complex emotions of White guilt in order to experience the joy of full restoration. It starts with asking questions, listening for answers, and asking more questions, like: What is it like to be you? What is it like to be a minority in a majority-White culture? What do you see about me that I don't see and you don't want to tell me?

And it doesn't stop there. It means giving up the power to always do what's most comfortable for us. It means deliberately sharing culture-shaping power with Black pastors and lay leaders. Majority-White churches must ask ourselves: What aspects of our worship services, or other activities we do together, could be changed or supplemented to more fully reflect the glorious diversity of the kingdom of God? Remember that the Bible was written by people who for most of their history were an oppressed cultural minority. Think about how much we miss or misinterpret because we don't study it with the unique perspective of cultural minorities! Who will stand up like the men of Ephraim, not armed with fear of God's wrath, but with confidence that the wrath of God was laid on Jesus, so that we might taste more of heaven now?

To my Black brothers and sisters

Your hurt and anger is more justified than I can fully understand, and the earthly debt to you can never be repaid. But Jesus showed you the way, too. On the cross he prayed, *"Father forgive them, for they know not what they do."* White Christians, myself included, have sinned against you both knowingly and in ways of which we are woefully ignorant. In the name of Jesus, please forgive us. And do not leave us in our ignorance; by the power of the Holy Spirit, help us! When we say or do asinine things regarding ethnicity, please love us enough to tell us the truth. And don't keep the hard-won riches of your particular Black culture from us. Where we are ignorant of Black theologians, scholars, entrepreneurs, authors, or artists, please share them with us. If your worship playlist at home includes songs White people have never heard, teach them to us.

To all of God's family

I have only scratched the surface of this vast subject, and there is so much more to learn. At minimum, I hope this article has helped you to want to learn more, because the Gospel demands it, and Jesus's whole church has treasures we have only begun to experience. What if our churches became leading lights in building comprehensively integrated communities of all ethnicities, all cultures, and all socioeconomic classes? What if your church could have the privilege of being one small part of that? If God in his kindness grants us this privilege, the non-believing world will no longer look at us as a religious social club of demographic sameness, but a mystery that only makes sense because the Gospel of Jesus is true.

Chapter 14

Loving Our First Neighbors Well

Rev. Chris Granberry

Chris Granberry serves as Pastor of Hope Fellowship on the Yakama Reservation in Washington, where he also ministers through Sacred Road Ministries. He studied at Samford University (BA) and was ordained by the Pacific Northwest Presbytery. Chris and his wife, Mary, have four children.

Being Native American and living in the United States feels like our indigenous peoples are an old grandmother who lives in a very large house. It is a beautiful house with plenty of rooms and comfortable furniture. But, years ago, some people came into our house and locked us upstairs in the bedroom. Today our house is full of people. They are sitting on our furniture. They are eating our food. They are having a party in our house. They have since unlocked the door to our bedroom but now it is much later and we are tired, old, weak and sick; so we can't or don't come out. But the part that is the most hurtful and that causes us the most pain, is that virtually no one from this party ever comes upstairs to find us in the bedroom, sits down next to us on the bed, looks us in the eye, and simply says, "Thank you. Thank you for letting us be in your house."[1]

Like family

The first time I ever came to the Yakama Reservation in Washington state I was a youth director from Birmingham, Alabama, traveling with my high school youth group. We were going to live and serve on the Rez for one week. We

---

1 Mark Charles, "Reflections from the Hogan," *The Grandmother in the House*. Accessed February 2, 2016. http://wirelesshogan.blogspot.com/2012/05/grandmother-in-house.html.

knew we would be roofing and painting homes for elderly people and single moms who were living in poverty. We would also be hosting backyard Bible clubs for children in the housing project in the little town of White Swan.

When we arrived, I was overwhelmed by what we saw and heard. I was devastated to the point that I had a hard time functioning as the team leader (or in any other capacity). The level of brokenness, desperation, and hopelessness that we saw firsthand and heard about laid me low. Even sixteen years later, it is hard to explain or talk about without weeping. I had traveled to various Third World countries, including very remote parts of Indonesia and Guatemala and had spent a good bit of time working in the inner city, but I had never seen anything like the despair and grinding poverty of the Rez. On top of that, most of the kids who came to the backyard Bible club had never heard of Jesus, and there was almost no Christian presence in the town. In other words, there was no way of escape.

The week we were in White Swan, we roofed and painted a woman's home. She seemed nervous or even scared around us so we didn't interact with her. It was hot, hard work, but at the end of the week her little house looked great! It had a new roof, fresh paint job, and all the weeds and trash were gone out of her yard. But I was sad that I had not had the opportunity to pray with her or share the Gospel. I wondered if we were simply making her comfortable on her way to hell.

When it was time to leave, the students were loaded in the vans and we were about to pull out. I walked around the house one more time to make sure we didn't leave anything behind and then headed toward the van. When I was about halfway across the lady's front yard, I heard a noise behind me and looked back. To my surprise, it was the lady from the house. She was running to catch me, and she had tears streaming down her cheeks.

She said, "Why? Why would you do this? You came all the way from Alabama, paid for plane tickets, paid for shingles and nails, bought all the paint, and did all this work on my house for free! Why would you do that? My own family would not do that for me. You don't even know me!"

My life changed dramatically in that moment. I didn't know what to say. Then the Lord gave me the words. I said:

The answer to that question is kind of a long story but it's a good one. I want you to know there are many, many people in Alabama and all around the nation who would love to come and do what we have done. But the better story that we really want to share with you is about Jesus. He left his home in heaven (which is way better than Alabama) and came to earth for a lifetime (not just a week). He came to renovate hearts and lives, not just roof and paint homes. Also, he didn't just pay for plane tickets and shingles, he paid for everyone who loves and trusts him with his own blood! He paid the ultimate price for us! And now he offers us a family and a home in heaven that will never need a new roof or a new paint job. Whenever you see the work that was done on your house and think about this week, we want you to look right past us and remember Jesus and what he has done. That is the real story we wanted to share with you.

Now, I wish I could tell you that she fell on her knees and prayed to receive Jesus right there in her front yard. She didn't. But she did stand there, with tears streaming down her cheeks, and listen to me (a random White guy) share the Gospel with her. I realized, deep in my soul, that the way to love our "first neighbors" well and develop relationships and create opportunities to share the Good News effectively is to love them "like family."

I kept seeing the woman's face and hearing her words, "Why would you love me like family?" I became convinced that if our first neighbors were going to hear and understand the truth of the Gospel, it must be communicated as they experienced the love of Christ through us. To the modern day Native person, the Gospel makes no sense apart from being "loved well" by the church.

Love mercy and pursue justice

When I visit churches to talk about what the Lord is doing on the Reservation, folks frequently ask, "What are you doing out there? What is the plan?" A simple verse, Micah 6:8, is my answer. Think of a time when you needed mercy. Think of a time when you wanted justice. Was there a time when you looked at the world and the way things are and knew, deep down, that it was a "broken world," that things are not the way they should be.

Micah 6:8 says, *"He has told you, O man, what is good; and what does the LORD require of you but to do justice, and to love kindness, and to walk humbly with your God?"* This short passage instructs us to love mercy and pursue justice.

When we are on the receiving end, we all like the ideas of mercy and justice, but are our lives characterized by offering mercy to our neighbors who need it and pursuing justice for them?

We need to look at the world around us and say, "That is not right. That needs to change. That is not the way it ought to be." To do justice means we engage in the fight against injustice in a certain area. We pray and take baby steps in a just direction.

As we engage an unjust system, we meet people trapped in that system and offer them mercy. Justice is more general, at first; mercy starts off specific. As we offer mercy, we are reminded of the Lord's great mercy toward us. He fought for justice, for things to be made right on our behalf, for us to be made right and justified.

For the Old Testament believer, God showed his commitment to justice and mercy by setting them free from slavery in Egypt. For us, we see how Jesus has set us free from slavery to sin. He did this at great cost to himself. He paid the ultimate price, made the ultimate sacrifice so that we could go free. This understanding becomes more clear to us as we engage in mercy ministry and are humbled. This spurs us to join in his great plan to build his kingdom one life at a time.

Isaiah 58 calls us to "spend ourselves," or in another version to "pour ourselves out," for our neighbors who are in need. It's significant that we are not simply called to "spend our money" or "spend some time or energy" but to spend ourselves, to "pour out" our very lives for others. We do this by speaking up for those who have no voice, standing up for those who can't stand up for themselves, and fighting for the defenseless.

Our first neighbors

After my first visit to the Rez in the summer of 2000, I was disturbed by a growing awareness that all was not well in the "good ol' USA." I began to suspect that the American Dream (which I had been pursuing without admitting it) might not run parallel to the Gospel. But the idea of fighting for truth and justice sounded too much like a job for Superman, and since I wasn't a superhero, I figured Isaiah 58 and other such Scriptures didn't apply to me. But God kept directing me to return, which I eventually did.

In 1855, the Yakama people, along with thirteen other tribes and bands, signed a treaty with the United States government that established the Yakama Reservation at the foot of Mt. Adams in south central Washington state. Since that time, the culture, families, and dreams of the Yakama people have steadily disintegrated.

Among the people Sacred Road Ministries serves:

- Virtually all the children suffer from neglect and/or abuse
- 70 percent of teenagers are homeless
- 65 percent drop out of school before graduation
- 100 percent are deeply affected by drugs and alcohol in some way

One day, not long after my family moved to the Yakama reservation in 2003, I was visiting with the leader from the longhouse (the building where the traditional Native religion is practiced) in White Swan. He was talking happily about the short-term teams that had been coming to serve that summer. He said, "Chris, most of the time when White people come here to help they hang around until they feel better, then we never see them again. But you guys are different. You just keep coming back."

Matthew 22:39 says, *"You shall love your neighbor as yourself."* I would argue that the first neighbors of the American church are Native Americans. Yet of the approximately four million Native people in the US today, only 3 to 5 percent claim to be Christian.[2] Obviously, there has been a major breakdown between the American church and our first neighbors, and the onus is on us, not them, to bridge the void. God is calling us to love our first neighbors as ourselves. Let's think of how we may serve and learn from them.

---

2 "A Native American Christian Speaks on Why?" *Bindings: Reflections on Faith, Life, and Good Books*. Accessed February 3, 2016. http://blogs.christianpost.com/bindings/a-native-american-christian-speaks-on-why-5494.

Chapter 15

Forming Friendships Through Music: Why Style Matters

Rev. Kevin Twit

Kevin Twit has served since 1995 as the Reformed University Fellowship campus minister at Belmont University in Nashville, Tennessee. He also works as an adjunct professor at Covenant Theological Seminary and Belmont University, teaching classes in hymnody. He has lectured widely on topics of hymns and worship. Prior to being an RUF campus minister, he served as a pastor at Christ Community Church for eight years. In 1999 Kevin, with some of his students, began Indelible Grace Music, which has released nine CDs and one documentary film. He is a graduate of Berklee College of Music (BA) and Covenant Theological Seminary (MDiv). Kevin and his wife, Wendy, have three children.

In 2002 public controversy erupted concerning the music Indelible Grace was using for hymn texts. On the website PCAnews.com (maintained then by the Presbyterian Church in America, but now defunct), a letter to the editor complained about setting hymn texts to rock music. The author explained that he had attended an Indelible Grace hymn concert and was offended by the musical style used. His contention was that rock music was inappropriate for worship. I responded to him publicly, pointing out a number of fallacies in his argumentation, though I am pretty sure I failed to convince him and others.

But what was most enlightening to me about this controversy was something that occurred behind the scenes. I received numerous private emails from African American pastors in the PCA encouraging me to fight the good fight about musical style. They shared their concern that if the PCA could not accept rock music or any other musical styles outside of the classical musical tradition, then it was difficult for them to hope that their own rich African American musical culture would ever be embraced. These emails encouraged me to challenge some of the assumptions surrounding musical style, but also broke my heart.

No single pure cultural expression of the Gospel

The issue is still a live one and an important one. I still engage in discussions about appropriate musical style from time to time and am concerned that many have unwittingly embraced a view that is uncomfortably close to the Galatians heresy. While many think of Galatians as a letter about legalism and grace, it also has important implications for thinking about contextualization. One of the central points of Galatians is that there is no single pure cultural expression of the Gospel. Gentiles do not need to adopt Jewish cultural markers to be fully pleasing to God. If there is not one pure cultural incarnation of the Gospel, then we must be very careful that we don't elevate any one musical style (the musical expression of a particular culture) as the pure cultural expression of the Gospel. The Jerusalem Council in Acts 15 reinforced this point, and it was critical to the subsequent spread of Christianity.

The fact is, Christianity has been a cultural chameleon throughout much of its history. Unlike the assumption of many today, Christianity is not a "Western" religion in its origin nor has it been one for much of its history.[1] African Christian scholar Lammin Sanneh argues that one of the geniuses of Christianity is the fact that it is a cultural chameleon.[2]

In my work with college students through Reformed University Fellowship for the last twenty years, I have had to regularly wrestle with issues of contextualization and enculturation. Yet I must say, that in too many debates and discussions with other pastors and elders in my own denomination, I regularly hear naïve or even unbiblical statements about these issues. This is a

---

1 Philip Jenkins, *The Lost History of Christianity: The Thousand-year Golden Age of the Church in the Middle East, Africa, and Asia—and How It Died* (New York: HarperOne, 2008).

2 Lamin O. Sanneh, *Whose Religion Is Christianity? The Gospel beyond the West* (Grand Rapids, MI: W. B. Eerdmans Pub., 2003).

major barrier not only to outreach, but also to loving our neighbors. Thoughts regarding musical style can be a helpful indicator of our cultural biases, revealing our assumptions about culture and the Gospel.

For the 2013 PCA Global Missions Conference, I was invited to lead worship and deliver a seminar. I chose for my topic "Does Musical Style Matter? Aesthetic Barriers To Missional Ministry."[3] After my address, I was approached by someone who was concerned about the musical style of many of the hymns we had sung at the conference. This person said she was deeply disturbed that we had set hymn texts that were focused on God to the musical style of the nightclub.

The concerns raised were not new ones to me, but this time I heard them differently. This time, I couldn't help but wonder how the concerns sounded to my African American brothers and sisters because the bass player, an African American RUF student, was standing next to me, listening to the whole interaction. At one point, I asked the person with the concerns, "Should we expect those from an African American cultural context to sing hymn tunes from the Western classical tradition to praise God in the 'best' way?" The response was that while it was OK to do some Black Gospel music to attract people, our ultimate goal should be to elevate their musical tastes.

I was frankly shocked. But I was also deeply saddened because I don't think this perspective was unique to the person who came up to me. My African American friend held his tongue, but as we discussed the event later, he was baffled as he tried to understand where the person was coming from.

I honestly don't think the person who said this even realized the way the argument was steeped in cultural blindness; it just seemed like common sense. Many of our deepest assumptions seem like common sense, which is why they are so rarely challenged and why we need to hear perspectives from those outside our cultural assumptions. I want to testify to the way God has helped me, through wrestling with musical style issues, to appreciate and celebrate the fact that the Gospel is bigger than any particular cultural expression.

---

3 The full recording can be obtained from Barker Productions http://www.barkerproductions.net/shop.asp?action=details&inventoryID=283177&catId=26729.

The problem with "The Great Tradition" view of music

> If I were to walk onto a platform to give a piano recital and introduced the evening by telling the audience that I was about to help them tune into the order of the cosmos, that some of the pieces I was about to play were more cosmically in tune than others, and that the best pieces would help them be finer people and bring them that much closer to the Creator, the audience might well conclude I needed therapy…. Yet for centuries in the West, this thinking, or something like it, was the norm. Indeed it was so dominant and persistent it is sometimes called "The Great Tradition."[4]

It is fascinating to me that in the fifteen years since the release of the first Indelible Grace CD, virtually all of the criticism about the musical style of the project has been from conservative Reformed folks. There are many in conservative Reformed Evangelical churches who argue that good and bad music can be determined from certain laws of music based on the created order made by God. The argument then typically proceeds to "prove" that the Western Classical tradition in music is superior to all other musical styles because it reflects this created order better than other musical styles.

Sometimes it seems that to challenge this view is seen as challenging the Bible itself. The links in the mind of many between the Bible and the Western Classical tradition of music (what has been called "The Great Tradition") are troubling to say the least. I would contend that this way of thinking is untenable and presents a significant barrier to reaching people from other cultures and helping them to glorify God in their own way.

Is it true that we can derive musical standards from the created order? No, because music is not just about physics and acoustics—it is human cultural interaction that works upon the stuff God has made, bringing out aspects of the God-glorifying potential he has built into his world. The description of the world with regard to music affirmed by those who contend the Western tradition is superior to all others is not accurate.

Without getting overly technical for this context, suffice it to say that when strings vibrate they also create sympathetic vibrations that follow a certain pattern called "the harmonic series." The harmonic series (also called the natural

4 Jeremy Begbie, *Resounding Truth: Christian Wisdom in the World of Music* (Grand Rapids, MI: Baker Academic, 2007), 78.

overtone series) is built into the created order of God's world. Yet the natural overtone series does not result in the twelve-tone Western system of tonality. In fact, the so-called "blue note" (somewhere between the sharp second and flat third in the Western twelve-tone system) is part of the natural overtone series. Yet, this note cannot be played on a piano keyboard. So if you want to argue that the tonality of the Western classical tradition is the one that reflects the actual created order, you would be wrong. In fact, the blue note that is central to many musical styles in the African American tradition is part of the natural created order, built into the way strings vibrate.

Also, we use well-tempered tuning today in Western classical music. That means what sounds "in tune" to your ear is actually a little bit out of tune according to the physics. Pianos are tuned this way so they can play approximately in tune in all twelve keys, allowing for musical modulations (key changes) within a particular piece of music.

The point is, what sounds consonant and dissonant to your ear is not simply a matter of reflecting the created order. It is actually a complex process rooted in the created order, your own embodiment, and your social context. When you hear a piano that sounds in tune, it is not actually in tune according to the created order and the laws of physics (the third of a chord actually has to be tuned a little flat in order to sound in tune to our ears). Yet I have heard numerous church leaders make the argument for the superiority of Western classical music in reflecting the created order based on what chords sound consonant and dissonant when played on a piano. This simply is not true!

This is not to argue that we can make no judgments about music at all. But we must be careful because the world is more complex than we often acknowledge. We must be careful about taking so-called rules of music theory from one type of music and using them to evaluate all other types of music. God did not give us a tune book when he gave us his Scriptures, and the music the Psalms were originally sung to would sound very strange to modern Western ears. Rodney Clapp asks, "Does our corporate worship reflect the atmosphere of a concert hall or a jazz club?"More importantly, he asks us to consider why we might consider one more appropriate than the other.[5]

---

5 Rodney Clapp, "That Glorious Mongrel: How Jazz Can Correct the Heresy of White Christianity," in *Border Crossings: Christian Trespasses on Popular Culture and Public Affairs,* 185–202 (Grand Rapids, MI: Brazos Press, 2000).

Exploring the God-glorifying potential of music

No culture has fully explored all of the God-glorifying potential in the creation with regard to music. Remember, Acts 2 does not present a monocultural vision. The people there praised God in their own tongues; they do not all adopt one pure cultural expression. The Holy Spirit does not conform the people from various languages into one cultural expression.

Neither does the Book of Revelation present a monocultural vision. Instead, it looks to a day when people of every race, tribe, and tongue will worship together and the kings of all the earth will bring their splendor, the best of their culture, into the heavenly city! Yet, I had a pastor tell me several years ago he believed we would only sing Bach in heaven because Bach was the greatest music ever written. Bach is superb music, but he did not explore all the God-glorifying potential that God has built into his creation! Ted Turnau says:

> There is nothing made by humans that is without flaws and yet nothing that fails to reflect God's glory in some way because the creation declares His praise (Psalm 19), and thus everything used to make music and culture interacts with the stuff God has made and stamped with meaning. We need to realize that every musical style has cultural baggage.[6]

Gene Veith and Thomas Wilmeth, in their book *Honky-Tonk Gospel*,[7] point out that every indigenous American musical form— jazz, blues, bluegrass, and rock and roll—was invented by poor people from the South. And it is true that many of our most-beloved hymn writers—like Watts, Newton, and Cowper—intentionally toned down their poetry to the level of the common people. So isn't it ironic that so many of our hymn texts are set to tunes that are associated with the upper class? It is easy to see musical style baggage in other people's music, but we must realize that our own musical styles have baggage as well. I love what Marva Dawn said one time, "If our congregations really reflected the

---

6 Theodore A. Turnau, III, "Reflecting Theologically on Popular Culture as Meaningful: The Role of Sin, Grace, and General Revelation." *Calvin Theological Journal* 37 (2002): 270–96. http://www.calvin.edu/library/database/crcpi/fulltext/ctj/88090.

7 Gene Edward Veith and Thomas L. Wilmeth. *Honky-tonk Gospel: The Story of Sin and Salvation in Country Music* (Grand Rapids, MI: Baker Books, 2001), 9.

kind of diversity that they should, then everyone should expect to sing some songs that they don't like."[8]

Similarly, Brian Wren suggests, we should seek to sing our songs, and other people's songs. We should sing our songs, the songs of our own culture and tradition, because Jesus came as a particular man in a particular culture, and God has situated us in a particular cultural context as well. But, we must sing other people's songs, the songs of other cultural traditions and other generations, because we must give expression to the fact that the church of God is bigger than any one cultural expression.[9]

The way we work this out in my Belmont RUF group is that out of the four songs we sing at our meeting each week, two are retuned hymns that have come out of this movement in RUF circles. But, we also sing one hymn to a traditional hymn tune, and we sing one modern praise song. I want my students to know that God has birthed a movement from within our midst of retuning hymns, and we celebrate this. But I also want them to know that the church is bigger than people that sing like us and talk like us.

How should we judge music?

Rather than making overarching judgments about art and music, the Bible encourages us to take a multiple-criteria approach, seeking to commend whatever we can.[10] Making broad judgments like "this is good art and this is bad art" is not very helpful. Philippians 4:8 says:

> *Finally, brothers and sisters, whatever is true, whatever is noble, whatever is right, whatever is pure, whatever is lovely, whatever is admirable—if anything is excellent or praiseworthy—think about such things.*

---

8 Marva Dawn, "Rethinking Worship For The New Millennium." Course lecture, Regent College, Vancouver, Canada, 1999.

9 Brian A. Wren, *Praying Twice: The Music and Words of Congregational Song* (Louisville, KY: Westminster John Knox Press, 2000), 192.

10 Kevin J. Twit, "Criteria For Judging Rock Music," Indelible Grace Music. *Indelible Grace Hymnbook.* Accessed January 7, 2016. https://www.google.com/url?q=http:// hymnbook.igracemusic.com/resources/criteria-for-judging-rock-music-by-rev-kevin-twit&sa=D&ust=1452173139210000&usg=AFQjCNEQ4_h9py57vZUL95xMMKZX0sBgFg.

So, for example, we can commend certain aspects of Bach's tremendous music, but we can also commend aspects of jazz and blues and Black Gospel music, too. Harold Best, former Dean of Wheaton's School of Music, rightly argues that there is no universal aesthetic. "Just as there is no universal music, there is no universal aesthetic. The trick is in locating and defining quality amidst the plethora of legitimate musics."[11]

There are some notable examples of strange musical decisions by theologians. For example, John Calvin opposed singing Genevan Psalms in harmony (i.e., in parts) in public worship as a violation of the principle of the unity of the body of Christ, although harmonized versions were published very early in Geneva for use at home. Calvin also believed when each of the 150 Psalms had been set to a suitable tune that we would need no other new church music. In fact, Louis Bourgeois was imprisoned for changing one of his own tunes![12]

While I believe these to be strong arguments, ultimately I believe one of the best ways to come together on these issues is through cultivating friendships with those outside our cultural tradition. I have seen how friendship and community is built around seeking to really understand and appreciate someone else's music. This can be a great step in loving our neighbors and welcoming them.

Heal Us, Emmanuel: The story behind the recording

In his preface to the Olney Hymns (from which we get such classic hymns as "Amazing Grace" and "Let Us Love And Sing and Wonder"), John Newton wrote that the collection was "intended as a monument, to perpetuate the remembrance of an intimate and endeared friendship."[13] The Olney Hymns were never intended as merely a collection of new hymns for people to sing. The project grew out of the deep friendship between Newton and the poet William

---

11 Harold M. Best, *Music through the Eyes of Faith* (San Francisco: Harper SanFrancisco, 1993), 9.

12 Charles Garside. *The Origins of Calvin's Theology of Music: 1536–1543* (Philadelphia: American Philosophical Society, 1979).

13 John Newton and William Cowper. Preface to *Olney Hymns in Three Books. Book I. On Select Texts of Scripture. Book II. On Occasional Subjects. Book III. On the Progress and Changes of the Spiritual Life* (London: Printed and Sold by W. Oliver, 1779).

Cowper, and thus it broke Newton's heart when Cowper was unable to complete his portion because of mental illness. In fact, Newton almost gave up on the project when the original design of a monument to their friendship was unable to be realized.

I have long thought of the Indelible Grace recording projects in a similar way. They are a testament to the bond of friendship God wrought between my former Belmont RUF students and myself, nurtured through our common love for old hymn texts. When I was able to present the Indelible Grace Hymn Sing at the historic Ryman Auditorium in Nashville in 2010, the emotion that filled my heart was pride for my former students (now dear friends), singing and playing so beautifully. I felt like a proud father, and the friendships that have been built and nurtured around these Indelible Grace projects are precious to me.

It was thus with great joy that I presented some of my friends on the latest project, *Look To Jesus: Indelible Grace VII*. In particular, I want to tell you the story of how the song "Heal Us, Emmanuel" came to be.

In 2005, our family began attending a new PCA church plant, City Church of East Nashville. One day, Craig Brown, the pastor, asked me how the Indelible Grace concept of setting old hymn texts to new music might look in an African American musical context. Part of my exploration of this question resulted in the songs "Hear Our Prayer, Hear Our Cry"[14] and "In The Hours"[15] from our recording *Wake Thy Slumbering Children: Indelible Grace V*. As I began to develop a friendship with the African American worship leaders at the church, I learned not only to appreciate the Black Gospel musical tradition,[16] but also learned about the barriers that musical style could present in seeking to welcome neighbors in East Nashville to be part of City Church. When RUF

14 Indelible Grace Music. *Wake Thy Slumbering Children: Indelible Grace V*, "Hear Our Prayer, Hear Our Cry." Kevin Twit. Accessed January 6, 2016. https://www.google.com/url?q=https://indeliblegrace.bandcamp.com/track/hear-our-prayer-the-litany-song-feat-emily-deloach&sa=D&ust=1452289994780000&usg=AFQjCNFt-Zikuy9oCRrnrUp37wnidwNngg.

15 Indelible Grace Music. *Wake Thy Slumbering Children: Indelible Grace V*, "In The Hours." Kevin Twit. Accessed January 6, 2016. https://www.google.com/url?q=https://indeliblegrace.bandcamp.com/track/in-the-hours-feat-emily-deloach&sa=D&ust=1452289994777000&usg=AFQjCNEhS9fUyEWxyPvJdKpiQc6Q40vcFw.

16 Robert Darden, *People Get Ready!: A New History of Black Gospel Music* (New York: Continuum, 2004).

began a work a few years later at Jackson State University, a nearby historic Black university, the question continued to press on me.

As the JSU RUF campus minister, Elbert McGowan, began to bring his students to RUF conferences, he and I began to talk about these issues. Elbert was seeking a way for his students to both celebrate their rich musical culture—the music of the Black church—while also celebrating being part of the RUF culture of singing retuned hymns. As we were discussing these issues, a beautiful opportunity developed. At the national RUF Summer Conference, Elbert and I arranged for the Belmont RUF group and JSU RUF group to try leading worship together. The music that night was glorious! The next year we merged the bands on the other nights as well. Working together our friendship grew, and our respect for each other as musicians grew as well.

I had been working with the William Cowper text "Heal Us, Emmanuel" (from the Olney Hymns) for many years. I wrote a tune in 1999, and some churches have been singing it since then. But I felt the tune wasn't quite right, so I had never recorded it on an Indelible Grace project. Since then, I have continued to nurture a love for Black Gospel music and have become a student of the history of this music. Somewhere along the way I thought that maybe "Heal Us, Emmanuel" needed to be set in a Gospel music style. I worked on tweaking the tune with Lucas Morton (my very talented RUF worship leader), and we came up with the Gospel feel the text needed. For me, "Heal Us, Emmanuel" felt like it should be sung in a Black Gospel voice because musically and historically the African American church has sung some of the most powerful songs of lament, the "sorrow songs" as W. E. B. Du Bois famously called them.[17]

When Ferguson, Missouri, erupted in 2015, this song seemed the right song for the right time. It also seemed appropriate to set a William Cowper text to a Black Gospel tune because Cowper was a very outspoken critic of the slave trade and a champion for the plight of Africans in the eighteenth century. In fact, he challenged the slave trade before either Wilberforce or Newton engaged the issue publicly.[18]

---

17 W. E. B. Du Bois, "Of The Sorrow Songs." In *The Souls of Black Folk* (Chicago: A. C. McClurg and Co. 1903).

18 George Melvyn Ella, *William Cowper: Poet of Paradise* (Durham, England: Evangelical Press, 1993), 487–93.

Part of the role of producer is finding the right sound and the right people for each part on our recordings. I knew we needed a Gospel choir for this song, and my dream was to figure out a way to involve the Jackson State RUF group. I thought it would both be a testament to the friendship God had developed between us and a way for them to share their gifts with the wider community that Indelible Grace can touch.

It was more difficult to schedule the recording with JSU than I had anticipated. In the end, my wife and I ended up flying down to Florida for a day to record the JSU RUF group singing the song and for my wife to capture the event on video.[19] I couldn't imagine the song without their voices.

I am proud to offer this hymn to the church. It still seems like the right song at the right time, and I am so proud of the way my Belmont students (current and former) and the Jackson State students came together to produce this track. As we mourn the brokenness of race relations in our country, and in our churches, we need a song that gives corporate voice to our cries.

There are lots of people with advice about what to do, but I think the best place to start is with a cry to the Lord to bring healing. "Heal Us, Emmanuel" is a powerful text giving us words to use to cry out together to our Father. But I will also always think of it as a testimony to a dear friendship the Lord built between Elbert and me, and between the Belmont and JSU RUF groups.

---

19 See the video at https://www.youtube.com/watch?v=uyNmG07BtSM.

Chapter 16

I Am Racist

Rev. Doug Serven

Doug Serven is a pastor at City Presbyterian Church in Oklahoma City, Oklahoma. Doug graduated from the University of Missouri-Columbia (BJ) and worked for The Navigators for four years before going to Covenant Theological Seminary (MDiv). After seminary, he was the campus minister for Reformed University Fellowship at the University of Oklahoma. Doug's books include TwentySomeone, The Organized Pastor, *and* Ecclesiastes: Everything Is Meaningless? *He and his wife, Julie, have four children.*

As she got up from the table, Brianna muttered under her breath, "I wouldn't say that out loud."

We had been talking over coffee about how I, a White Anglo Saxon Protestant male, had been waking up to the fact that I had many cultural advantages that most people of color did not. I told her about my interactions and new friendships with people who didn't look like me. I told her about our denomination's recent annual meeting that included resolutions, prayer, and confession.

Brianna was not impressed. She asked why it had taken so long for these things to happen.

"Better late than never," I said.

That's what drew her ire. Later, after I asked her why she was so disgusted, she told me that my comment sounded so patronizing, so condescending. In fact, here is what she said in her email to me (used with permission):

It seems to me that you wouldn't have said that ["Better late than never."] to a person of color who has experienced systematic marginalization by our country. It seems like the kind of thing you would only say to another White person with a shrug to say: we're working on it. I would hope that as you continue to explain the reasons for why you want to engage in racial reconciliation with your church members, community members, members of other churches, people of color, etc., you would find words to say that were more reflective of the journey that led you to believe this was a core issue. "Better late than never" says to me, we missed the Civil Rights Era, etc., but now we're here to figure out how to encourage more people of color to join in on our worship. ANYTHING else would seem better to me. "We have woken up to the deep, systemic injustices that separate all God's children from living in faith with each other." "We have arrived at a troubling and late conclusion that there is brokenness in the way that we value and treat one another on the basis of skin color." "We praise God that he is patient and gracious with us as we slowly have come around to the reality that so many of our neighbors, our brothers, and sisters have known for their entire lives, and we pray that they would forgive our blindness to their suffering as we move forward promising to learn and grow toward racial reconciliation."

I'm glad I can reflect on this painful commentary on my words—and repent again. I need it. I am still waking up. Thank you, Brianna.

Doing my own White thing

I was born in 1970 in Detroit, but my parents moved to southwest Missouri when I was five. I lived in a small town of fewer than 5,000 people. When I graduated from high school in 1989, there was one African American kid in our whole school district K-12, and he was in second grade so I didn't know him. There were no Hispanics or other ethnicities either. I don't remember anyone in our school who was gay that I knew of. It was a monolithic culture.

Then I went to college at the University of Missouri-Columbia, and I met many people who expanded my cultural horizons significantly. After college, I moved to Stillwater, Oklahoma, to work for the Christian parachurch ministry The Navigators at Oklahoma State University. Oklahoma is not known for its diversity and progressive race relations. I remained in my predominantly White bubble.

I later spent four years at Covenant Seminary in St. Louis, which is a racially diverse city. However, there wasn't much diversity at the seminary or in my life. I suppose it was better than what I had been used to, but I didn't choose to attend the churches that were intentionally seeking racial diversity. I was more interested in my studies, my community, my family, and myself.

After graduating, I served for ten years on the campus of the University of Oklahoma with Reformed University Fellowship. I was back in Oklahoma in a college that was in a city largely filled with educated, White Protestants.

So I came by my racial obliviousness honestly; it was what I knew. God would have to intervene to change me into someone who would see, care, and embrace all the people he made in his image.

Walking a different path

This change began in earnest in 2011 when I began the process to start City Presbyterian Church in downtown Oklahoma City. Bobby Griffith, the other pastor, and I researched the city. We walked the city. I started to understand and know about the cares of the city. We defined our space and tried to get to know the people in it.

The people in it included White, hipster, young professionals, all of whom were thrilled by the revitalization and rebirth of downtown. I got to know many of the young marrieds and young families who were buying houses in or near downtown. They were educated and motivated to help start a new church. I got to know the business professionals by attending meetings and organizations for urban design and entrepreneurship enterprises. This was fun stuff! These were my people!

But I was troubled. My people weren't fully the same as Jesus's people. I realized I didn't like to go to the places where Jesus would have gone. I didn't know the poor in the area. I didn't ever naturally hang out with the marginalized or distressed. I just kept self-selecting into my same demographic.

After I realized this, I tried to confess, repent, and walk a different path. I didn't know where I was going or how it would turn out, but I think that's when I started to wake up to this part of the heart of God for his people.

I began to wander into the nearby alternative public high school for pregnant girls, young mothers, and at-risk boys. I began to talk to the staff at the

Homeless Alliance and the Good Shepherd Health Clinic. I began to notice our state and city's problems with mental illness, with incarceration rates, with addiction, with poverty, with food deserts, with foster care, with education. And I began to understand that so many of these (not all) were connected to issues related to race. I was picking up the clue phone, I suppose.

I became friends with several Black men who helped me. I started attending a weekly breakfast where we'd discuss the news and our faith. We talked about Ferguson, the various police incidents, Charleston, and the Confederate flag.

I started reading books and watching movies and documentaries about race. I started noticing. I started having more conversations. I started blogging to process my thoughts.

And from all of that, it's taken me a long time to be able to admit this: I am racist.

It may be true to call this condition racial prejudice instead. It may be more palatable to myself, my congregation, and my denomination if I back up and say that I can't think of (many) blatant or noticeable or egregious instances of racism in my life. But does that mean as an American White male I'm not racist? While it is tough to say about myself, I think I am not only racially prejudiced, but also racist.

My tendency then is to think about how what I have done is not that bad, at least not comparatively. And that's my out—that word "comparatively." I'm not that bad. I'm not that racist. But we can't evaluate everything about ourselves in this comparative way. As a Christian and as a pastor, I am forced to accept what Jesus says. He says I am that bad. In fact, in Matthew 5, Jesus says that if I have hated, then I am a murderer. Jesus also says that if I have lusted, then I am an adulterer.

Because Jesus teaches me to say that I am a murderer because I hate and that I'm an adulterer because I lust, I think I have to say that I'm a racist because I judge people based on the color of their skin. I don't know why I do. I don't think I was explicitly taught this way. But I grew up in America, and we're struggling with this issue all over our nation. I was at least implicitly taught racism in America.

For what does your heart break?

I was hit with a two-by-four when I preached a sermon series on the book of Nehemiah at our church. Nehemiah, a godly leader, goes back to Jerusalem to rebuild the wall. It's obvious to highlight his strategic planning and implementation, which are incredible attributes that get this public works project finished. However, I was captured by the reason all of this leadership starts in the first place. When Nehemiah—a cupbearer for the king in Persia—gets the news about the trouble and shame in Jerusalem, we read, *"As soon as I heard these words I sat down and wept and mourned for days, and I continued fasting and praying before the God of heaven"* (Neh. 1:4).

Nehemiah then risked bringing this heartbreaking news to the king to ask if he could go and repair a place for a people who were not exactly his. Nehemiah had never lived in the city of Jerusalem. We don't know if he'd ever been there. He was all set in the king's service. He'd attained a high position of influence. Yet he still cared for God's people in Jerusalem. When he heard the news, he wanted to do something for them. His heart was broken, and he wanted to rebuild those walls and make their lives better.

During the Nehemiah sermon series at City Pres, we didn't focus as much on leadership and technical abilities—we asked God to show us where our hearts should break and what we might do about it together. We asked God to give us his eyes so we'd weep when we heard the news of tragedies and broken down walls in our city and nation and world. We wanted Nehemiah hearts instead of our normal, calloused, jaded ones.

God gives those types of hearts. He can give all of us a more broken heart for those who have been treated poorly because of sin and injustice. He cares. Do we care?

In 2015 alone, did your heart break for Charleston, South Carolina? A young man walked into a church for Bible study. The church welcomed him and prayed for him, and he gunned them down because he wanted to start a race riot. And yet the families all forgave him. Did that break your heart?

Did your heart break for the situation in McKinney, Texas? A police officer pulled his gun on a crowd of teens standing in bathing suits. One Black girl was thrown to the ground and sat on. Does that break your heart? Do you think that is uncommon? Do you think that is justified?

Did your heart break for the Black, pregnant woman arrested in the altercation in the parking lot in California? Did it break when you saw the dashcam video of Laquan McDonald shot in the street in Chicago? Did it break for a city culture that would hold that video for more than a year? Did it break when you saw the news in Ferguson? In Baltimore? Does your heart break when you realize the cycles of poverty and privilege are powerful, often unseen, and a challenge to break out of?

Every week we hear of something that our Black friends tell us has been happening for decades, but we hadn't noticed before. Do we care?

We're not OK in our society. Race relations are not fine. Racism is not over. Terror and fear still rise up. We need to pray and work to make this better.

The church needs Nehemiahs who risk and lead. But we need them to do so with broken hearts of love and compassion, along with their resolute work. We need a redemptive way to help others who have great trouble and shame, much of which we have directly or indirectly caused. We need their forgiveness, and we need to stop pretending that we have worked for all we've gotten and they have gotten all they deserved. We need to own up to our sins and the sins of our forefathers and do whatever it takes to make this a better world for everyone, not just better for people like us.

Nehemiah confessed this himself when he prayed:

> Let your ear be attentive and your eyes be open, to hear the prayer of your servant that I now pray before you day and night for the people of Israel your servants, confessing the sins of the people of Israel, which we have sinned against you. Even I and my father's house have sinned. We have acted very corruptly against you and have not kept the commandments, the statutes and the rules that you commanded your servant Moses. (Neh. 1:6–7)

We confess the sins of racism, indifference, sloth, pride, greed, hate, envy, arrogance, blame-shifting, silence, and the misuse of power. We're taught to confess like this when we read through the Ten Commandments portion of the Westminster Larger Catechism. The Westminster Divines were very thorough in their confessions! We should be thorough as well. We've got to be aware there is a lot to confess for all of us and that includes the sins of racism, whether we realized them consciously or not.

We confess that those have been the sins of our fathers and of our nation, but they've also been OUR sins because we are a covenant, connected people. We have to admit this not only in our own lives, but also in our churches and denominations.

Some of our grandparents, fathers, mothers, uncles, and aunts actively stood against Civil Rights. They had their reasons. They had their arguments. They had their blindnesses. They weren't bad people in every sense. They stood for truth and love in many areas in their lives. However, we must confess this more shameful part of our and their history, too, because it truly happened, and we are truly sorry. We take these sins seriously and want to stop hiding them.

Some of our heroes, whatever their reasons, stood on the side of slavery as a viable and reasonable institution to fight for and defend. They were deluded. They were perhaps fooled, or at least foolish. They believed it was right to hate this way. We still honor their statues and valor to fight for something so evil. It's confusing.

Some still hold on to symbols of hatred, claiming they don't mean what they mean. We fly our "heritage" Confederate flags without caring what that might mean to others. Perhaps some of us do not truly know what this heritage communicates and entails, but some do and wish it were that way again. Either way, it is an abomination, and we confess this and wish to remove the offense.

Our racism certainly isn't limited to African American issues. We still cling to words and mascots like Redskins with pride. We still resist the removal of these racial slurs through tricky arguments like tradition and honor and private ownership.

Many didn't actively display racist speech or actions. Instead, we did nothing.

We didn't actively participate in anything; we passively did nothing. We didn't notice. We didn't speak up. We didn't stand with. We didn't walk with. We did nothing, and we do nothing. We keep quiet in our lives and pulpits. We hide behind procedures and our own privileged cultural logic (just like our forefathers did). We refuse to let our hearts break.

This is also shameful. It's wrong. It's something to confess.

Shocking forgiveness

Thankfully, praise Jesus, there is forgiveness for all of these sins!

It was startling to watch the forgiveness expressed to Dylann Roof in Charleston, especially from the family members on the day he was charged in court for his crimes. It was incredible to then watch the nation's reaction to that forgiveness. It was something people weren't quite sure what to do with. The newscasters appeared befuddled as they reported on the story. Although this was and should be the church as usual, it sadly hasn't been. Forgiveness became newsworthy. The Black church showed us the way.

The way of forgiveness is love, justice, and mercy. It's the way of the Cross. It's the way of the saints who are used to being martyred and marginalized for their faith. It's the way of those who have let their killers into their midst in love. It's the way of Jesus. And that is amazing! We serve a loving God of justice and mercy, who shows compassion for his enemies, who came and lived and died and raised again. We have the hope to see these saints again together with Jesus.

Lord, help us to love like the families of your precious slain saints in Charleston. May we reach out to each other in a forgiving love that mystifies CNN and the world. May we forgive when we or those we love have been offended, mistreated, or even killed. May we find love instead of hate. May we find compassion instead of judgment. May we work on the wall together for your glory, for you are great and mighty, compassionate and merciful, powerful and intimate.

O Lord, let your ear be attentive to the prayers of your people, who delight to fear your name, and give us success. Give us mercy in your sight and in the sight of those who have the power to help us make these changes. We are your so-often unfaithful servants and your people, whom you have redeemed by your great power and by your strong hand. Amen (adapted from Nehemiah 1:10–11).

I'm admitting my need for Jesus in this area. I'm confessing my sins. I'm also confessing the sins of my fathers and forefathers. I need this forgiveness. We need this forgiveness. Heal us, Emmanuel.

Racism is real. It's both overt and covert. It's wrong in every way, and most people don't ever want to admit it. It's real in Ferguson, in Charleston, in Oklahoma City, and all over the country and the world. It's real in my heart. Heal me, Emmanuel.

Historical and Theological Perspectives

Chapter 17

The Theology of Race in the South

Rev. Bobby Griffith

Bobby Griffith is a pastor at City Presbyterian Church in Oklahoma City, Oklahoma. He is an Adjunct Professor at Mid-America Christian University, where he teaches US History, US Government, and the History of Christianity. Bobby has degrees from Pensacola Christian College (BS), West Virginia University (MA), and Covenant Theological Seminary (MDiv) and is working toward his PhD from the University of Oklahoma. He and his wife, Jennifer, have one son.

One of the aims of history is honesty. When we are open and honest about history, only then can we move forward. This story is about failure. It is about the failure of White Christians to love their neighbors as themselves.

Our story begins in Massachusetts. When the Puritans came to North America, they soon established a law that granted them the right to take "strangers" as slaves because they saw it as permitted in the Old Testament, though slavery of Christians was forbidden (Lev. 25:44–46). This created a warped view of people based on race. In the minds of the Puritans, natives and Black Africans were not a Christian people; they instead were property. This passage in the Old Testament law became a weapon for the first legal enshrinement of race-based slavery in North America.

The period up to the American Revolution also saw White New England Christians carrying marriage laws from the church into the civic arena. John Wood Sweet's Bodies Politic shows how the fear of interracial marriage and Black reproduction led to the creation of laws that reserved marital rights only to White couples. Blacks were permitted to marry only on rare occasions. Northern cities introduced segregation codes to prevent contact between the races in public space. Basically, public space was White space.

While there was some measure of slavery in the North, too, Southern slavery was more comprehensive since tobacco and cotton production required intensive labor. The free labor of slaves meant lower costs and higher profits for landowners. How did this happen in a largely Christianized society? The answer is theology.

A theology of race

We may often think that theology adapts to practice, but it is not that simple. Sometimes, the complex interaction between culture, belief, economics, and social practices works in such a way that incorrect ideologies are promoted by even the most pious Christians. Such is the case with race and slavery in the South. Race is not simply a biological category, but a socially constructed one. Racial labels carry distinctions with them. That was the case in Virginia, and it spread throughout the Southern colonies.

For example, when English colonists poured into Virginia during the 1600s, they carried with them a legal tradition that suggested that membership in the church granted people access to civil rights.[1] If you were not Christian in Virginia, you were without rights. In time, the colonists passed laws that prevented slaves from being baptized—either as infants, the standard practice of the Anglican tradition, or as converts. Later, an ideology of Christianity as a civilizing force became the argument to evangelize slaves. To be Black was to be uncivilized, cursed, and ignorant. This ideology of race found its grounding in the Scriptures during the 1600s and, unfortunately, is still used by many White American Christians to explain race.

Christians repeatedly used theology to justify slavery, prevent baptism, and forbid sexual contact. Yet what plagued the South throughout the 1700s was the issue of evangelism. In heavily Anglican parts of the Southern colonies, planters and missionaries made a biblical connection between heathenism, race, and perpetual slavery. Later, though, Anglican officials charged their ministers to

---

1 Rebecca Goetz, *The Baptism of Early Virginia: How Christianity Created Race* (Baltimore: Johns Hopkins University Press, 2012), 1–20.

evangelize slaves, by reassuring planters that any salvific change would not result in a social change.

The Great Awakening affected not just the Northern colonies, but also the Southern ones. In the 1730s and 1740s, religious revival swept across the British Colonies. One of the most famous revivalists was English evangelist, George Whitefield. Whitefield believed that while the races were not equal, the souls of mankind were.[2] This became the mantra of the Great Awakening arguments to Christianize slaves. Whitefield, like so many, believed God allowed slavery to Christianize "the heathen Africans" and, in fact, Whitefield became a slave owner in the late 1740s.

Here lies the crisis of the Great Awakening. If African Americans were deemed incapable of embracing Christianity, how did a White Christian reconcile the fact that they converted in droves? If Christianization equaled civilization, then the White power structure would need to allow for literacy, education, and Bible training for African Americans.

Yet even most of the early White abolitionists held to the value that all humans are equal in a social sense. They taught that people were sinful and needed redemption regardless of race, but also that racial inequality and social hierarchy were the norm and God-ordained. In fact, one argument concerning God's allowance of slavery was to Christianize the "heathen" and send them back to colonize their homeland with European civilization and Christianity.[3]

Slavery and the early republic

Though the Founding Fathers were made up of professing Christians, yet they kept slavery. Their view was that because the budding Union was fragile, they could not ascribe human dignity to "property." When the South later shifted its mode of production to crops, thus began the days of plantations and chattel slavery. Unfortunately, this most brutal form of slavery had its defenders and propagators within the church.

---

2 Edward Blum and Paul Harvey, *The Color of Christ: The Son of God and the Saga of Race in America*, (Chapel Hill: University of North Carolina Press, 2012.), 55.

3 John Saillant, "Slavery and Divine Providence in New England: The New Divinity and a Black Protest," *WMQ*, 68.4 (Dec, 1995): 586–587.

Within the South, the notion of spiritual equality with racial and social inequality helped to propagate the chattel system. Pro-slavery Christians were "biblical literalists." They taught that the Bible never ended the prohibition on slavery, so the practice was accepted by God. They also said that Christ never addressed the issue of humans seeking to improve their social condition through political means. The lynchpin for many Southern Christian thinkers was that to advocate abolition was to take something from the sacred realm into the political, so it was unbiblical to take spiritual issues into the civic arena.[4]

This idea that the institutional church must reject political means is a theological concept called the spirituality of the church. This teaching, unique to American Presbyterianism, took particular hold in the South. Simply put, the church must not delve into political matters. Southern theologians Robert Lewis Dabney and James Henley Thornwell are credited as two of the most important teachers of this ideology.[5] With this view tied to the deeply held belief that non-Whites were inferior to Whites, they argued to preserve the institution of race-based slavery.

Another problem for institutional White US churches was that the revivalist movements were fostering allegiances detached from ecclesiastical bounds and authority. The Second Great Awakening and the intensification of individualism effectively pitted abolitionist societies against denominations. Between 1830 and 1860, Presbyterians split, Baptists split, and Methodists split. In each case, the divisions were sectional and over the issue of slavery. The United States entered into a war that was in large part over slavery, and which fundamentally reshaped life thereafter.

After the Civil War

When the war ended, Reconstruction of the South began. With it came the expansion of racism and the beginning of Jim Crow. One theme that loomed large over White Southern Christians after the Civil War was that of divine judgment. Was the South judged for breaking covenant with God? Preachers across the Deep South taught that their defeat was akin to that of the Southern

---

4 Blum and Harvey, 107–109.

5 Mark Noll, *America's God: From Jonathan Edwards to Abraham Lincoln* (New York: Oxford University Press, 2002), 420.

Tribes in Israel, and since God was on their side, the South would rise again and bring back the former institutions, including slavery.

White Southern pastors created a theology based on the myth that the war was a noble effort for honor. Churches began to ascribe religious significance to Robert E. Lee, Stonewall Jackson, and Jefferson Davis. In fact, Jefferson Davis's birthday became known as the "Sabbath of the South." Furthermore, the mythical images of Lee and Jackson became attached to phrases like "religious saints and martyrs."[6] The "peculiar institution" of slavery was seen as a good thing.

A prime example of this way of thinking is in Robert Lewis Dabney. He served in the Civil War as a chaplain. He also never changed his mind on race and slavery even after the war. Dabney, a Virginian who later moved to Texas, argued that Southerners should encourage the northern migration of Black women. He said this out of his fear that Reconstruction allowed Blacks the capacity to produce innumerable offspring that would eventually destroy the racial makeup of the South. Dabney also stood before his denomination's General Assembly in 1867 and argued that Blacks should not be allowed to be ordained as ministers within the Presbyterian Church because it violated the God-ordained separate spheres of operation for races.[7] Instead, he wanted a separate Black church that was not equal.

Such ideas, sometimes also referred to as the Lost Cause, combined with generations of racial theology of White supremacy, set the stage for segregation and Jim Crow. Soon after the Southern states regained control over their jurisdictions after Reconstruction, there came the rise of legal, enshrined segregation and lynchings—all in the most churched part of the country. White churches did not speak out against this system, and groups like the Ku Klux Klan enjoyed support of church leaders throughout the Deep South.

---

6 Charles Reagan Wilson, *Baptized in Blood: The Religion of the Lost Cause, 1865–1920* (Athens: University of Georgia Press, 1980), 13–28.

7 Robert Dabney, *Ecclesiastical Relation of Negroes Against the Ecclesiastical Equality of Negro Preachers in our Church and Their Right to Rule Over White Christians* (Richmond, 1868), 1–16.

A theology of segregation

Founded in 1866, the KKK quickly became a primary vehicle against civil rights for African Americans. The KKK was made up of churchgoing men who set out to preserve a White heritage. We know there are several incarnations of this group with the worst coming during the twentieth century. I am not going to spend a lot of time discussing the KKK except to say this: it would not have succeeded without the protection of churches, and its mission was to preserve a certain White Protestant vision of Southern and American culture.

As chattel slavery gave way to segregation after the Civil War, segregationists had a more difficult time biblically defending their practice than slaveholders had. The biblical justifications were thin and rooted more in culture than the text. However, one common theme in segregation theology was that of refutation. The common argument against segregation was that Paul said there is neither Jew nor Greek, therefore segregation is wrong (Gal. 3:28). But many segregationists said that the text "cannot be used to require indiscriminate integration."[8] They said Paul was making a spiritual point, not one of literal race.

Another theme for segregation theology was boundaries. Dr. G.T. Gillespie said the Bible does not contain commands for segregation but inferences of it.[9] He referenced the separation of Cain in Genesis 4, the intermarriage of the sons of God and line of Seth in Genesis 6, the divisions after Noah's flood in Genesis 9, the Tower of Babel and Abraham's call to be separate in Genesis 12. He looked to the Mosaic Law that forbade interreligious marriages and called those interracial.

Other segregationists looked to Paul's speech in Acts 17 for theological justification. They honed in on the last part of verse 26, which says God *"decreed how long each nation should flourish and what the boundaries of its territories should be."* This view became popular during the late 1800s. Again, during the modern Civil Rights Era, key church leaders in the South promoted this view. Dr. W.M. Caskey, a professor at the Baptist institution, Mississippi College, in

---

8 David Chappell, "The Religious Ideas of the Segregationists," *Journal of American Studies* 32.2, 240–246.

9 Ibid., 246–248.

1960 said "Southern segregation is the Christian way."[10] The *Baptist Standard* said "God created and established the color line in the races....we have no right to try and eradicate it."

In 1954, the Supreme Court decision Brown v. Board of Education which forbade discrimination set off a theological firestorm. Throughout the South, White Christians obsessed over integration, both social and sexual. In fact, many protested the Court's decision and said that Christianity never addressed segregation, though it addressed discrimination. Furthermore, segregation, according to this line of thought, fit the biblical norm of God's boundaries and actually promoted racial harmony. One pastor wrote that "birds of a feather flock together" and so should the races.[11]

During the Civil Rights Era, the *Southern Presbyterian Journal* dealt with integration and civil rights. First, it argued that integration was a political maneuver for a power grab that went against God-ordained spheres of race. Second, the *Journal* took a strong stand against interracial marriage. Various authors argued that God set apart the races and that marriage between Blacks and Whites was a violation of his boundaries. Third, the *Journal* endorsed the KKK on numerous occasions.[12]

Regarding the role of institutions, Bob Jones College, later Bob Jones University, was founded by a segregationist who was funded by the KKK. This institution played a key role in defending segregation and maligning racial unity. Bob Jones is known for his sermon "Is Segregation Scriptural" in which he argues that it is a clear biblical teaching.[13] In fact, when MLK was assassinated,

---

10 Joseph Crispino, *In Search of Another Country: Mississippi and the Conservative Counterrevolution* (Princeton: Princeton University Press, 2007), 65.

11 Dwyn Mounger, "Racial Attitudes in the Presbyterian Church in the United States, 1944–1954," *Journal of Presbyterian History* 48.1, (Spring 1970): 44–46.

12 L. Nelson Bell, "Some Needed Distinctions," *The Southern Presbyterian Journal 16* (June 5, 1957): 2, and G T. Gillespie, "A Southern Christian Looks at the Race Problem," *The Southern Presbyterian Journal 16* (June 5, 1957): 11–12.

13 Bob Jones, "Is Segregation Scriptural?" (Greenville: Bob Jones University Press, 1960), 1–32. You can find the transcript of the sermon at http://www.drslewis.org/camille/2013/03/15/is-segregation-scriptural-by-bob-jones-sr-1960.

Bob Jones students cheered.[14] They also had a strong policy that forbade interracial dating all the way until 2000.

There is evidence that race and the Civil Rights Movement played a role in the founding of Reformed Theological Seminary, in Jackson, Mississippi. One of the founding professors, Morton Smith, wrote public defenses of segregation using rhetoric that made the case that "God brought diversity, so who are we to tear it down?"[15] My own denomination, the Presbyterian Church in America, has a past connected to pro-segregationists.

Practical repentance

Racial difference and racism as we know it in the United States is due, in large part, to the theological justifications of White Christians who allowed slavery and promoted racism in nearly all aspects of life. The fruits of slavery were the Civil War, Reconstruction, and Jim Crow laws. Yet many White Christians clung to racial stereotypes and hatred, using the Bible, tradition, and Southern honor to support their views. After losing the battle against civil rights, some White Christians surrendered; others created new institutions and never addressed the issues over their role in the Civil Rights Movement. Instead, they retreated into an ecclesiastical and theological world where races did not interact. They lived, worshipped, and ministered as if their White privilege gave them the right to address the problems of African American culture and even the decline of the Black family unit while never taking responsibility for the part their past and heritage played.

So today, we do not have many racially united churches. We do not have political cohesion or social cohesion. Black Christians and White Christians seem to talk past one another, largely because White privilege blinds White Christians from true dialogue and partnership. How do we move beyond this sordid history?

First, we need public confessions of repentance at denominational and institutional levels on the part of those whose history played a role in

---

14 Edward Babinksi, *Leaving the Fold: Testimonies of Former Fundamentalists*, (Amherst: Prometheus Books, 1995), 39.

15 Morton Smith, "The Racial Problem Facing America," *Presbyterian Guardian*, (October 1964): 125–128.

propagating racism. I realize this is not a popular stance, but in the book of Nehemiah, the Jewish people repented of the sins of their forefathers. This has to happen. I believe in denominations, and I believe denominations need to move beyond generic statements and toward the pain, because pain is honest, and repentance will bring the seeds of reconciliation.

Second, we need honest stories. When Propaganda's rap "Precious Puritans" was released, some White Christians went ballistic that he talked about the reality of Puritans and race.[16] Yet academics have long talked about the racist views of White Southern church leaders. Academics have told us about sexual, cultural, and physical brutality. We need honest stories even when they are uncomfortable.

Third, we need honest conversations and cross-cultural, cross-racial friendships and dialogue. We will never move past the sins of the past until we are willing to talk about them. I need to hear stories of my friends who get pulled over for "driving while Black." I need to hear stories about my friends whose parents and grandparents faced discrimination. I need to be told how my own privilege prevents me from understanding the world of my African American friends. I need to know. We need to talk about hard things.

We need a resurgence of prophetic Christianity, which always challenges the status quo and speaks boldly. Prophetic religion is not Left or Right or Black or White, but it is hungry to show that change is needed and that change is possible. I believe that prophetic Christianity will breathe life into the American church, awake her from complacency and captivity, and persuade believers to heed the radical words of Christ to each take up our cross and follow him.

---

16 You can see an example on Dr. Joel Beeke's blog post addressing the issue, particularly in the comments section. http://www.joelbeeke.org/2012/10/propaganda-giving-the-puritans-a-bad-rap.

Chapter 18

Telling the Truth

Rev. Dr. Sean Michael Lucas

Sean Michael Lucas is the senior minister at First Presbyterian Church, Hattiesburg, Mississippi, and professor of church history at Reformed Theological Seminary in Jackson, Mississippi. He received his degrees from Bob Jones University (BA, MA) and Westminster Theological Seminary (PhD). He has previously served congregations in Louisville, Kentucky, and St. Louis, Missouri, and also taught at Covenant Theological Seminary. Sean and his wife, Sara, have four children. His books include What Is Grace? *and* For a Continuing Church.

In some ways, I was an unlikely candidate to bring the Personal Resolution on Civil Rights Remembrance to my denomination's annual meeting in June 2015. For one, I am a relatively new Presbyterian. I joined a Presbyterian Church in America congregation in Louisville, Kentucky, in 2002 and was ordained as a pastor in 2003. I didn't grow up in the PCA and so don't have a natural reason to feel the weight of its history.

Also, though all of my people are from Virginia, going back to the 1680s, I was actually born in New Jersey, just across the Delaware River from Philadelphia, Pennsylvania. And though we hightailed it back to Virginia two weeks later, growing up, I moved around the country and across the ocean: Manchester, England; Williamstown, New Jersey; Spring, Texas; Westfield, New Jersey; and finally, Reston, Virginia, where I went to middle and high school. I have Southern roots, but the leaves of my tree are variegated.

On top of all this, I was raised in a middle-upper-class family in the suburbs. I don't recall having any Black friends as I was growing up—lots of

White Jewish and Catholic friends, especially in New Jersey; lots of White fundamentalist Baptist friends, especially in Virginia; even a Korean-American girlfriend, whom I dated very seriously for a year and a half; but not any Black friends.

In hand with this, my family was very politically conservative. My dad used to joke that politically he was right of Attila the Hun and also that he thought political liberals were simply illogical. Because our household subscribed to The Conservative Digest, I soon learned that Martin Luther King Jr. was one of these political liberals who was actually a closet Communist. To a kid growing up in Reagan's America, to be a Communist simply put someone outside the pale of acceptability.

If you take all of this together, the idea that I would help to write, present, and defend such a resolution calling for civil rights remembrance in my denomination would not be obvious. And so, the obvious question then is: Why did I?

Personal history

Undoubtedly, a significant personal reason comes from where I went to college. I attended Bob Jones University, the fortress of the faith in Greenville, South Carolina. If you aren't familiar with BJU, it is the citadel of Baptist fundamentalism. In 1990, I transferred to BJU from Liberty University because I was convinced that they would enforce the rules—unlike Liberty, where they couldn't because they were hamstrung financially from building the basketball arena and the football stadium at the same time.

While I was a preacher boy at BJU—I majored in pastoral studies as an undergrad—I was forced to reckon with the easy merger of conservative religion, politics, and social mores represented at the college. At one level, that merger didn't bother me much. After all, I had grown up with the assumption that conservative religion and politics went together hand-in-glove. I was a College Republican, supported Pat Buchanan in 1992, felt that our world was under siege when Bill Clinton became president, and never really questioned the "God and Country" alliance of my alma mater.[1]

---

1 For a telling of BJU history, see Mark Dalhouse, *An Island in a Lake of Fire: Bob Jones University, Fundamentalism, and the Separatist Movement* (Athens: University of Georgia Press, 1996).

Except—I couldn't reconcile that with the Civil Rights Movement. I wasn't really rebellious at BJU. My rebellion was connected to three things: I would sneak kisses from my girlfriend (now wife) on campus; I bought an NIV Study Bible; and I read Martin Luther King Jr.'s collected writings and the first volume of Taylor Branch's trilogy on the King years. And as I read about Dr. King and Civil Rights, it was hard to reconcile what I was told with what I was reading. It struck me that African Americans were protesting an unjust society in the only ways available to them and that, for all his flaws, Martin Luther King Jr. was profoundly heroic.

That began to shake my assumed worldview in which conservative religion, politics, and racial views merged together. As I began to probe how these things merged in my own life as well as for other conservative Evangelicals, God led my wife and me to Westminster Theological Seminary where I came under the influence of the historian D. G. Hart.

When I got to Westminster in 1994, Hart was one of the brilliant, though cantankerous, men on the faculty. I had originally gone to Westminster to write a dissertation on Jonathan Edwards, who had helped me transition from nearly being a Free Will Baptist preacher to a want-to-be Presbyterian. But under Hart's influence—especially, his insistence that "Confessionalism" represented a better and more faithful expression of Christianity than the activistic, politicized Evangelicalism and fundamentalism out of which we both came (Hart's parents are BJU grads)—I began to explore more thoroughly the interconnections between conservative religion, politics, and racial views. And this, in turn, would lead me to the Southern Presbyterians as a test case.[2]

As a result, in 2001, I wrote my dissertation on Robert Lewis Dabney, the great nineteenth-century Southern Presbyterian theologian. I decided to explore Dabney's "public theology," his theological engagement of the public environment—the economic, political, cultural, and social spheres of his times. That meant that among the topics I had to consider was how Dabney engaged on slavery and race.

If you have read Dabney's *A Defence of Virginia: And Through Her, of the South*, you know that for him the only possible form of slavery is race-based

---

2 See D. G. Hart, *The Lost Soul of American Protestantism* (Lanham, MD: Rowan and Littlefield, 2002).

slavery: only Black people can be slaves; only White people can be masters. In addition, he did not even deal fairly with all of the biblical material and the overarching trajectory of the Gospel itself, which is toward freedom, not slavery.[3]

But the entire project forced me to examine again the intersection of conservative religion, politics, and racial views. And I was trying to understand how someone like Dabney—with whom I agreed theologically and whom I viewed to be brilliant in so many ways—could be so wrong when it came to race. That led me toward a way of writing history that is called "cultural history": recognizing that our theological commitments are one of several deep commitments that shape our cultural systems. Sometimes, our theological commitments break free and serve to judge our commitments to class or race, gender, or education. At other times, though, our theological commitments remain captive to our class, race, or region. For Dabney, then, his theological commitments were ultimately trumped by and held captive by his identity as White Southern gentry. His conservative worldview had a massive blind spot: racial injustice as represented by his defense of race-based slavery and segregation.[4]

But how do you tell this story? That was the question that confronted me, both with my dissertation and with my first book, *Robert Lewis Dabney: A Southern Presbyterian Life*. I decided to take Wendell Berry's advice, given in connection with a piece he wrote on the Southern agrarians, and apply it to Dabney:

> The enterprise of political correctness deals in the political merchandise of general categories, invoking judgment without trial, whereas critical discourse must try to deal intelligently with the fact that people who are wrong about one thing may be right about another.[5]

---

3 Sean Michael Lucas, *Robert Lewis Dabney: A Southern Presbyterian Life* (Phillipsburg, NJ: P&R, 2005), 122–128, 143–150.

4 I outline my approach in two places: "Presbyterians in America: Denominational History and the Quest for Identity," in *American Denominational History*, ed. L. Keith Harper (Tuscaloosa: University of Alabama Press, 2008), 50–70, and "Church History as a Pastoral Discipline," in *The Pure Flame of Devotion: The History of Christian Spirituality*, ed. G. Stephen Weaver Jr. and Ian Hugh Clary (Toronto: Joshua Press, 2013), 15–24.

5 Wendell Berry, "Still Standing," *Oxford American* (January/February 1999): 65.

Surely, this was true for Dabney: telling the truth meant saying that he was wrong about one thing, but right about many other things. That's how I tried to tell his story.

Presbyterian history

Right as I was finishing my dissertation and graduating from Westminster, I was working at the Southern Baptist Theological Seminary, where the merger of conservative religion and politics was alive and well; I was still wrestling with my fundamentalist past; and I had just finished researching and writing about Dabney. On top of all this, my family was transitioning to the PCA. And so, a new set of questions was emerging for me. What has God called me to be and do? What is this Presbyterian body to which God had led me? How could I take a look at the more recent past and tell the story of American Evangelicalism and fundamentalism through the history of the PCA?

Thus, in 2002, I started researching the book that eventually became *For a Continuing Church: The Roots of the Presbyterian Church in America.*[6] And I knew from my work on Dabney that the PCA's history was tied up with conservative theology, politics, and racial views.

The first place I went to research was First Presbyterian Church, Jackson, Mississippi. The session graciously let me read session records from 1934 until 1974 and to work in the church's history room. One of the things I realized through that initial work was this: the conservative leadership in the Presbyterian Church United States (from which the PCA split in 1973) were incredibly heroic, and on the matter of race, tragically flawed.[7]

The question had come again, like it did when I worked on Dabney—how should I tell the story fairly, sympathetically, and yet truthfully? My decision was to simply tell the story to my best ability and let things play out from there. What made this difficult, even painful, is that the pages of the *Southern Presbyterian Journal*, the main magazine for Southern Presbyterian conservatives, are filled with full-throated defenses of segregation from the journal's founding

---

6 Sean Michael Lucas, *For a Continuing Church: The Roots of the Presbyterian Church in America* (Phillipsburg: P&R, 2015).

7 The history of First Presbyterian Church Jackson was published as: Sean Michael Lucas, *Blessed Zion: First Presbyterian Church, Jackson, Mississippi, 1837–2012* (Jackson: First Presbyterian Church, 2013).

in 1942 until 1959. And even after Aiken Taylor took over as editor in 1959, the opposition to the Civil Rights Movement was consistent.

How do we understand this? How could so many of these men—theologically sound, ardent and articulate defenders of orthodoxy, heroic in their stances and their willingness to leave a church they loved and knew—defend segregation as the Southern way of life? That was the question I had to ask. My answer was the same as with how I handled Dabney: this was a place where their theological commitments and insights were held captive by their commitment to White superiority and racial inequality.

We need to pause here and say that, by the founding of the PCA in 1973, a division emerged. A younger generation, led by Don Patterson, Frank Barker, Kennedy Smartt, Jim Kennedy, and others, and influenced by Billy Graham and Bill Hill, began to understand that it was not possible to be passionate for evangelism and missions and still to defend segregation. And so, these leaders included in the "Declaration of 1969" a commitment to racial inclusion in the plans for the "Continuing Presbyterian Church." Likewise, they worked behind the scenes to mitigate the influence of those who were more determined to maintain the Southern way of life when it came to race. However, these exceptions don't outweigh the preponderance of evidence that many, if not most, of the PCA's founding generation stood for continued segregation.[8]

But what does that mean? Should we consign them all to the dustbin of history? Shall we try to airbrush them out of the story? No—both because that is not possible and also because it is not desirable. It is not possible to consign everyone who has such painful, demonstrable blind spots to the dustbin of history—because we would all end up there. John Calvin and Philip Melanchthon, Martin Luther and John Agricola, Jonathan Edwards and John Davenport, Charles Hodge and Charles Finney, Robert Lewis Dabney and John L. Girardeau, L. Nelson Bell and E. T. Thompson—they and we are all flawed, captive, sinful human beings. If we wrote them all out of the story, there would be no story to tell.

The Good News, however, is that even with all our sin and failure, our blindness and captivity, while we were enemies and ungodly, Christ died for us.

---

8 I tried to make these distinctions here: http://www.thegospelcoalition.org/blogs/justintaylor/
2015/02/06/jim-crow-civil-rights-and-southern-white-evangelicals-a-historians-forum-sean-
michael-lucas.

And if he died for us, he surely died for all the other flawed, captive, sinful human beings in the church's story. If we are going to forgive one another as God in Christ forgave us, we have to include our ancestors in the faith.

But if we are going to experience forgiveness through repentance, then airbrushing flawed human beings out of the story is not desirable. Because the only way we can move forward in repentance, the only way we can experience reconciliation with African American brothers and sisters, is by telling the truth about the past. I had this very conversation with my friend, Dolphus Weary, long participant in the Civil Rights struggle. He made the point to me that the way forward must start in the past—it can't stay in the past, but it must start there. White Christians must tell the truth about that past before reconciliation and partnership can happen.

And so, as a historian, I made the decision to tell the origin story of the PCA as faithfully and truthfully as I could. I explored the interchange between conservative religious, political, and racial commitments. It makes for painful reading at times; at many other points, we will nod our heads in hearty agreement with the stances the founders took. And yet, what I hope will emerge is a more honest telling of the past so that we can understand our own place and calling and become more faithful Gospel churches in our contexts.

Confess and repent

By the time I finished the book, in December 2013, I was more than a historian. Since 2003, I also have been a PCA pastor. I've now served three churches in Kentucky, Missouri, and Mississippi, and taught at two of the seminaries aligned with the PCA. And as I was finishing the book, my friend Steve Garber's question from *Visions of Vocation* haunted me, "Now that you know what you know, what will you do?" How would I pursue proximate love and justice in response to God's call founded on this knowledge that I've gained?[9]

It is not like I hadn't done anything. When I was an administrator at Covenant Seminary, I was involved in recruiting the first two non-Caucasians to our full-time faculty in its (then) sixty-year history. From the time I've been at First Presbyterian Church, Hattiesburg, Mississippi, I have sought to move our

9 Steven Garber, *Visions of Vocation: Common Grace for the Common Good* (Downers Grove: IVP, 2014).

church gently toward a more faithful relationship with our African American brothers and sisters. In 2010, we started worshipping two to four times a year with Ebenezer Missionary Baptist Church; we received our first Black members that same year; two years later, we had Mike Campbell preach our Bible Conference, the second time an African American had preached and the first time for our "premier" event. We've had several denominational leaders on racial reconciliation come to speak to us about what we could do in our city, examples from similar towns like Huntsville, Alabama, and Augusta, Georgia.

But both for us as a congregation and especially for us as a denomination, more could and needed to be done. It had always bothered me that the 2002 overture on racial reconciliation and the 2004 PCA position paper on the Gospel and Race had referenced the sins of 1861 but had ignored or vaguely referenced the sins of 1961. And yet, I knew both from my own historical research as well as from ten years of teaching at Covenant and Reformed seminaries, that it was those sins of 1961 that continued to be a very real stumbling block, both for our Black and White ministerial students as well as for our engagement with other Christians across denominations.

Consider, after all, how huge our failure has been in trying to recruit African American pastors. After forty-three years as a denomination (from 1973–2016), we have more than 4,400 teaching elders—only 51 of our PCA pastors (1.2 percent) are Black. This isn't because we haven't offered scholarships at seminaries or tried to start Reformed University Fellowships (RUFs) at historically Black colleges and universities. At some level, as an overwhelmingly White denomination that has failed to tell the truth about our past, our church is just not hospitable to Reformed African Americans. It is simply too difficult and too much of a sacrifice for them to join us and remain with us.[10]

Likewise, consider how our failure to tell the truth about our past hinders our involvement with other Christians. There is never a year of teaching that goes by where I am not asked by students: How did the theological liberals get it right on Civil Rights while the conservatives got it so wrong? That is the PCA's reputation.

---

10 There is a significant amount of literature on this point, but see Michael Emerson and Christian Smith, *Divided by Faith: Evangelical Religion and the Problem of Race in America* (New York: Oxford University Press, 2001).

I'll never forget when I was on a research fellowship at the Presbyterian Historical Society in 2004. One day, PHS hosted Joel Alvis, author of *Religion and Race: Southern Presbyterians, 1946–1983*, to speak on the issue of Presbyterian history and race. In the discussion that followed, countless older mainline Presbyterians stated unequivocally that the PCA started as a racist denomination[11]

While a fair telling of the story should emphasize that the main reason the PCA started was for theological faithfulness and missionary zeal—as stated in the motto, "Faithful to the Scriptures, True to the Reformed Faith, and Obedient to the Great Commission"—because it has never owned its past, that charge, which has a measure of truth, continues to carry a sting. And what will take the sting away, especially for our Black brothers and sisters in Christ? Telling the truth. Now that we know what we know, what will we say about it? What will we do?

And so, something needed to be done. But the thing that spurred me to work on the personal resolution was this larger sense that I too was a racial sinner. This wasn't simply Dabney's blind spot or Nelson Bell's blind spot: it was mine. Not only was I covenantally and generationally connected to and involved with this larger story—that included Dabney and Bell and so many others—but these same failures were manifested in my life. I've been complicit; I've been a hypocrite; I have sinned. Until I own this past as my own past, as a place where God's grace needed to meet me, there would be no way forward for me, for us.

Along that line, I won't forget taking a class on Karl Barth at Louisville Presbyterian Theological Seminary in 2000. We were talking about Barth's defense of the Jews during the Holocaust, and one of my classmates wondered aloud, "What issues of injustice or atrocity are we missing today? Where are we so captive that we are blind to injustice?" My mind went quickly to one issue in particular: abortion. But just as quickly a voice echoed in my head, "All right, Lucas: but what about you? Where are you blind?" Over the last fifteen years, I've learned the answer: I too have been blind on matters of racial injustice and prejudiced in my own heart and life.

---

11 Joel L. Alvis Jr., *Religion and Race: Southern Presbyterians, 1946–1983* (Tuscaloosa: University of Alabama Press, 1994).

And so, taken all together, this was the heart behind the personal resolution: it came from someone who was, from his upbringing, unlikely to even see these issues as significant or as tests of Christian faithfulness. Through God's providence, God has brought me through a range of experiences to where at this point in my life and our church's life, we are confronted by what we know about our church and ourselves. What should we do? Tell the truth. Confess and repent. Bring forth fruits of repentance. And seek for ways that our church might increasingly reflect the vision of Revelation 7: "a great multitude that no one could number, from all tribes and peoples and languages, standing before the throne and before the Lamb.... And crying out with a loud voice: 'Salvation belongs to our God who sits on the throne, and to the Lamb!" Amen. Amen, indeed.

Chapter 19

Toward a Compelling Theology for Unity

Rev. Dr. Craig Garriott

Craig Garriott planted Faith Christian Fellowship in urban Baltimore in 1980. Craig continues to serve as pastor of the multiethnic, socioeconomically diverse church. He has degrees from Virginia Tech (BS), Covenant Theological Seminary (MDiv), and Westminster Theological Seminary (DMin). Craig and his wife, Maria, have five children and three grandchildren.

In his final, high priestly prayer, Jesus promises that our holy unity will yield fruitfulness. In John 17:23, he says:

> *I in them and you in me. May they be brought to complete unity to let the world know that you sent me and have loved them even as you have loved me.*

The resolve of many within my denomination, the Presbyterian Church in America, to move from a predominantly White, culturally Anglo church to a multiethnic church that reflects the growing demographics of our nation calls to mind the paradigm shift of the New Testament homogeneous church of Jerusalem to the multiethnic church of Antioch. While my specific examples will pertain to the PCA, which is my context, the principles may be applied to other monoethnic churches or denominations seeking to mirror the expansion of the kingdom.

In order to move more diligently and strategically toward an ethnically diverse church, I propose three applications that could be framed as theological, ecclesiological, and doxological in nature. The process will not be easy, and it won't come without great prayer, persistence, and the power of the Gospel of grace.

Theological: Embrace a compelling theology

Many of my brothers and sisters in Christ struggle with culturally conformist movements that seek to grow the church but are weak on theology. This is a valid concern. Fortunately, Presbyterian and Reformed history has produced an arsenal of missional theologies that address many of these questions.[1]

Yet while we must encourage fresh, contextual theology, we primarily need the power and discipline to apply the truths we have already affirmed. We have a strong body of biblically and theologically faithful documents related to these missional questions. We need to mine them, confirm them, and then figure out how to apply them.

One example of theological clarity has come from Dr. Vern Poythress, Professor of New Testament Interpretation at Westminster Theological Seminary. Poythress highlights the magnitude of the related cultural barriers we face today when he examines Ephesians 2:14, which reads, *"For he himself is our peace, who has made the two one and has destroyed the barrier, the dividing wall of hostility."* Poythress writes:

> It (the religious/cultural difference between Jew and Gentile) was the hardest barrier between people in the first century.[2]

In commenting on how God brings reconciliation between people and himself and between Jew and Gentile, Poythress adds:

> Old cultural attachments must die for everyone who is united with Christ. When it says he made the two one, nobody stays the same. Nobody has the luxury of clinging to his old upbringing and old culture.... The new man is one new man, not pre-Christian Jew or Gentile. But in the process Gentiles are not required to become Jews or

---

1 http://www.pcahistory.org/pca/race.html.

2 Vern Poythress, "Lessons from the N.T.; Lessons from the O.T.," Lecture presented as part of the "Racial Tensions Racial Reconciliation" at the Second Annual Conference on Contemporary Issues, Westminster Theological Seminary, Philadelphia, PA, March 9–11, 1993.

visa versa. Both retain a good deal of their former cultural identity... this struggle (of cultural and ethnic conflicts) runs throughout the pages of biblical history.[3]

Poythress continues to address the root and remedy of racism today. He says:

> Racism and ethnic tensions are nourished by root sins—idolatry, love of self and comfort, money, and power. The comfort of my own upbringing from that of those radically different from me. What is the remedy? He has triumphed. He will triumph. God is triumphing. "He has made the two one."[4]

Ecclesiological: Empower a diverse leadership team

How do we build a united leadership culture among diverse brothers and sisters? We need to encourage various representatives to speak wisdom and truth into our structures and help us do church better. How do we eliminate an "us and them" mentality church culture so that it is only "we and us"? How do we create a church where those who are different from the present majority culture do not feel like an overwhelmed minority but like beloved, valued brothers and sisters?

Acts 6 displays a healthy church government structure that expanded to ensure that various people groups would not be overlooked in the process of advancing the Gospel. Because the leadership power base was in the sole hands of the dominant Hebraic group, there was a tendency to overlook the needs of the sub-dominant group. *"The Grecian Jews among them complained against the Hebraic Jews because their widows were being overlooked in the daily distribution of food"* (Acts 6:1). The Twelve immediately took action. They realized that injustice in the fellowship would be a scandal, disgracing the name of Jesus and impeding the expansion of the church. The disciples then chose seven men, most if not all of whom were from the Hellenistic group—all the names listed are Greek names. The power base grew, *"So the word of God spread. The number of disciples in Jerusalem increased rapidly"* (Acts 6:7).

---

3 Ibid.

4 Ibid.

Note that in the act of expanding the leadership base, biblical standards were not diminished. The candidates had to be *"known to be full of the Spirit and wisdom"* (Acts 6:3). This was not a superficial racial quota that diminished the qualifications or standards of leadership. In this regard, the church was above the reproach of paternalism or cheap social action. Theological unity would not be compromised for cultural diversity. Not only was the Jerusalem church becoming diverse, but the Apostles were consciously affirming leaders among its subcultures. The believers were one in Christ, and they affirmed the cultures of the diverse subgroups.

Yet it should also be noted that the early church wisely did not find a token representative here and there to speak and act on behalf of their "own kind." Such single representation becomes a heavy burden that no one should carry alone. Such representative leadership is also prone to be overlooked and marginalized by the well-intended dominant leadership culture. The early church established a force, a team of culturally connected leaders who joined en masse and became fully incorporated and interdependent within the larger leadership team. This is not a complex principle to apply, but it results in a significant power shift or more accurately, a redemptive leadership sharing. God reveals for us the fruit of such faithful leadership adjustment: the number of disciples in Jerusalem increased rapidly.

Dr. John Frame captures well "the ideal thing" in how the church should function as we grow together in Christ. This principle also applies to how we govern the body as a diverse team of leaders. The ideal situation (a pre-Fall situation) would be for the whole human race to work as a team, seeking out all the mysteries of the creation together, trusting one another, collaborating peacefully on a great edifice of learning, each contributing his part to a body of knowledge far larger than any individual could build. This is what God intends for his church. He wants us to grow together toward a knowledge of him that is broader than any of us (Eph. 4:15).[5]

---

5 John Frame, *The Doctrine Of The Knowledge Of God* (Phillipsburg, NJ: P & R Publishing, 1987), 159.

Doxological: Experience the soul language of united worship

How do we keep the unity of the Spirit in our corporate worship with diverse peoples? The worship of God by the united people of God is not only a most visible witness to the reality of Christ's presence in the world (John 17), it is also a vital worship prescription in how we glorify and give praise to God.

Paul makes this clear in his exhortation to the Roman believers:

> *May the God who gives endurance and encouragement give you a spirit of unity among yourselves as you follow Christ Jesus, so that with one heart and mouth you may glorify the God and Father of our Lord Jesus Christ.... as it is written: "Therefore I will praise you among the Gentiles; I will sing hymns to your name." Again, it says, "Rejoice, O Gentiles, with his people."* (Rom. 15:5, 9,10)

The Apostle Paul instructs the historically alienated and culturally separated Jews and Gentiles of Rome to bear with one another and to receive each other as dear friends. The whole of the Scriptures speaks not only to the movement toward the climactic united worship celebration of all God's peoples gathered *"from every tribe and language and people and nation"* (Rev. 5:9), but also to practice this sacred calling of united worship now to the best of our abilities.

In this struggle for united worship, Paul gives us the model and motive to advance this Gospel. *"Accept one another, then, just as Christ accepted you, in order to bring praise to God"* (Rom. 15:7). Acceptance here is not mere toleration that allows for emotional disconnection but rather granting heart access to one another just as Christ has entered into our world and embraced and loved us completely.

Cultural and personal preferences of worship were therefore subordinated to the priority of family unity in which God delights. God-pleasing worship requires that I consider and support what will help brothers and sisters who are culturally different from me enter into the worship of the Father in Spirit and truth. This will take work and effort. This will require some dying to self. But out of that effort for unity and burial of self will arise a kingdom-seeking, Christ-centered worship experience that will reflect and resonate with the soul worship in heaven. God's people will recognize it and be filled with even greater praise.

This united worship is not just for the edification of the present church. It also becomes a clarion call to lost sons and daughters who are looking for the signs of a kingdom not of this world. In united worship, Christ's visible presence is intensified and his glory more revealed. Paul captures this witness in his encouragement to the diverse church of Corinth when he exhorts them to use understandable and accessible language so that an unbeliever won't feel like a foreigner but would rather be compelled to worship God saying, *"God is really among you!"* (1 Cor. 14:25).

Unity declaration

In 2000, Faith Christian Fellowship PCA adopted a Unity Statement that was the fruit of three years of devoted labor and prayer by a multicultural group of church members who participated in the congregation's ongoing Reconciliation Task Force. It clarifies and expresses a commitment to celebrate diversity while maintaining unity. At the same time, it speaks to the world concerning the urgent matters of racial justice and reconciliation. I include it here to show what one church has said regarding the essential need for unity in the body of Christ. The declaration reads as follows:

Unity Declaration Statement 1: Our Fundamental Identity

We declare that God our Father, in His great love, has redeemed us by sending His Son Jesus Christ and united us as people, by His blood, from diverse cultures into one family through the Holy Spirit committing to us the message of reconciliation. John 17:20–24; 20:17; Eph. 2:13,14;19–22; Rev. 5:9,10; Col. 3:11; Gal. 3:26–29; Eph. 4:4,5; Acts 2:5–12; 2Cor. 5:19.

Unity Declaration Statement 2: Cultural Affirmation

We declare that God's truth transcends culture and speaks to all cultures. We affirm the biblical value, dignity and distinctions of our varying cultures because God uses culture to communicate His truth and grace and receives glory from our cultural expressions. Yet we acknowledge that God declares the fallen condition of all people and their cultures. We claim a personal and corporate responsibility to evaluate and bring Christ-centered reformation to our cultures and society by the Word of God in dependence on the Holy Spirit. Gen.1:26,28; Gen. 2:15,19; Rom. 8:18–25; Rom. 1:18–32; Rom. 3:9–20; Rev. 21:24; 1 Cor. 9:19–23; Acts 17:16, 22–31; John 17:15–19; Matt. 5:27–43.

Unity Declaration Statement 3: Repentance and Forgiveness

We acknowledge that great transgressions based on race, gender, class and faith have tragically marked our life together as a human family throughout the history of the world and this nation. While the church has pursued justice and reconciliation, regrettably it has often participated in this sin through active support or indifference. We join with those believers who confess that true reconciliation cannot be realized without a commitment to repentance, forgiveness and the pursuit of justice. Neh. 1:4–11; Dan. 9:4–19; Eph. 4:1–6, 32; Phil. 2:1–11; Acts 6:1–7.

Unity Declaration Statement 4: Necessity of Grace

We seek to apply God's grace to our lives. His grace enables us to love God with all our being and our neighbor as ourselves. God's grace provides the only means to conquer our fears, remove our guilt, resolve our anger and give us the strength to persevere as one family where Jesus Christ is Lord. We declare that the Holy Spirit is our only source of power for true unity in the Body, and that He strengthens us through daily repentance, prayer and the cleansing power of the Word. Matt. 22:37–40; Eph. 3:14–19; Eph. 4:1–5; Eph. 5:1,2,15–21; Eph. 6:10,11; Heb. 2:14,15; 1 Pet. 4:19.

Unity Declaration Statement 5: Cultural Awareness

We commit ourselves to acquiring greater cultural awareness and sensitivity, starting first with our own cultural bias and prejudices, recognizing that we live in a multicultural city and world. We believe that cultural awareness is foundational to the way in which we develop leaders, conduct worship, equip the body for evangelism and discipleship, and promote justice and community development.1 Cor. 9:19–23; Acts 15:19–21; Acts 17:16–34; Acts 26:28,29; Rom. 15:1–4.

Unity Declaration Statement 6: Leadership

We commit ourselves to modeling the reconciliation of culturally diverse believers before the world in our church and ministry leadership. We promote reconciled leadership which understands and values church membership, the unity of the church, spiritual accountability, the benefit of ethnic diversity, shared servant leadership, cross-cultural skills, strategic service, sound theology, godly character, spiritual renewal, and discipling emerging leaders. Luke 6:12–16; Acts 6:1–7; 13:1–3; Gal. 2:2; Isa. 56:1–8; Rev. 21:24.

Unity Declaration Statement 7: Worship

We declare that as a reconciled community in Christ we work in our worship services to represent God's kingdom in our local context. We work to offer God our most precious and valuable expressions of devotion from our varying cultures. Such worship requires the pursuit of excellence as we glorify God in a Christ-centered, believer edifying and seeker welcoming service. Rom. 15:5–11; Isa. 19:23; Zeph. 3:9; Ps. 22:27; Rev. 7:9,10; Rev. 21:24.

Unity Declaration Statement 8: Evangelism

We commit ourselves to work together as a multiethnic body to proclaim Good News that communicates Christ to people in their particular cultures with biblical integrity through culturally sensitive means. 1 Cor. 9:19–23; 1 Cor. 10:33; Matt. 20:26–28; Rom. 1:14; 2 Cor. 4:5; Prov. 11:30; Rom. 11:14; 1 Pet. 3:1.

Unity Declaration Statement 9: Discipleship

We declare that as we disciple one another toward Christian maturity, we must obey Christ's command to love our neighbors as ourselves. We do this by keeping the unity of the Spirit, who indwells believers of diverse and historically separated cultures, in the bond of peace. Eph. 2:11–22; Eph. 4:1–4;11–16; Phil. 2:1–5; Col. 3:5–14; John 17:23; Rom. 14:17–19; 1 Cor. 1:10; 2 Cor. 13:11.

Unity Declaration Statement 10: Justice and Community Development

We declare that the church is called to be the redemptive presence of Christ by proclaiming Good News which is demonstrated through concrete deeds of mercy and justice. This Good News affirms dignity, cultivates an environment of hope, and restores people to God through Christ and to service in God's kingdom. Micah 6:8; Luke 4:18,19; Acts 6:1–7; Gal. 2:10; James 2:1–9.

An opportunity

Our increasingly ethnically diverse communities, the emerging generation, and our post-Christian, postmodern, postsecular, posteverything world is not compelled by abstract theology. However, there is a hunger for Good News manifested in concrete realities. The spiritual and functional practice of holy unity is the key Gospel reality that compels people to Jesus Christ (John 17:20–26).

The church possesses this glorious, transformative Gospel. Yet we stand at a missional crossroads. Will we become captive to old cultural patterns that impede our growth, or will we do the hard work of the theology, ecclesiology, and doxology for this holy unity? Let us by God's grace be like the tribe of Issachar, *"who understood the times and knew what Israel should do"* (1 Chron. 12:32).

Chapter 20

Deconstructing the Racialist Framework

Rev. William Castro

William Castro serves as Assistant Pastor for Hispanic Outreach at Mitchell Road Presbyterian Church in Greenville, South Carolina, and helps Calvary Presbytery with Hispanic outreach in Upstate South Carolina. He has degrees from University Seminary Evangelical of Lima (BA, MDiv) in Peru and from Greenville Presbyterian Theological Seminary (ThM). He and his wife, Judy, have three daughters.

I want to state from the outset that I am not an expert on race, nor am I an expert on American church history, including the Presbyterian history that is my denominational heritage. I write as a pastor who has been working on Hispanic ministry for several years, praying, reading, preaching, and talking with many friends of different backgrounds. My desire is to help the conversation move forward with regard to how majority-White denominations can have an effective Christian outreach to Hispanics in America.

Nobody can deny today that America is becoming more diverse and that the Latino/Hispanic population is growing. This can be confirmed by complex statistics or by practical things like visiting an elementary school or superstore in some of our towns. However, if we visit a Reformed Christian congregation on Sundays, we won't see many Latino/Hispanic people present.

Why aren't there more Latino/Hispanic people in Reformed denominations? This is due to a confluence of factors. One important reason is because American Christianity has become captive to a racialist framework that unintentionally makes our denominations unwelcoming to Hispanic people and perhaps for other minorities. If we want the church in America to partake consistently of the Abrahamic promise (Gen. 12:3, Matt. 28:19), we need to not only engage in actively reaching minorities, but also to undermine the racialist framework that pragmatically overrides our biblical call for unity. While my examples are from the Presbyterian and Reformed traditions, similar factors have influenced other majority-White denominations in America as well.

Before we go any further, we must make an important distinction between racism and racialism. Racism is hostility to other races based on their supposed inferiority. Racialism is the use of racial categories to provide forms of order to human existence. Racialism is not necessarily something negative from the outset, but as many scholars on race have said, in America it has become problematic.[1] While many today are preoccupied with the impact of this racialism in social and political arenas, my concern is how racialism undermines our efforts for diversity and unity in the churches of America.

The racialist framework

Racialism in America has produced a framework that underlies the way we think, talk, and react toward people and groups of people. This racialist framework provides a strong sense of identity that makes us see ourselves and our group as different from others. We tend to see the topic of race as something static and usually in terms of White and Black people. Many White and Black people have the tendency to see and feel their own races as "pure races" that have experienced no or minimal mixing.

Further, this framework sees racial identity or racial categories as somehow ingrained in our human nature, to the point that we consider racial separation in society and church as "natural" instead of "unnatural." The racialist framework has become the norm in the way we plan and work in terms of church and missions. It encourages and rewards what is called the "homogeneous unit principle," which states that if churches want to grow and be effective, they need to target people in society who are like themselves—ethnically, culturally, and economically. Thus, in order to have successful churches and ministries, we are moved to perpetuate this racial framework and postpone our biblical commitments for unity.

---

1 Lucius T. Outlaw, *On Race and Philosophy* (New York: Routledge, 1996), 8–11.

The racialist framework prompts us to justify our homogeneity. When justified from a theological view, this is usually seasoned with the idea of God's providence. Someone might say God's will is that we are a predominantly White congregation or denomination. When spoken of from a secular perspective, this is usually seasoned with an air of scientific or sociological flavor.

This is a major problem. Few Christians today would defend the principles of Jim Crow and apply them to their congregations. Few would explicitly speak in favor of segregation. However, one can be against racism and even desire diversity, but at the same time justify separation and inadvertently undermine racial reconciliation and unity, postponing biblical commitments in the process. This justification is present in many articles, videos, and books that hold partially true statements, but in the end sacrifice the idea of unity on the altar of pragmatic issues.

Churchmen who justify racial and ethnic separation of churches in America are not necessarily Kinist or racist, but they cannot overcome the racialist mindset. John Frame, Professor of Systematic Theology at Reformed Theological Seminary-Orlando, offers some interesting examples of a moderate expression of this tendency. Frame is a godly man and a sound Reformed theologian. However, he is dependent on the strong historical racial outlook of American Christianity.

When asked, "Why is it that Blacks and Whites worship in separate churches?" Frame says:

> Churches tend to belong predominantly to one race or another, because worship is one of those times in which it is important to understand one another on an intimate level. The church is like a family . . . much of its ministry involves communication; and communication is almost always better within ethnic limits. Blacks and Whites tend to speak different languages in worship—a difference that is evident in their choice of music and of preaching style.[2]

---

2 John M. Frame, *The Doctrine of the Christian Life* (Phillipsburg, N.J.: P & R Pub, 2008), 673–678. Almost exact quotes we can find in http://frame-poythress.org/racisms-sexisms-and-other-isms. As an ordained teaching elder in the Presbyterian Church in America, I am deeply indebted to him as a fellow churchman. I've enjoyed corresponding with him about this topic; this piece is submitted to this work with his encouragement.

While Frame is in favor of churches welcoming all types of people regardless of their race or ethnicity, he suggests we should not be surprised when a church body is not diverse. According to Frame, this separation is mainly because of "our natural tendency to want to be with people like ourselves." He adds:

> With your own people, it is usually easier to let your hair down, to joke, to cry, even to worship. With people very different from yourself, you . . . are never quite sure when something you say or do will be found offensive, so you tend not to intrude too far into the emotional space of the other group. It is no accident that Blacks refer to one another as "soul brothers." It is not that people outside one's ethnic group have no souls, but it sometimes seems like that. The outsiders seem stiff and formal, or their language of friendship seems incomprehensible.[3]

I think many readers in our predominantly White congregations will find no problem with these statements. Many Black believers in America will agree as well. Even more, it is true that associating with people like ourselves is the easiest tendency. However, many Hispanic/Latino, especially first-generation, will find these statements problematic.

The problem with the racialist framework

Two seemingly contradictory influences frequently impact Latinos who have recently arrived in the United States. On the one hand, they are impressed by how much progress America has made regarding racial integration in society in comparison with their countries of origin. On the other hand, they are struck by how separate the descendants of African slaves are from White people in terms of church and worship. Many Latino people feel uncomfortable with this separation because even though in their countries of origin racial jokes and discrimination are openly displayed, such divisions are supposed to be blurry in church life.

Most would agree we should not force people to worship together. African Americans and White people in this country have developed a different culture of worship and community through the years. However, we all know that the

---

3 Frame, 672.

cause of this separation is not necessarily, using Frame's words, the "natural human tendency" but also the unnatural traumatic experience of slavery. I don't pretend to understand all the implications of that history, but as Rev. Sandy Wilson has said, the Ferguson unrest reminded us how unresolved those traumas are and how much we need the love of Christ to bring people together to the table of communion in order for the church to be the salt and light in society.[4]

In that regard, not only White people (the majority), but also Asian, Black, and Hispanic people need to recognize our need for change. I am sympathetic to those who want to achieve reconciliation in society, but how will we do this if we don't proactively practice this example as individuals and congregations? Racial reconciliation is more than ethnic diversity, but it does begin with ethnic diversity and rarely can be achieved without transcultural and interracial interactions.

The shaky foundation of the racialist framework

Even though the racialist framework has a strong dominance over the church in America, it is not built on a solid foundation. This lack of a solid foundation becomes evident when we contrast this framework against both special revelation and general revelation. This faulty framework needs to be reevaluated in light of the vast fields of biblical and theological studies, as well as the areas of the study of nature, societies, and history.

With regard to special revelation, many have written about biblical truth, including my colleagues' essays in this book. It is safe to say that the Bible does not use the concept of race as a category to divide humanity, much less the church. On the contrary, the Bible contains many verses that call us to reach those who are not like us and that tell us that being in Christ blurs such divisions (Luke 14:12, Acts 14: 8–18, Rom. 12:16, Gal. 3:28). Hence, there is no biblical justification for demarcations on the basis of races or ethnicity, nor for maintaining the racial separations of churches in America or considering them "natural."

While the racialist framework provides tranquility of conscience and emphasizes freedom of association, the Gospel calls us to see ourselves as

---

4 https://vimeo.com/113336162. Accessed May 3, 2015.

"debtors" of other ethnicities and races (Rom. 1:14). Yet many Bible readers, some even serious scholars, use a strong racial outlook to read homogeneity into the biblical text.[5] Many approach the Bible as if it were written from their personal cultural framework, which then leads to a self-perpetuating blindness. On the one hand, reading the Bible in the context of a homogeneous community won't enrich our vision of church because we are not diverse. On the other hand, we won't be diverse because we will read the Bible from a homogeneous perspective.

We see an example of this circular influence in John Frame's writings. While Frame is not advocating that one race is generally superior to the other, he does find in places such as Romans 12 and First Corinthians 12 the suggestion that humanity is composed of many races and that some races are superior to others in some aspects. While we may agree with Frame that individuals are not equal or do not have the same abilities, Frame insists that this inequality of individuals can be applied to human racial groups as well. He says:

> . . . the biblical teaching about the differences of supernatural gifts in the body of Christ (Romans 12; 1 Corinthians 12) suggests a similar way of looking at the natural gifts in the human race in general. No individual, no race, has all possible human abilities. And the "lesser" abilities are just as necessary to the whole society as are the "greater". . . . It is not wrong, in my view, to believe that some races generally excel others in some particular respects . . . . It is very unlikely that one race is "generally" superior to another in any meaningful sense. But it is just as unlikely that all races are equal in every particular ability. The diversity of gifts I mentioned above would suggest that neither individuals nor races or nations are equal in every human ability or skill.[6]

Frame stretches the analogy of the body and its members and applies it to the racial arena. His intentions are good. However, he confuses the individual level with the racial level of the topic, and this affects his reading of the Bible.

There are not grounds for applying these passages about diversity of gifts in the church to groups that humans have made, named, and classified. The

---

5 J. Daniel Hays. *From Every People and Nation: A Biblical Theology of Race* (Downers Grove, Ill: InterVarsity Press, 2003), 25 -33.

6 http://frame-poythress.org/racisms-sexisms-and-other-isms. See also *The Doctrine of the Christian Life*, 669.

pronouns in the text of Romans 12 and First Corinthians 12 show clearly that Paul is talking about Christian individuals in relation to one group, the church. The analogy of the body in Romans 12 and First Corinthians 12 speaks against the idea of racial division because it speaks of the church as one body integrated by individuals regardless of origin.

The interpolation of the word "race" in this analogy is unfortunate as it opens the door for serious misunderstanding. Can we say that one race excels over others in its ability to prophesy or lead? Can we say that in America one race excels in its ability to teach or write theology? While Frame would not go so far as to say the Bible suggests this, there have been others who would draw such conclusions.[7] Of course, if we are comfortable seeing society and church marked by separation of race or ethnicity, then we may be inclined to see suggestions like this in the Bible at the same time that we paradoxically attempt to advance unity, value, and respect for all groups.

The same is true when we come to contrast this framework with general revelation. There are vast amounts of material in terms of history, social studies, and natural sciences concerning human beings that can make us rethink the idea of race and racial issues. While a detailed study of this material is beyond the scope of this writing, I will mention a few.

For one, our categories of races shift over time. Take, for example, the German people, who:

> For a thousand years they had been the sons and daughters of the ancient Romans. With the fall of the Empire they needed to find a common lineage. The English in the 16th century began to nurse the fetish of Anglo Saxonism, which unites them with the Germanic and separates them from the Roman past.[8]

Historians tell us that what we call White people is the conglomeration of Celts, Picts, Iberians, Etruscans, Romans, Latins, Huns, Slavs, Tartars, Gypsies, Arabs, Jews, Hittites, Berbers, Goths, Franks, Angles, Jutes, Saxons, Vikings,

---

7 For example: http://www.holysmoke.org/sdhok/reggie.htm. Accessed May 3, 2015.

8 Jacques Barzun, *From Dawn to Decadence: 500 Years of Western Cultural Life, 1500 to the Present* (New York: Harper Collins, 2000), 108, 694–695. See also Jacques Barzun, *Race: A Study in Superstition* (New York: Harper & Row, 1965).

and Normans.[9] Further, there is a definite lack of clarity as to what the racial boundaries are. In one sense, the phrase "White people in America" is not reduced to the color of the skin. For example, Irish people were not considered White in the past, and even today many poor light-skinned people are considered "not quite White."[10] The reality is that the concept of White race is fairly new and continues to change.

Similarly, Blacks in America, are actually a mixture of several peoples from Africa brought from different places, violently uprooted from their cultures and nations, and immersed in the common world of slavery. African Americans constructed their racial pride and cultural identity with great effort. Today, it seems normal to speak in terms of the Black church, Black theology, or Black America. It is true these phrases are widely used among African American theologians. But one may justifiably wonder to what extent the idea of Blackness is a product of an imagined community.[11]

There are not sufficient grounds to defend the racial American framework, and there is not even clarity with regard to what terms such as "race" or "ethnicity" mean. These terms are difficult to define because they are not the static reality that we so often think.[12] Race is a slippery idea that we tend to confuse with other categories. We see a constant confusion of race, ethnicity, nation, and culture in our conversations, articles, and books. For instance, John Frame, when writing about race and diversity, avoids defining race and uses the terms "race" and "nation" interchangeably.[13]

---

9 Barzun, *From Dawn to Decadence*, 694–695.

10 Frank D. Bean, Jennifer Lee, and James D. Bachmeier. "Immigration & the Color Line at the Beginning of the 21st Century," Daedalus, 123–140; Noel Ignatiev, *How the Irish Became White* (New York: Routledge, 1995); David R. Roediger, *Working Toward Whiteness: How America's Immigrants Became White* (New York: Basic Books, 2005); and Matt Wray, *Not Quite White: White Trash and the Boundaries of Whiteness* (Durham: Duke University Press, 2006).

11 Bernard Bailyn, *Sometimes an Art: Nine Essays on History* (New York: Alfred A. Knopf, 2015), 7–12. Concerning the diverse ethnicity of African descendants in South America, see the work of Manuel M. Marzal, S. J., "La evangelizacion de los negros americanos segun el de instauranda aethiopum salute" in *Esclavitud, economía y evangelización: las haciendas jesuitas en la América virreinal* (Lima: Pontificia Universidad Católica del Perú, Fondo Editorial, 2005), 26–27.

12 Guido Bolaffi, *Dictionary of Race, Ethnicity and Culture* (London: SAGE Publications, 2003).

13 Frame, 650–653, 662.

This does not mean race is unreal or unimportant. Categories such as race and ethnicity are useful for pragmatic issues and as social constructs of our modern society. Further, how can we avoid talking about race in America if there is high racialist division? How can we ignore the reality of White churches and Black churches? The problem is that racialism has made racial and ethnic distinctions shape the way we organize society, and even worse, how we do ministry and build the church in America.

The lack of clarity in terms is important to note when we say many denominations are monolithic or homogeneous. This cannot be reduced only to phenotypal differences or skin color. For instance, when I say the Presbyterian Church in America, my denominations, is mainly "a White denomination," I am not necessarily saying that it is full of light-skinned people. I am saying that most of our churches are integrated by certain types of people who have some cultural and socioeconomic elements in common that make up the concept of "Whiteness" in this context. Hence, the problem of race is also the problem of socioeconomic differences in America, and we need to work not only to bring other races to our denominations but also people from other socioeconomic backgrounds.

The uncritical acceptance of racialism in America is so shallow and without proper foundation that if a Christian person without knowledge of history were suddenly brought to visit American churches, he or she could easily ask why we ended up so divided? We need to recognize the painful truth—because of the brutality of the past, we have developed a racial framework that we are not willing to give up and that we keep feeding and perpetuating in our society and, unfortunately, in our churches.

Latino/Hispanic ministries and the racialist framework

How does this racialist framework undermine the efforts to reach Latinos? First, the racialist framework may hinder or discourage people from reaching Hispanics at all. Second, it may encourage people to reach them from a distance.

I don't think this is intentional. For instance, during the Reformation in the sixteenth century, godly men made significant advances in terms of human rights and tolerance, but, as historian Heiko Oberman said, these ideals bypassed a whole group of people, the Jews.[14] The past thirty years, there has been a Calvinist revival in America, but the impact of this revival in the growing Hispanic population is thus far insignificant. Many Reformed Christians almost seem to bypass Latinos/Hispanic immigrants as though they were invisible.

In short, most of the plans for our congregations to reach the city or world do not include Hispanics. When most plans speak of the city, they really mean the White middle-upper-class city. We need Christians who will rise above contextual limitations. We need to let our theological commitments break free and serve to judge our commitments to race, ethnicity, and culture.

The second impact of the racial framework is that it hinders non-Hispanics evangelicals from developing relationships with Hispanics. People may reach them, and keep them, only in the peripheries of the church rather than accepting them into the core of activities. Frame, when providing an example of how to minister to Latino/Hispanic communities in America, did not recommend that a White congregation "barge into the Hispanic neighborhoods and bombard them with English gibberish." He said it would be better if they showed their love and concern for the salvation of Latino/Hispanic people by seeking "partnership with a Spanish-speaking congregation, providing resources, teaching, and encouragement where needed."[15]

Also, Frame believes the tactics used by White churches for missions overseas when they plant "tribal churches in areas new to the Gospel" should be applied to the Latino/Hispanic communities in America. Just as our missions install indigenous leadership who know "the Gospel and the basics of the Bible," the same would be with Latino/Hispanics because "educational expectations differ greatly" in these communities. However, for Frame, it makes sense to thoroughly prepare senior pastors of White suburban churches, but it does not make sense to prepare as thoroughly the pastors of Hispanic migrant farm workers.[16]

Initially, someone may find Frame's suggestions inspiring, and in some cases and contexts his proposals may work well. However, these types of well-intended suggestions ignore the concept of *Latinidad*, the various attributes that

---

14 Heiko Oberman, *The Impact of the Reformation* (Grand Rapids, Michigan: Eerdmans, 1994), 81.

15 Frame, 674. See also http://www.frame-poythress.org/minorities-and-the-reformed-church.

16 Frame, 680–681.

are shared by Latin American people and their descendants without reducing those similarities to any single essential trait.[17] In addition, Frame's idea of partnering with churches seems to lean toward a "handout" concept of ministry that tends to see the relationship with Hispanics as only a matter of giving resources to their poverty and teaching to their ignorance. Above all, however, is that this is an expression, precisely, of the racialist framework that encourages us to help other races, cultures, and socioeconomic groups from a distance.

This framework moves us to speak of diversity for our denominations, but we do not practice it in our congregations. This is one of many reasons why we get excited about reports of missions in Mexico but not quite as excited to welcome Mexicans in our own congregations. We are excited about Hispanic Christians planting separate churches. However, the same excitement is not shared in reaching Hispanics and bringing them to our own congregations. We must honestly ask ourselves: What is the initial reaction that our congregation would have if several Black or Latino/Hispanic families began attending our church?

John Frame provides an example of a White pastor who visited a Black family that began to attend his church and suggested that the family "might feel more comfortable" at a predominantly Black church some distance away. For Frame, that pastor "had the best of intentions," because "people tend to prefer worship with others like themselves." Frame however recognized that, at least from the perspective of the Black family, this was taken as an unwelcoming attitude.

Theologians and pastors need to realize that it is not possible to be passionate for evangelism and missions and overlook our failure to overcome these racial, cultural, and socioeconomic divisions. If Reformed denominations want to intentionally and seriously reach the Latino/Hispanic community, they need to create a pipeline of leadership for educated Hispanics with a heart for ministry. Creating this is challenging because many of these educated Hispanics are assimilating into mainstream society. Even if they retain a desire for Hispanic ministry, the current approach to race and ethnicities may discourage them from pursuing this ministry within the bounds of a White-majority

---

17 José Luis Falconi, José Antonio Mazzotti, and Michael Jones-Correa, *The Other Latinos: Central and South Americans in the United States* (Cambridge, Mass: Harvard University Press, 2007).

denomination. Well-intentioned mission proposals, with signs of racial, ethnic, and socioeconomic demarcation, may remind some educated Hispanics of the practice of *reducciones*, a type of indigenous Apartheid practiced by well intentioned Jesuit missions in the history of the colonies.[18]

Latinidad and the White American church

If we desire to reach Latinos, it is crucial that we grow in mutual understanding. Predominantly White denominations such as the PCA need to begin to acknowledge the heterogeneity of Latinos/Hispanics.

First, the word "Latino" or "Hispanic" assembles a disparate range of individuals of all sorts of origins, races, and ethnicities, which in some cases have few things in common. Latino or Hispanics "are a pan-ethnic group with roots in nineteen Spanish-speaking Latin American countries and Spain."[19] "Only about one-quarter (24 percent) of Hispanic adults say they most often identify themselves by 'Hispanic' or 'Latino'" and many of them, such as some Cuban-Americans and Puerto Ricans, reject the category with bitterness[20] "About half (51 percent) say they identify themselves most often by their family's country or place of origin." Even if they accept the label Latino or Hispanic, they are prouder of their country of origin than of their Latino identity.[21] Whether the word Latino or Hispanic be taken as race, ethnicity, or culture, it is not strong enough to mark a line of identity.[22]

---

18 *Reducciones* were a type of indigenous Apartheid practiced by Jesuit missions in different parts of the Spanish colonies, moved initially by a mixture of pious desires and a paternalist protectionism of the indigenous people. Stelio Cro, *The Noble Savage: Allegory of Freedom* (Waterloo, Ont: Wilfrid Laurier Univ. Press, 1990), 7. See also Stelio Cro, *The American Foundations of the Hispanic Utopia (1492–1793)* (Tallahassee, Florida: The DeSoto Press, 1994), and Peter Lambert and R. Andrew Nickson, *The Paraguay Reader: History, Culture, Politics* (Durham and London: Duke University Press, 2013).

19 Idelisse Malavé and Esti Giordani, *Latino Stats: American Hispanics by the Numbers.* 2015; XI.

20 See http://www.pewhispanic.org/2012/04/04/ii-identity-pan-ethnicity-and-race/ accessed May 3 2015.

21 Marshall C. Eakin, *The History of Latin America: Collision of Cultures* (New York: Palgrave Macmillan, 2007), 282–283.

22 Jorge J. E. Garcia, *Race or Ethnicity? On Black and Latino Identity* (Ithaca, NY: Cornell University Press, 2007).

Ministry to Latino/Hispanics is challenging not only because Reformed denominations are homogeneous but also because the churches tend to look at Latino/Hispanics as if they were a homogeneous population. We plan and structure missions and churches placing Hispanic ministries in parallel with Korean and African American ministries. The heterogeneity of Hispanics needs to be acknowledged.

In addition, it is important to seriously consider demographic studies that show a difference in the destinations of the new immigration wave in contrast with the traditional destinations.[23] Some of Frame's comments may be useful for traditional destinations of immigration. However, if members of White churches visit neighborhoods where Hispanic people live, they will find that even the least literate immigrant dreams of learning English, and many of them will view friendship with people from other races, ethnicities, and cultures as a positive thing. They will find that in those Latino/Hispanic families there are children who speak English fluently and surprisingly identify themselves as Americans. Predominantly White churches should acknowledge that the majority of Latinos were born in the United States and that three out of four of all Latinos are US citizens.[24]

Visiting the Hispanic neighborhood is something we should encourage. In the interaction of American Christianity and *Latinidad* we must deal with some paradoxical realities. We must concede, to those who think like John Frame, that there are important differences between the majority of Latino/Hispanic people and predominantly White churches. Paradoxically, one of these differences is how believers and the church react to cultural differences. What makes a church welcoming? What is Christian hospitality? How do we apply the communion of saints to different groups in America?

It is true that most people, including Latino/Hispanics, want to be with people like themselves. However, Latino/Hispanics are not as prone to racial or ethnic separation as White Christians are. Dealing with these issues will require patience and moving past our initial reactions. One helpful thing to improve our understanding of this difference between Whites and Hispanics is to consider that many of our approaches to race and ethnicity lie in our different histories, especially in the different histories of North America, Central America, and South America.

---

23 Helen Marrow, "Assimilation in New Destinations," *Daedalus* 142:3 (Summer 2013): 107–119.

24 Idelisse Malavé, *Latino Stats*, 1–2.

Latin American countries have strong divisions, of course, including racism that is often expressed more openly than in the United States. Nevertheless, the strongest divisions are in terms of the deep inequality of wealth. In spite of this, churches in Latin America tend not to perpetuate divisions because of the radical concept of communion.

The risk for new Latino/Hispanics coming to our congregations is that they will perceive the attitudes of White and Black Christians as in opposition to genuine Christian communion and react toward them in a judgmental way. It is the duty of the pastors, from all backgrounds, to help Hispanics joining the church develop an understanding attitude toward this.

On the other hand, it is the duty of pastors and elders to honestly promote hard and loving conversations in our congregations, denominations, and courts to determine whether their commitment to diversity and integration is greater than their commitment to race, class, and culture. Is our commitment to missions stronger than our commitment to American values of success, such as numerical size and financial security? Is Anthony Bradley correct in saying the PCA "is primarily a place to gather people who share similar cultural norms that fit within White conservative political and social customs and, in city centers, the norms of White and Asian elites"?[25] If so, Latino/Hispanic Reformed Christians will follow their own path and either partner with other denominations who are doing a better job of breaking racial and ethnic divisions or begin a parallel Latino Reformed denomination. If they take that road, though, it would mean giving up efforts to be a truly diverse denomination. I think a better alternative and hope is before us.

Alternatives and hope for Reformed denominations

I am optimistic that the PCA can be a diverse denomination and reach Latino/Hispanics. To do this, we must first work to deconstruct the racial framework and undermine ideas and practices that justify, defend, and promote (openly or euphemistically) racial, ethnic, and socioeconomic separations in our churches. This cannot be done without courage and sacrifice. We need to use the great resources of our theology to address and confront ideas that may help perpetuate un-Christlike separation in future generations. We need to point out,

---

25 Anthony B. Bradley, "The PCA: A Clustering of Political and Social Conservatives and City Center Elites. Part One: Setting forth the premise." Accessed May 3, 2015, at http://theaquilareport.com/the-pca-a-clustering-of-political-and-social-conservatives-and-city-center-elites-part-one-setting-forth-the-premise.

in love, that the racialist framework is not neutral but instead works to perpetuate a problem that is pervasive in American Evangelicalism. This change needs to begin in the heart in the way we see our cities and the world. It is a change of worldview or mindset. We should not conform to the flow of this racialist world, but we must renew our hearts and our congregations to confess our complicity with this racialism.

Second, we should value and empower the current efforts of people and congregations that are walking on the path of integration. We need to listen to congregations with integrated staff who are currently working in the context of integrated ministries.[26] We should keep stressing the urgent need to cross barriers, but also stress the beauty of doing so. We need to highlight that integrated ministry is biblically missional, consistent theologically, is a practical application of incarnational missions, can unite Christians working toward racial reconciliation, can help us impact our society and the world concretely, and will help us achieve a diverse denomination that goes beyond mere rhetoric or intention. Of course, every approach will present challenges and difficulties, but I think the needs addressed by integrated ministries are some of the most urgent faced by our churches and denominations today.

Third, we should move toward a biblical worship that reflects cross-cultural hospitality. I am not suggesting you transform your congregation into a hodgepodge of multiculturalism. However, there can be consideration and hospitality. James K. A. Smith says:

> Worship should be an occasion of cross-cultural hospitality. Consider an analogy: when I travel to France, I hope to be made to feel welcome. However, I don't expect my French hosts to become Americans in order to make me feel at home. . . . And I know that this will take some work on my part.[27]

In this regard, we need to promote a better understanding of what minorities really want. I think many Latino/Hispanic people long for a "radical welcoming heart" in worship instead of a radical change of music style. Many young pastors may be comfortable applying Smith's challenge when it comes to

---

26 "Igniting Your Heart For Integrated Ministries." http://pcamna.org/wordpress/wp-content/uploads/2014/07/Igniting-your-Heart-for-Integrated-Ministry.pdf.

27 James K. A. Smith, *Who's Afraid of Postmodernism? Taking Derrida, Lyotard, and Foucault to Church*, (Grand Rapids: Baker Academy, 2006), 78.

White postmodern millennials. They may struggle more to apply it to immigrant cultures as well.

Fourth, we should proactively work with the children of today, welcoming them and their families, in order to have a better future for our churches. We need to disciple and provide the means of grace for the first, second , and third generations. We need to think of children and their future roles in our denominations. We need to think ahead and work today to leave a legacy for the future generations of unity and reconciliation that begins in the playground of churches and the Sunday Schools of our congregations. I am sympathetic to my colleagues in this book who stress the fact that reconciliation needs to start with the past, but I want to add that the present now will later be the past. A faithful preaching of the Bible will open our eyes to see our blind spots of today for which we will be responsible before future generations and above all to our Lord and King.

Fifth, let's promote friendship with people from different backgrounds. The best way to break the prejudices and misconceptions of others is to work side-by-side. I think many misconceptions of the Hispanic community would disappear if individual Christians would simply get closer to Hispanics. Conversely, Hispanics would dispel misconceptions about White brothers and sisters if they got close to them.

I want to encourage my brothers and sisters in majority-White denominations to emphasize the need for crossing barriers at all levels—individual, congregational, and denominational. Let's keep a sense of urgency in the need to break the grip of the strong racial and ethnic mindset that is our historical burden. I believe our future can be one of greater unity.

Chapter 21

Are Segregationist Hermeneutics Alive in the Church Today?

Rev. Gregory A. Ward

Greg Ward is the Cedar Park Site Pastor of Redeemer Presbyterian Church in Austin, Texas, and Adjunct Professor of Biblical Languages at Redeemer Seminary. He is a graduate of Louisiana State University (BA) and Reformed Theological Seminary-Orlando (MDiv). He has done graduate work in Hebrew Bible and Semitic Languages at Hebrew University in Jerusalem, Israel, and the University of Texas in Austin. He and his wife, Sarah, have two children.

Biblical proofs for segregation were widely in use in the 1950s by White Southern Protestant churches, including Southern Baptists, Methodists, and Presbyterians.[1] However most today would expect that such interpretations of the Bible would have dissipated since the Civil Rights Movement. But what if

---

1 Paul Harvey refers to this widespread phenomena as "segregationist folk theology." See Paul Harvey, *Freedom's Coming: Religious Culture and the Shaping of the South from the Civil War to the Civil Rights Era* (Chapel Hill: University of North Carolina Press, 2007), 218–245. For examples of various proponents see David L. Chappell, *A Stone of Hope: Prophetic Religion and the Death of Jim Crow* (Chapel Hill: University of North Carolina Press, 2004), 108–117; Carolyn Renée Dupont, *Mississippi Praying: Southern White Evangelicals and the Civil Rights Movement, 1945–1975* (New York: New York University Press, 2013), 79–85; Stephen R. Haynes, "Distinction and Dispersal: Folk Theology and the Maintenance of White Supremacy," *Journal of Southern Religion* 17 (2015): accessed April 7, 2016, http://jsreligion.org/issues/vol17/haynes.html; Sean Michael Lucas, *For A Continuing Church: The Roots of the Presbyterian Church in America* (Phillipsburg: P & R Publishing, 2015), 112–126; and Mark Newman, *Getting Right With God: Southern Baptists and Desegregation, 1945–1995* (Tuscaloosa: University of Alabama Press, 2001), 48–64.

such rationalizations of segregation from the Bible are still present in our churches? If such is the case, we need to clearly reject such thinking.

In the following essay I will engage the hermeneutic of segregation used by Dr. Morton H. Smith in his article entitled "The Racial Problem Facing America"[2] to demonstrate his errors in interpreting the Bible to support racial segregation. I have chosen this particular theologian and his hermeneutic for several reasons.

First, Smith's use of Scripture is a good representative of the proofs typically used by other Southern theologians. In fact, Smith's argument is more thorough and nuanced than most of his predecessors.[3]

Second, compared to others, Smith's argument is relatively recent, having been penned in 1964, when most of the others date to the '50s. Surprisingly, Smith's thoughts never received a full response.[4]

Third, though Smith is not well known outside of Reformed and Presbyterian circles, he is well known and highly regarded within Southern Presbyterianism. Smith is an Emeritus Professor of Biblical and Systematic Theology at Greenville Presbyterian Theological Seminary, one of the founders of Reformed Theological Seminary,[5] and was Stated Clerk of the Presbyterian Church in America from 1973 to 1988. Smith is renowned as a churchman and teacher of the doctrines of the Reformed faith. No doubt, many pastors have

---

2 Morton H. Smith, "The Problem Facing America," *The Presbyterian Guardian* 33 (1964): 125–128. Accessed Jan. 7, 2016, http://opc.org/cfh/guardian/Volume_33/1964-10.pdf.

3 I do not mean to suggest that Smith treats every Scripture proposed by others, but that overall he is more thorough than most. Further his argument is more mature in that he avoids problematic passages like arguments based on the curse of Canaan in Gen. 9:22–27. Even still his hermeneutic for interpretation is similar to his predecessors. Compare for example the sermon given by Methodist minister Rev. J. C. Wasson in Itta Bena, MS, in 1953: Dupont, *Mississippi Praying*, p. 82 and Rev. G. T. Gillespie, D. D., "A Christian View on Segregation." Address made before the Synod of Mississippi of the Presbyterian Church in the U. S., November 4, 1954. Accessed April 7, 2016, http://clio.lib.olemiss.edu/cdm/ref/collection/citizens/id/725.

4 Randy Nabors denounced Smith's article in a blog post, but it was not a thorough treatment of Smith's argument. Randy's Rag, July 23, 2012. Accessed January 7, 2016, http://randysrag.blogspot.com/2012/07/talking-about-racism-in-pca.html.

5 I am a graduate of Reformed Theological Seminary in Orlando. As such, even though I have never met Dr. Smith, I owe a debt of gratitude to him for his life and ministry of which I am at least an indirect beneficiary.

benefited from Smith's years of faithful service in ministry. However, it is also likely he has influenced current pastors with his hermeneutic of segregation.

Fourth, Smith's teaching in this article is cited by at least one modern segregationist website, demonstrating his influence in this area continues.[6]

The goal of Smith's article

Smith's intent[7] in the article is to show that the Bible teaches that "ethnic pluriformity is the revealed will of God for the human race"[8] and that a "principle of segregation as such is not necessarily sinful in and of itself."[9] He goes on to suggest that such segregation should continue and that integration is unbiblical. In other words, Smith's goal is to demonstrate that racial segregation and purity is normative in the Bible and should be preserved in the church and society. Smith says:

> The mass mixing of the races with the intent to erase racial boundaries he (Smith) does consider to be wrong, and on the basis of this, he would oppose the mixing of the two races in this way. Let it be acknowledged that a sin in this area against the Negro race has been perpetrated by godless White men, both past and present, but this does not justify the adoption of a policy of mass mixing of the races. Rather, the Bible seems to teach that God has established and thus revealed his will for the human race now to be that of ethnic pluriformity, and thus any scheme of mass integration leading to mass mixing of the races is decidedly unscriptural.[10]

His use of the term "pluriformity" is peculiar and deserves some attention. "Pluriformity" simply means having multiple forms, and it should be a synonym

---

6 *Tribal Theocrat*, March 2014. Accessed January 7, 2016, http://tribaltheocrat.com/2014/03/dr-morton-h-smith-the-racial-problem-facing-america.

7 Smith states his preliminary goals as to "set forth what I understand the Bible has to say about the unity and diversity of the human race" and "examine the question of whether segregation per se is necessarily sinful." Smith, "The Problem Facing America," 125. However, he clearly goes beyond these simple objectives as he makes his case.

8 Smith, "The Problem Facing America," 126.

9 Smith, "The Problem Facing America," 126.

10 Smith, "The Problem Facing America," 127–28.

for diversity. However, Smith seems to use the term with some distinction. Smith's use of "pluriformity" appears to be related to his desire to argue that God intends for certain forms, or races, to remain distinct from one another through his principle of separation.

The reason this particular use of pluriformity is important is that although integration and intermarriage would blur the lines between certain races and reduce the particular pluriformity Smith argues we should maintain, they would not necessarily reduce diversity in mankind. On the contrary, intermarriage and integration multiplies diversity. For the sake of clarity, I do not see a problem with ethnic and racial pluriformity in mankind because God intended it to be that way. Rather, Smith argues that some sort of status quo of pluriformity[11] by means of the separation of races should be maintained through segregation.

As we work our way through Smith's use of Scripture, we will see three problems that lead him to his incorrect conclusions about segregation. First, he is often imprecise and vague. He makes generalizations without careful consideration of the passage at hand, and he uses terminology carelessly. Second, he exercises poor exegesis in handling passages, missing the point, and reading in his own presuppositions. Third, he uses poor hermeneutics. He fails to take into consideration broader scriptural and historical context. All of this either comes from, or leads to, poor theology.

The Bible and ethnic diversity

Smith begins his discussion of the matter with an observation of the unity of mankind having descended from Adam first and later from Noah. This is all well and good, but he then moves to consider a few verses from Paul's speech to the Athenians, a passage to which both integrationists and segregationists were appealing in his time. In this passage, Paul seeks to connect the Athenians of the Areopagus to the God of the Bible. In Acts 17:26 we read, *"And he made from one man every nation of mankind to live on all the face of the earth, having determined allotted periods and the boundaries of their dwelling place."* Smith

---

11 It is worth noting that nowhere does Smith define which races, ethnicities, or nations (except Israel) God endorses as necessary forms within the ordained pluriformity and therefore should be maintained through his "principle of separation" which we will discuss later. However, it seems clear from his discussion of racial issues in the South later in the article that he at least believes there should be a principle of separation between White people and Black people. See above quote.

concludes that God is sovereign over all national distinctions, and by logical extension over all racial distinctions. But saying that God in his providence is sovereign over all the variations and distinctions of mankind is unhelpful and a bit misleading.

There are several problems. First, it is not Paul's point to demonstrate that God has deemed all of these divisions good. He is merely describing the world as it is and connecting it to God, so that he can connect his hearers to God. Smith tacitly acknowledges this reality in his own terminology. He observes that the verse "teaches the basic unity of the human race, but it also speaks of the diversity of mankind…. "[12] The difference between what Scripture teaches and what it speaks to is no small thing, but Smith is focused on the latter. Worse still, he neglects to mention that the purpose of all this is so that "they should seek God" and that "he is actually not far from each of us" in Acts 17:27. Paul is speaking to pagans from whom he is traditionally distanced, both spiritually and physically, in an effort to establish connection to them. But Smith is focusing on ways to better find separation in the Bible. In sum, Smith misinterprets the verse, because he fails to read it in context and understand the intent.

Further, this is an example of where he is theologically careless. When Smith takes his point from an issue the verse speaks to but does not teach, he subtly attributes to God an intention in his sovereign providence over the nations. In other words, if God is sovereign over the nations and their seasons and boundaries, then he also approves of all divisions regardless of their potential connection to, and involvement with, sin.

This goes completely against the judgments that God pronounces on the nations repeatedly in the Old Testament prophets. If the distinctions were good, why judge the nations? God "determined allotted periods" and "boundaries" for all nations to accomplish his purposes of calling mankind back to himself. However, it does not follow that the nations, their boundaries, and their ethnic distinctions are necessarily good. Yet that is what Smith implies and argues. Smith is confusing the decretive will of God with the preceptive will of God. Paul is describing the former, while Smith is suggesting the latter is in play.

Smith acknowledges that the Acts 17 passage is focused more on national than ethnic distinctions, so he seeks to establish a principle of ethnic

---

12 Smith, "The Problem Facing America", 125.

pluriformity in other passages. For instance, he observes that the Tower of Babel (Genesis 11) and the genealogy of Noah's descendants (Genesis 10) are possible biblical explanations for the origins of races and nations. While Smith uses terms like "seems" and "may," he assumes the connections are valid without exploring the difficulties. The reality is that the genealogy is essentially useless for establishing any sort of endorsement by God of different ethnicities. Certainly there are names of tribes, nations, and people groups in the list, but this is at most etiologically descriptive. There is no reason to think this explanation of the origins of these groups is by God's special prescription or positive endorsement.

Smith's treatment of the Tower of Babel in Genesis 11 is more disconcerting. He gives a brief summary of the passage and then focuses on God's action to disperse mankind from Babel. He rightly describes God's action both as divine judgment and as a form of common grace, "Thus God, by his common grace intervened, and by his act of judgment intensified the diversity or pluriformity that was inherent in his creation."[13] There are several problems here.

First, God did not intensify ethnic or racial pluriformity. He intensified linguistic diversity. One may argue that this then resulted in ethnic, or racial, diversity, but the two are not the same thing and should not be assumed to coincide. We have numerous examples in the modern world of different races that speak the same language and conversely of people of the same race who speak different languages. It does not follow that just because God intensified linguistic diversity that he necessarily caused an increase in ethnic or racial pluriformity.

Second, Smith assumes that just because God has acted in a gracious way to restrain sin, the result of this is ideal, or at least worth preserving. He says:

> If from this we may conclude that ethnic pluriformity is the revealed will of God for the human race in its present situation, it is highly questionable whether the Christian can have part in any program that would seek to erase all ethnic distinctions.[14]

---

13 Smith, "The Problem Facing America," 126.

14 Smith, "The Problem Facing America," 126.

However, God's acts to restrain sin are often in degrees. While they may prevent a situation from being as bad as it could be, his actions do not necessarily make the situation as good as he desires it to be. For example, consider the provision for divorce in the Mosaic law in Deuteronomy 24:1. Jesus makes it explicitly clear in Mark 10:2–12 that we may not conclude from this that divorce is a good, or ideal, state we should preserve simply because there is provision for it in God's law. In the same sense, just because God pronounced a judgment on the sin at Babel, it does not follow that the results of that sin and judgment should not be overcome by the Gospel.

One might wish to object since Jesus explicitly clarifies the issue with respect to divorce, so where would such a clarification come from for the Tower of Babel? The confusion of tongues at Babel is addressed at Pentecost in Acts 2, where the Gospel transcends ethnic and linguistic divisions, which Smith acknowledges. However, he does not see that this reversal nullifies the necessity of ethnic pluriformity he concludes is implied by God's judgment. Smith fails to grasp the significance of the Gospel with respect to race because he reduces the impact of the universality of the offer of the Gospel to the spiritual realm. I will deal with this problem later. For now, suffice it to say that Smith has not proved his premise that "ethnic pluriformity is the revealed will of God for the human race in its present situation."[15]

The Old Testament, segregation, and intermarriage

From there, Smith turns to demonstrating a principle of ethnic, or racial, segregation in the Old Testament. Again, as has been his habit thus far, Smith describes the situation in the Old Testament as he sees it rather than engaging in detailed exegesis of the passages in view. This time his broad brush strokes are a bit more problematic, as he seems to misunderstand the Scriptures. In his defense, racial purity has been a focus of Judaism at different times, but in reality a close examination of the Old Testament reveals that race has never been a biblical criteria for participation in Judaism.

Smith begins his demonstration of a principle of segregation with the general observation of the intent of God to "create and preserve a peculiar

---

15 Smith, "The Problem Facing America," 126.

people unto himself."[16] Indeed God does this, and he does it by separation or segregation. This Smith rightly observes happening in the patriarchal narratives in Genesis, where Isaac and Jacob each take wives from Abraham's people rather than intermarrying with the Canaanites. In this much, we agree. However, the problem comes when Smith confuses this religious segregation with ethnic or racial segregation. To be fair, Smith acknowledges that God's purposes are religious when he says:

> It should be noted that this segregation of Abraham's seed was done by God ultimately for the purpose of preserving their religious purity, yet it was accomplished by means of a racial or ethnic segregation.[17]

However, we need to make a careful distinction here. The race of people that is Israel is more the result of this segregation rather than the means to accomplish it, as Smith maintains. More importantly, this result is mainly incidental to God's intent to have a special people rather than the goal of the segregation. The question is how can we demonstrate that this is the case and show Smith's error? The answer actually lies in Smith's treatment of the next parts of Israel's history.

Smith moves from Abraham to consider the sojourn of the people of Israel in Egypt. Curiously, he suggests that God moves Jacob and his sons from Canaan to Egypt because of their failure to remain separate in Canaan.

> His descendants failed to keep themselves separate from the people of Canaan, and God in his all wise providence brought them down into Egypt, where they were set apart by the Egyptians in a segregated area.[18]

However, separation is not at all the purpose given in the text. Rather Joseph is sent ahead to prepare the way to preserve the sons of Jacob (Gen. 44:5, 7), and the LORD clearly assures Jacob that he will make him a great nation in Egypt (Gen. 46:3–4). There is no indication that this sojourn in Egypt is for the purpose of ethnic, or even religious, purity.

---

16 Smith, "The Problem Facing America," 126.

17 Smith, "The Problem Facing America," 126.

18 Smith, "The Problem Facing America," 126.

What sort of segregation do we observe the children of Israel experiencing in Egypt? As Smith rightly observes, they are given a specific area in which to live, the land of Goshen. However, does this mean Israel was really isolated ethnically? They were separated from the Egyptians, or at least those of higher standing, but they were really being relegated to an area with all the other slaves in Egypt, some of whom were ironically probably Canaanites.[19] The great multitude that left Egypt was certainly not all descendants of Jacob, but before we consider the people that lived in Goshen and left in the Exodus, we should discuss Joseph.

Smith conveniently omits the fact that Joseph took an Egyptian wife, Asenath, who was given to him by Pharaoh. He leaves out that Joseph's two sons Manasseh and Ephraim, the fathers of two of twelve tribes of Israel, were of mixed blood. They were half Israelite and half Egyptian. Clearly ethnic segregation was not what God had in mind in this case.

But perhaps Joseph is an exception? Perhaps the rest of Israel maintained their ethnic purity in Egypt and during the Exodus? Not much is preserved of the four hundred years Israel spent in Egypt, except that what began as a great thing turned sour. They certainly managed to maintain a national identity, but did it come with ethnic purity and segregation? The latter seems unlikely because of some of the problems noted in the Exodus itself. Again, as with Joseph's wife, we are in territory that is largely uncharted by Smith right now.

After the tenth plague when the Israelites finally leave Egypt, their numbers are counted, and a curious group of people join them (Exod. 12:38). They are referred to by a particular Hebrew word, *'ereb*, which occurs in an expression usually translated something like "mixed multitude." The term occurs rarely (Exod. 12:38; Jer. 25:20; Jer. 50:37; Ezek. 30:5; Neh. 13:3), but it is clear from these other occurrences that it refers to "other people" or "foreigners." Presumably, these foreigners are the other slaves that lived in the same area as the Israelites and benefited from their association with them.

These people come up again later in the wilderness wanderings in Numbers 11:4. Here they are referred to by an even rarer term, *'sapsup*, which is usually translated "rabble." In this case the rabble that is with, but distinct from, the

19 See James K. Hoffmeier, *Israel in Egypt: The Evidence for the Authenticity of the Exodus Tradition* (New York: Oxford University Press, 1997), 54–68.

Israelites is complaining about the manna God had provided and not having meat to eat like they did in Egypt. Again it is not clear exactly who these people are, but it is clear that they are part of the Exodus. God not only delivered his covenant people from slavery, but also others who joined them.

If this is not proof enough that there were foreigners among the Israelites during the Exodus, consider that the Passover meal was explicitly restricted to those who had been circumcised (Exod. 12:43–49). But further, it seems likely that these foreigners integrated into the tribes of Israel because Joshua had to circumcise a number of the second generation of Israelites, which had not been circumcised during the wanderings, in order to make sure all the people were circumcised (Josh. 5:2–7). The passage mentions explicitly that this effort to circumcise all the people is occurring a second time. In other words, there was both need and opportunity to circumcise the foreigners that originally joined Israel in the Exodus, and further at least some of them were not diligent to circumcise their children, which required the second round of circumcision.

The bottom line in all of this is that neither ethnicity nor race was key for defining who was a part of the tribes of Israel or who participated in their defining communal ritual, the Passover. Rather, circumcision was the key for defining who was a part of Israel during the Exodus, the wanderings, and the settlement of the Promised Land.

Smith's next interaction with the Scripture is with the Mosaic law, where he maintains that segregation was the intent of Deuteronomy 7:3. "The people were commanded not to intermarry with other peoples. This was to preserve their racial integrity, and especially their religious integrity."[20] However, the prohibition of intermarriage with the peoples of Canaan has nothing to do with racial integrity. The reason for the prohibition is given explicitly in the very next verse, and it is only about religious purity. Smith goes on in the same paragraph to reference Genesis 6 and Second Corinthians 6:15 as reasons for prohibiting the people of God to intermarry with unbelievers, but this rationale has nothing to do with racial intermarriage at all.

Finally, Smith references Ezra 9 and 10 and Malachi 2:10–16 as further proof that the people of Israel are to remain racially pure and not intermarry with the peoples of the land. But again the problem is that neither of these

---

20 Smith, "The Problem Facing America," 126.

passages are about racial purity. In both cases the issue is that they are intermarrying with people that worship other gods (Ezra 9:1; Malachi 2:11). Intermarrying with these people that are not faithful to God has made them unfaithful to God. If they had taken wives from the neighboring peoples that had converted to Judaism and united themselves to God, this would not have been a problem. In neither case was this about racial purity, but rather about religious fidelity.

How can we be sure that this last assertion is true? These passages are pretty strong in their condemnation of intermarriage with the other peoples of Canaan. Is it possible that the Old Testament is concerned with more than just religious purity? In order to falsify this, we need to demonstrate positively, that people of foreign blood were welcome to join Israel.

First, we will consider Rahab, the prostitute of Jericho, that helped the spies. In Joshua 6:22–25, Joshua famously spares Rahab and her family while destroying the rest of the city and everyone in it. But Rahab is not just spared and sent on her way, she actually *"lived in Israel to this day"* as stated in verse 25. Further, not only does Rahab live with Israel, but she intermarries and becomes part of the most prestigious bloodline in the entire Bible. She is the wife of Salmon and the mother of Boaz, which means she is an ancestor of both David and Jesus (see Matt. 1:5). She even makes the faith hit parade in Hebrews 11:31. All this can be said of a woman of the blood of the peoples of the land that Israel was prohibited from intermarrying with in Deuteronomy 7:3. The issue was not her bloodlines. It was her faithfulness to God. She was faithful; the others were not.

Second, consider Ruth the Moabitess. The point of the book of Ruth, the reason for its preservation and entrance into the canon, is to argue for the legitimacy of David's bloodlines and right to the throne. In Deuteronomy 23:3–6 Moses explicitly prohibits Moabites to *"enter the assembly of the LORD forever,"* because of the treacherous ways in which they dealt with Israel during the wandering in the wilderness. This would surely ban intermarriage and the offspring of any such marriage. Yet Ruth's faithfulness to Naomi and to the Lord (Ruth 1:16–17) gain her entrance into Israel by marriage to Boaz. And she, like Rahab before her, bears a child in the royal bloodline, Obed, the grandfather of David (Ruth 4:21–22), which in turn also places her in the line of Jesus (Matt. 1:5).

But perhaps these two are exceptions that prove the rule? Do we find a principle elsewhere in the Old Testament that would lead us to expect people of foreign bloodlines might become part of the people of God? Indeed we do. Isaiah 56:3–6 speaks of the *"foreigner who has joined himself to the LORD"* and how he should not fear that the LORD will separate him from the people of God. Isaiah goes on to prophesy about these foreigners who join themselves to the LORD, so long as they keep the covenant and the Sabbath, *"these I will bring to my holy mountain."* So again we see that entrance into the community of God is a function of covenant and religious fidelity, not bloodlines. The only segregation that the LORD instituted in the Old Testament was for purity of religion, not purity of race or blood. Smith's assertions and insinuations are scripturally invalid.

The New Testament, segregation, and intermarriage

Next, Smith turns his attention to the New Testament and wisely acknowledges that it seems to overturn the principles he believes he has found in the Old Testament. Smith says:

> The question may be asked as to whether or not the New Testament sets aside this principle of separation. With the coming of Jesus Christ and the completion of his work on earth, we have the close of the period of particularity, in which God openly revealed himself to only one nation. With the giving of the Great Commission, we have the opening of a new period, namely, a period of universality. This is a time in which God offers his grace and mercy to the whole world. Ultimately, the death of Judaism came with the death of Jesus Christ on the Cross.[21]

Smith mentions a number of passages, including the aforementioned Pentecost event of Acts 2, several Pauline passages about the ingrafting of the Gentiles into the Jews, and even a few interactions between Jesus and Gentiles. He also considers a number of passages that focus on distinctions and differences between Jewish and Gentile Christians and men and women. It is these differences and distinctions he wishes to emphasize in order to focus on diversity. His argument is essentially that since there is diversity in the church,

---

21 Smith, "The Problem Facing America," 126.

there should also be a continuation of the principle of segregation he errantly found in the Old Testament.

The key to his argument is his treatment of Galatians 3:28, *"There is neither Jew nor Greek, there is neither slave nor free, there is no male and female, for you are all one in Christ Jesus."* His comment on this verse is as follows:

> Paul is speaking of the essential spiritual unity that we all have in Christ Jesus, and yet it can hardly be maintained that he meant to imply that there were no longer any distinctions or differences within the church. The Christian faith does not demand the erasure of all diversity between men. Rather, it teaches a unity in diversity and a diversity in unity.

In other words, Smith appears to be taking Paul's language here as hyperbolic, or perhaps eschatological. Both are common ways to understand this passage. Indeed, it is difficult to imagine there should be no differences or distinctions at all between individuals this side of heaven. However, just because we acknowledge unity in diversity or the fact that neither we nor Paul can or should dissolve all differences and distinctions, it will not do to simply reduce Paul's point here to apply only to spiritual unity.[22] To do so is to ignore Paul's historical context and rob this verse of its spiritual conviction and practical impact.

Paul is countering creedal sayings of both Greeks and Jews. The historian Diogenes Laertius attributes to both Socrates and Thales the saying that he is thankful "that I was born a human being and not a beast, a man and not a woman, a Greek and not a barbarian."[23] The Talmud is even closer to Paul's language. It says:

> R. Judah says, A person must recite three blessings every day: "Praised are you, O LORD, who has not made me a Gentile," "Praised are you, O LORD, who did not make me a boor," and "Praised are you, O LORD, who did not make me a woman." (T. Ber. 6:18)

---

22 Paul was not interested in doing so either, at least in the case of male and female. Compare his teaching on husbands and wives: 1 Cor. 11.3; 14.34–35; Eph. 5.22–24; Col. 3.18; 1 Tim. 2.12; Titus 2.4–5.

23 Diogenes Laertius, *Lives of the Philosophers*, 1.33. This saying is also attributed to Plato by Plutarch in *Marius* 46.1 and Lactantius in *Divine Institutes* 3.19.17. With such a diversity of attributions, this was obviously a widespread quotation.

Another rabbi substitutes "slave" for "boor" in this prayer in B. Men. 43b–44a.

When this historical context is taken into consideration, it becomes clear that Paul is not seeking to erase distinctions, but to unite the church, and not just spiritually. He is counteracting bigoted notions that would cause divisions between Jewish Christians and Greek Christians. This verse is polemical, and it would have daily, practical impact on their social interactions. It simply cannot be reduced to spiritual unity.

The same is true of all of Paul's teachings on the unity of Jews and Gentiles. He is in the trenches with real-life scenarios. He is uniting disparate people in one faith. This has implications for all of their lives. Segregation would be antithetical to all that he was trying to accomplish. Diversity does not limit or restrict the extent of the impact of the Gospel, but rather it is the context in which the Gospel shines and brings practical social and physical unity, not just spiritual unity.

And what of intermarriage? Was Paul concerned with maintaining separation between Jews and Greeks in marriage? To be united religiously in the Greco-Roman world was to be united socially and culturally and even professionally.[24] Under those circumstances, it is hard to imagine that intermarriage would not occur in the early church, particularly given that historically when Gentiles entered the Jewish faith, they intermarried. So, if Paul wanted to prevent the dissolution of this particular racial distinction, one would expect him to prohibit it. However, when Paul addresses the issue of whom a Christian should marry, race seems to be the furthest thing from his mind. In an extensive discussion of marriage in First Corinthians 7, the issue of racial intermarriage never comes up, and again in First Timothy 5, when discussing the issue of the remarriage of younger widows, concern for racial intermarriage is lacking. Further, in Second Corinthians 6:14, when Paul says, *"Do not be unequally yoked with unbelievers,"* the concern is about faith, not race.[25]

---

24 This was in large part due to the guild systems in place. See for example Ben Witherington III, *Revelation*, The New Cambridge Bible Commentary (New York: Cambridge University Press, 2003), 98.

25 In fairness, it should be noted that Smith observes the same. However, he connects this "religious integrity" inappropriately with "racial integrity," because he brings this verse up in the context of his misguided discussion of Deuteronomy. 7:3. See above.

This really should not be surprising given that the Old Testament concerns over intermarriage were the same.

Conclusions

First, while the Bible does describe an ethnically and racially pluriform world, it does not prescribe a particular pluriformity. God does not endorse a particular set of ethnic and racial divisions, nor is there any indication he wishes us to preserve what divisions are there.

Second, it is clear in the Bible that God is constantly at work in history setting apart a people of his own. In the Old Testament, this is the nation of Israel, which is intended to be separate geographically and religiously. The intent of this separation was to maintain religious purity or fidelity to the Lord and had nothing to do with race, ethnicity, or blood. The proscriptions of intermarriage with the nations around Israel were also about religious fidelity, and intermarriage was allowed once a person of foreign descent pledged fidelity to the Lord. The Jewish nation has never been a nation of truly pure blood, and blood was never a barrier to joining Israel.

Third, the ethnic and racial diversity of the world is seen in the New Testament as an opportunity for the Gospel to bring unity amongst diversity. While there is indeed great diversity manifested in the New Testament church, the goal of Jesus[26] and Paul is to bring unity of a social and physical nature, and not just a spiritual unity to the diverse members of the church.

Further there are no proscriptions of interracial marriage in the New Testament or suggestions that ethnicity or race should be a consideration for Christians in marriage. Rather, just as in the Old Testament, the emphasis is on not marrying outside of the faith.

In sum, we should say that any suggestion that the Bible offers principles of separation or segregation based on ethnic or racial lines is false and a misrepresentation of Scripture. Further, any teaching that Christians should be about the business of promoting or supporting such segregation is antithetical to the Gospel of Christ.

---

26 I have not taken the time to pursue Jesus's teaching on this, but cursory consideration of his teaching on the Good Samaritan in Luke 10, or the implications of the command to "Love your enemies" (Matt. 5:44; Luke 6:27, 35) in the midst of an Israel dominated by foreign reign, or his willingness to enter the home of the centurion in Luke 7, indicates that the Gospel is intended to transcend racial and ethnic divisions.

Confession and Reconciliation
Are Necessary

Chapter 22

Reconciliation Is About Obedience

Rev. Barry Henning

Barry Henning is the founding pastor of New City Fellowship of St. Louis, where the church has been working toward racial reconciliation and justice since 1992. Barry has degrees from William Tyndale College (BS) and Westminster Theological Seminary (MDiv). He and his wife, Ann, have four children and twenty grandchildren.

What kind of new obedience will be required to accompany genuine repentance in the area of racial reconciliation?

What would it look like if our churches were more successful in reaching the diverse cultures of North America, and what changes would have to take place? Where do we see God already at work, and how can we build on that and learn from that?

As God has formulated my thoughts on these issues during the past 25 years of ministry, I hold absolute conviction that the righteousness we long for can only come by grace through faith in Christ and the work of the Spirit. But the need for specific action is real. The body of Christ suffers when we remain divided.

Reconciliation versus diversity

I do not ask for these only, but also for those who will believe in me through their word, that they may all be one, just as you, Father, are in me, and I in you, that they also may be in us, so that the world may believe that you have sent me. The glory that you have given me I have given to them, that they may be one even as we are one. (John 17:20–22)

I am going to start with the presupposition (from John 17, 1 Corinthians 12, Ephesians 1, Colossians 1, 1 Pet. 2, 1 John 1) of a needed, Christ-purchased, Jesus-prayed-for commitment to a God-imaged reconciliation in the church. This is not simply or merely diversity. And it's not only ethnic or racial reconciliation. It is racial, gender, social, and economic reconciliation that is needed. Universities and workplaces are often diverse, but not necessarily reconciled. The United States as a country is unbelievably diverse, but still without much deep reconciliation.

True reconciliation involves an actual in-the-flesh embracing of one another, where we learn to love one another deeply and reflect the true humanity God created us to be. This humanity includes placing a high value on each other. We are meant to value the differences God created in us. We are meant to function in a way that truly acknowledges we really need those differences—ethnic and socioeconomic.

Thus, we humbly learn from and submit to the image of God in one another as equal members of the body with differing gifts and functions, all from the same Spirit and all in the same family. It also means we constantly forgive one another, exercise grace for one another, bear one another's burdens, and honor one another above ourselves. It is so much like being married and being a family that Paul uses marriage as one of the greatest images of the reconciled church, and the rest of the Apostles regularly use direct family language in describing the people of God.

For real diversity to occur, there must be reconciliation. However, I do not think it is possible to address past or present sins of racism without facing the fundamental need for a paradigm shift toward intentional reconciliation that is both ethnic and socioeconomic in scope.

To do this, we will need new structures to foster meaningful reconciliation. Consider Jesus's words, *"And no one puts new wine into old wineskins. If he does, the wine will burst the skins—and the wine is destroyed, and so are the skins. But new wine is for fresh wineskins"* (Mark 2:22).

Deep repentance will lead to many changes in our current wineskins. We will need to humbly work toward genuinely becoming a multiethnic, multi-socioeconomic worshipping and kingdom-focused community of churches, with multiethnic, multi-socioeconomic leadership.

Evidence of new wineskins would mean local churches would be increasingly multiethnic and multi-socioeconomic both in their membership and their leadership. Elders, deacons, and pastors in local churches would come from the Black, White, Asian, African, Latino, American Indian communities, both rich and poor, and so would worship, discipleship, community, and other ministries. Publications and curriculum would address the perspectives and concerns of immigrants, refugees, minorities, and the poor as well as reconciliation issues—described and addressed without a dominant-culture spin. We would begin learning from and being instructed by our brothers and sisters in minority cultures instead of always being in the position of giving instruction.

At present, too many churches are culturally, financially, and even theologically entrenched in a White-upper-middle-class power system that no one will easily let go of. What makes it doubly hard is that some elements of our Christian practice are interlaced with cultural Christianity that has been given a theological covering that produces a near-impossible grid to break through. Nothing short of a cataclysmic shaking will likely change this.

But in response to the preaching of the Word and the conviction of the Spirit, we can repent and change. If not, the good news is that God is in the business of bringing the cataclysmic changes necessary to move his church along (Acts 1:8 becoming a reality through Acts 8:1, for example). What would it take to see repentance-based changes and significant new obedience? I believe we need both a theological change (always reforming) and a commitment to system-wide structural changes (always willing to create new wineskins) in our churches and denominations.

Theological changes

We need a theological/practical embracing of reconciliation as a covenantal obligation. Consider Paul's words:

> *But when I saw that their conduct was not in step with the truth of the Gospel, I said to Cephas before them all, "If you, though a Jew, live like a Gentile and not like a Jew, how can you force the Gentiles to live like Jews?"* (Gal. 2:14)

If we do not see the call to reconciliation as a fundamental, moral, and covenantal obligation of the church that Christ has both called us to and will himself equip us for, we simply won't do the hard work to make it happen. If not careful, we can read the Scriptures with heavy cultural blinders and plug in the perspectives and dynamics of an all-White, Western, middle-class, dominant-culture church point of view and believe we can understand and apply these Scriptures to ourselves and to every other ethnic group as well, fully and adequately.

We can keep on ignoring the historic realities of an early church doing its theology, given to us in the New Testament letters, in a context that included sworn enemies and totally opposing worldviews and cultures all being called to humbly, lovingly embrace one another in local congregations under the lordship of Jesus the Messiah. Our cultural points of view help shape what we are sensitive to and see in the biblical narrative, and the more narrow our cultural point of view, the easier it is to "screen out" the call and need for the practical reconciliation of the nations in the body of Christ.

Currently, it seems many pastors are overwhelmed with the needs of their congregations and think that a commitment to reconciliation is not really necessary for them to be a faithful church. They also think of it as something their busy, hectic, already struggling congregations simply do not have time for. They think adding such a commitment is unrealistic.

But the great freedom of the Gospel and the kingdom allows us to die to self and lay our agendas aside and trust God to take up his agenda and find the expression of eternal life we were looking for all along. While I am not naively suggesting that embracing reconciliation and justice are either easy or a cure-all for the self-absorbed struggles with sin in our churches, reconciliation does powerfully help put many other things in perspective that our Christian communities constantly stumble over. These include:

1. The use of wealth as a covenant blessing to help others versus storing up wealth for ourselves (1 Tim. 6)
2. The need for the Spirit's vision and gifting in every member of the congregation to bring God's righteousness and justice to the nations (Acts 2), and the deeper equipping of the body for significant ministry that leads to laying down our lives for our enemies (Romans 8, Ephesians 4)
3. The context of worship that is meant to be inclusive of all God's people and not bound to one culture (John 4)

4. The purpose and focus of education and career—namely, to be equipped to seek justice and do good to express the glory of God in all aspects of life, which is the only "calling" the Bible actually talks about and applies to everybody (Ephesians 1)
5. The assessing of life decisions being tied to an eternal kingdom of righteousness and reconciliation that has already begun and being confident that all our labors are not in vain because they lead into this coming kingdom at the return of Christ (Colossians 1, 1 Corinthians 15)
6. The accompanying confidence that the darkness of the world's problems will not defeat the kingdom of light.

The theological and practical lack of focus and commitment to reconciliation and justice means our energies go elsewhere. That elsewhere, if it's not toward the poor and for reconciliation, eventually ends up being some version of "I can have my best life now." Some form or other of the Prosperity Gospel is simply the natural offspring of any church that refuses to focus on the poor and reconciliation.

We need a theological and practical embracing of the good news of the kingdom for the poor as seen by Jesus's own words and actions:

> *The Spirit of the Lord is upon me, because he has anointed me to proclaim good news to the poor. He has sent me to proclaim liberty to the captives and recovering of sight to the blind, to set at liberty those who are oppressed, to proclaim the year of the Lord's favor.* (Luke 4:18–19)

> *And he lifted up his eyes on his disciples, and said: "Blessed are you who are poor, for yours is the kingdom of God.* (Luke 6:20)

One of the major contributing factors that has provided us with the theological rationale to function as a church without genuine reconciliation has been a redefinition of the kingdom of God to fit a majority-culture and individualistic culture point of view. We have too often conflated the *"good news of the kingdom of God"* with only personal salvation and justification. That has left us reading passages about the kingdom for the poor and kingdom justice as simply and only a reference to an attitude of the heart of the individual sinner seeking personal salvation and a standing of forensic righteousness in Christ. We have actually exchanged the amazing announcement of the kingdom of God and the anointing of the Messiah to bring his actual (not only forensic) justice

231

and righteousness to the nations of the earth (Isaiah 42) and to announce good news to the poor and to set the captives free (Isaiah 61, Luke 4) as the means for seeing his kingdom come into this world, to a gospel of only personal, individualized salvation.

This redefinition and individualizing allows us to be complicit in the cultural sins of racism, oppression, and economic greed on both a personal and structural level, while still leaving us convinced we can effectively disciple the culture into the kingdom through an intellectual exercise in personal discipleship and Bible study without actually enacting the lifestyle of Jesus and the Apostles.

Structural changes

Closely tied to this is the history of the White, Western church as part of the dominant culture. Because the history of White, Western Christianity became entangled with the majority-culture power structures, including during the Reformation and later in the founding of the United States, we have increasingly stumbled over the nature of the kingdom of God. We have accepted all along the "natural ethnic division of the church" as a practical reality—Dutch Reformed, German Lutheran, French Catholics, Scots Presbyterian, English Episcopalian.

The lure of cultural power within those nation groups helped rationalize this reality. Perhaps the highest expression of an ethnocentric, dominant culture church in the Protestant tradition that we still extol today as the model we all aspire to, was the work embodied in the life of Abraham Kuyper. That model has left us too often with a working definition of the nature of the kingdom of God in its greatest expression, as primarily focused on shaping worldviews through the systems and structures of the culture—including the arts, science, politics, economic structures, and educational institutions.

While all these things are certainly meant to be redeemed, the unchangeable fact that God has called the weak and lowly and the despised things of this world to be the source of confounding the wise and strong is lost on us. The ministries of Jesus and the Apostles and many church leaders around the world today, and even in the immigrant church in the US, would find it hard to fit in the structures and aspirations of many current denominations.

As the Scriptures are read from the perspective of the poor, oppressed, and excluded minorities, the obvious (to their eyes) dramatic expression and even the scandal of the power of the kingdom in the life and ministry of Jesus and the Apostles and the early church is that the kingdom rule and reign of the Messiah confronts, tears down, and redeems all those structures by walking directly with the poor and oppressed of the earth and without discrimination. It makes everyone who has faith in Jesus the Messiah, regardless of ethnicity or social status, an equal member of the family of God.

The side effect of that kind of embracing love and obedience indirectly—but forcefully—challenges those systems. We can get so focused on changing the culture that we actually neglect the very things Christ has called us to humbly do that will, in God's good time, change the look of things. The nature of the rule of God is that it is actually focused on the poor and oppressed who look to God for their help. The purpose and promise of the kingdom rule of the Messiah is directed their way. Oppressor and oppressed, rich and poor are all saved by grace through faith in Christ, but the kingdom rule of the Messiah is an intentional care for the poor, the widow, the fatherless, the immigrant, and the oppressed.

Our continued and increasingly segregated churches over the past fifty years, both ethnically and socioeconomically, has produced a Christianity in many of our congregations that is simply ethno-socioeconomic-centric and self-absorbed. And two self-absorbed people simply won't reconcile. Unless all ethnic groups seeking reconciliation are committed to such a kingdom vision, real reconciliation will not work. Attempting deep, long-term reconciliation among different groups who are vying for their own agendas of the kingdom, without accepting the call of God for a deep reconciliation as a covenantal obligation that focuses on the poor and oppressed of the earth, is a recipe for more entrenched segregation. The best-case scenario is a Plessy v. Ferguson church culture of "separate but equal," where the dominant group controls the agenda.

Instead, the biblical picture in the early church ought to help us know the Gospel is powerful enough to see that rich and poor, slave and free, Black, White, Latino, Asian, American Indian, formally educated and street educated can all be called to be members of the one family of God. And we are all called to the same sacrifices and service—to forgive and love one another in a community that is constantly embracing one another and the outcast and broken and shows this same love for the world, even our enemies. What is it that has kept us from such practical, real expression of the reconciling love of God for one another except cultural pride and self-protection?

Next steps

The good news of the Gospel is that real change is always available, at any moment in time, if we truly repent and do the things God has called us to do. So, where do we begin?

There must be an intentional commitment to be a welcoming, embracing community in every aspect of church life, for the powerless and poor, as well as those from every ethnic group in our communities. The flow of the ministries of the church, as well as the allocation of resources must move in their direction.

In addition to asking forgiveness, White, dominant-culture leaders, must also confess that we do not know how to make this reconciliation work on our own. The established White leadership cannot effectively figure out how to do reconciliation on its own, on any level. The very nature of paternalism is to try and resolve these issues without equal input from other groups. The good news is that many of our churches are in changing neighborhoods. Immigrants, refugees, and other long-standing minority groups in our culture keep invading the suburban community. These are tremendous opportunities to embrace the richer, fuller focus of the kingdom as we learn to humbly partner with one another.

We need to make use of the non-Anglo, non-upper-middle class contacts we already have, as well as other willing brothers and sisters. We need to let them help us reconsider our theological training, worship styles, leadership structures, outreach focus, and regional and denominational structures.

We must also theologically and practically embrace the humble circumstances necessary to express the kingdom. Paul calls us to:

> *Have this mind among yourselves, which is yours in Christ Jesus, who, though he was in the form of God, did not count equality with God a thing to be grasped, but made himself nothing, taking the form of a servant, being born in the likeness of men. And being found in human form, he humbled himself by becoming obedient to the point of death, even death on a cross.* (Phil. 2:5–8)

The paradigm of our culture and of a great many of our churches is one of educational and financial power, personal efficiency, task accomplishment, and sometimes a rather naive idea that we are the change agents for the whole world. We can hardly talk about starting a project without turning to questions of "national model" and "global impact" within a few sentences.

The model and teachings of Jesus, the Apostles, and the early church is that the kingdom moves forward in humble circumstances. It's not just individually that God's power is made known in weakness, but also corporately. The one church that is the most pitiful in John's letter-message from Jesus is Laodicea. It is the one with the most cultural power and the biggest blinders.

The theme of God choosing to lead his people in humility runs all the way through the history of Israel (Deut. 17:14ff, 20:1ff) and into the fullness of the expression of the kingdom in the life of Christ, the Apostles (1 Cor. 4:1ff, 4:16), and the church (1 Cor 1:26ff). The fundamental reasons for God directing his people into these humble, dependent conditions are centered on the issue of Israel being a people "for the poor" and then, when the full expression of the kingdom comes in Christ, the church pursuing a kingdom that is focused for the benefit of the poor and oppressed.

When we come to the poor and minorities who are not part of the dominant culture, from positions of cultural power, we naturally tend toward paternalism. Which is one of the other reasons we have the need to imitate Christ and the Apostles by embracing humble circumstances: it is the boasting in human power that feeds division (1 Cor. 1:10ff). We must see this as a theological paradigm and something to practically embrace as Israel was called to and Jesus and the Apostles lived out. Otherwise, our paternalism will always be a barrier, and we will never experience large-scale reconciliation.

The implications are revolutionary, cataclysmic. Our colleges, seminaries, church buildings, pastor's salaries, missionary support levels, church planting strategies, and world mission endeavors would all change and include more of a deliberate move toward the poor, instead of seeking to bring the poor up to our standards and comfort level.

Currently White-majority churches and denominations are too often willing conspirators with the Western cultural abuses of wealth, power, and paternalism. However, if the church were to be in a humble, reconciled position, it would be a genuinely prophetic voice against those cultural abuses and a voice from the reconciled nations for God's glory in his justice and compassion. With these changes, the poor would be valued and genuinely embraced, deep reconciliation would be fostered, and there would be a real sense of the kingdom of God being lived out in the body of Christ.

I am convinced we need, as American Christians, to be provoked to repentance for any injustice we have perpetuated either through sins of commission or omission. The writer of Hebrews said, *"And let us consider how we may spur one another on toward love and good deeds"* (Heb. 10:24). Maybe some of that "spur" might be to confront ourselves with the truth of how we have treated and continue to treat one another across racial, ethnic, economic, and social lines. Is it possible we might humbly and honestly inquire whether there is any need for change in ourselves so that we might truly love our neighbors as ourselves?

Chapter 23

Reconciliation or Bust

Rev. Dr. Irwyn Ince

Irwyn Ince is a graduate of Reformed Theological Seminary (MDiv), Covenant Seminary (DMin) and the pastor of City of Hope Presbyterian Church in Columbia, Maryland. He serves on the Mission to North America permanent committee and has served as moderator of Chesapeake Presbytery. Irwyn's ministry passion is to see the Gospel message of reconciliation with God and among people lived out in the context of the local church. Irwyn and his wife, Kim, have four children.

> *For as many of you as were baptized into Christ have put on Christ. There is neither Jew nor Greek, there is neither slave nor free, there is no male and female, for you are all one in Christ Jesus. And if you are Christ's, then you are Abraham's offspring, heirs according to promise.* (Gal. 3:27–29)

I remember the first time I flew first-class in an airplane. I was around thirteen years old. My father and I were traveling to visit our family in Trinidad, and the airline had overbooked the flight. We had reservations, but in order for us to fly together they had to split us up. Since the error was theirs, they upgraded one of our tickets to first class. My father, being the man he was, insisted that I take the first-class seat. This was a brand new world to me.

Every time I turned around, the stewardess was asking me if I wanted something to drink, if I wanted something to eat, or if I was comfortable. At first it felt a little awkward to me. But then I thought, "This is nice! I want to fly like this all the time!" What I didn't realize, of course, is how much more money a first-class ticket costs.

I had at other times already in my young life experienced overt racism. Now, looking back, I see that time on the plane was my first awareness of the notion of privilege. The way people tend to use their privilege is like covert racism, a sneakier bias that feels much more palatable. The lesson that experience taught me is that in this life there are different and better levels of privilege in society that one can access depending on how much money you have, how many resources you have at your disposal, and what your social status is.

That's actually not news. We all know there are walls that separate us in society. It's also not news that those same walls exist in the church. Yet, the clear message of Galatians 3:27–29 is that there is only one class in Christ. The apostle Paul declares that the three primary categories where societal separation is most vividly seen—ethnicity, social status, and gender—are no longer valid reasons for separation when it comes to the church.

In Christ, ethnic, social, and gender distinctions are not obliterated. Rather, what is done away with is the sinful inequality that separates us from one another. My passion in pastoral ministry is to see the local church press toward a life where our differences, diversity, and distinctions are not elevated over our unity in Christ.

A new passion is born

My first experience with the Christian faith was at Hanson Place Central United Methodist Church in Brooklyn, New York. Hanson Place was my father's church until his death and remains my mother's church to this day. During my late teen years, however, it became clear that my parents' faith had not become my own. I rejected Christianity, and through my college years at City College of New York in Harlem, I came to view Christianity as "the White man's religion." I wanted no part of it.

The only expression of the Christian faith that had any interest to me was the Black church experience. This interest was driven by the reality that historically, in America, the Black church was the single most authoritative force in the Black community. Not only that, but the Black Christian worship experience represented an ongoing connection to the African worship experience. I was in full agreement with Dr. Molefi K. Asante, who asserted that this connection to African religious expression made the Black church "the most logical institution for the beginning work of instructing the masses concerning African customs, habits, and styles."[1] That's what I wanted to see happen.

The value in the Black church was seen in its ability to further the cause of the Afrocentric movement by political and cultural activism and by recognizing that it is the place where the religious aspect of the continuity of the one African cultural system is vividly seen. I did not view the Black church as a place where souls are saved and set free from the bondage of sin to worship the Lord Jesus Christ. Rather it was a place where, if it was done right, people could be saved and set free from the bondage of Eurocentric thought and oppression.

So, how does someone go from this view of the church to pastoring a multiethnic church?

I'm glad you asked! When my wife and I moved our family to Maryland in the mid-'90s, we began attending historic New Bethel Baptist Church in Washington, DC. We didn't attend because we had any interest in becoming Christians. We were invited by a family. We'd left all of our friends in New York and figured that it would be a good way to meet some decent people. Of course, if you fool around and start attending Bible studies and worship services you might just meet Someone Else. That's precisely what happened. My wife and I became believers in Jesus Christ.

A decisive shift in my worldview began to take place. While I could, like Paul, have a burden for my "kinsmen according to the flesh," the biblical vision of the kingdom of God was reconciliation and peace across the breadth of humanity. I couldn't yet articulate it, but there was a growing discontent with the state of monoethnicity in the church given the growing diversity in our communities.[2]

My pre-Christian understanding of humanity was that brotherhood was predominantly based on racial identity. The clear message of the Gospel is that the brotherhood God creates is based on union with Christ. I saw in the Scriptures not simply a message of reconciliation, but a declaration of immeasurably great power working in the church for reconciliation, unity, and

---

1 Molefi K. Asante, *Afrocentricity* (Trenton, NJ: Africa World Press, Inc., 1988), 74–75.

2 I don't intend to make an oversimplification here. I realize there are valid historic, indeed God ordained, reasons for the racial state of the American church.

peace (Eph 1:15–4:16). Yet it seemed the church was quite comfortable maintaining our divides.

Over the next four years at New Bethel, I had a growing sense of call to ministry. At the same time, I became exposed to Reformed theology through the Ligonier Ministries *Renewing Your Mind* broadcast. I enrolled at the Reformed Theological Seminary Washington/Baltimore campus and began taking courses in 2000.

Although I was taking courses at RTS and developing an understanding of covenant theology, my wife and I weren't looking for a new church. But I had a desperate need to be mentored in ministry. That need was met by Rev. Kevin Smith, an African American pastor in our area. Kevin had planted Mount Zion Covenant Church (PCA) in Bowie, Maryland. Our family joined Mount Zion in 2002, and I was now in the Presbyterian Church in America.

Mount Zion was a unique PCA congregation. The congregation was largely a mix of African American families and predominantly Anglo-American college students. Needless to say, there was a vast difference between our experience at a 100-year-old Black Baptist church and this four-year-old ethnically diverse church plant.

So, all of these factors—my pre-Christian worldview, conversion at New Bethel, RTS studies, and church life at Mount Zion—formed my passion to pursue multiethnic ministry in the local church.

From community to "ghetto living"

The theologian Herman Bavinck emphasizes the vastness of the image of God when he says:

> The image of God is much too rich for it to be fully realized in a single human being, however richly gifted that human being may be. It can only be somewhat unfolded in its depth and riches in a humanity counting billions of members. Just as the traces of God (*vestigia Dei*) are spread over many, many works, in both space and time, so also the image of God can only be displayed in all its dimensions and characteristic features in a humanity whose members exist both successively one after the other and contemporaneously side by side. Only humanity in its entirety—as one complete organism, summed up under a single head, spread out over the whole earth, as prophet proclaiming the truth of God, as priest

dedicating itself to God, as ruler controlling the earth and the whole of creation—only it is the fully finished image, the most telling and striking likeness of God.[3]

During seminary, the Lord began to add theological fuel to my passion in the form of covenant theology. There wasn't any particular emphasis or focus on the implications of the Gospel for pursuing diversity in the local church, but when I came across the above words by Bavinck, they immediately resonated with me as having deep implications for the local church.

Much of the Gospel message I had been used to hearing had been reduced to simply having "a personal relationship with God through Jesus Christ." In that way of expressing the Gospel message, there lies a radically individualistic emphasis on what it means to be a Christian. While no one would argue that the Lord saves individuals and reconciles them to himself, the Gospel is so much more than that. It must include the fullness of what it means to be made in the image of God. And Bavinck is right. The finished image, the most telling and striking likeness of God is the entirety of redeemed humanity.

In Genesis, the first words about humanity in the Bible come from the lips of God:

> *Then God said, "Let us make man in our image, after our likeness. And let them have dominion over the fish of the sea and over the birds of the heavens and over the livestock and over all the earth and over every creeping thing that creeps on the earth." So God created man in his own image, in the image of God he created him; male and female he created them.* (Gen. 1:26–27)

Covenant community is created. Male and female are covenantally bound to the Lord and to each other. Humanity's beginning was in covenantal community. This is as much an aspect of what it means for us to be made in the image of God as is our being rational, thinking, feeling beings created "in the virtues of knowledge, righteousness, and holiness."[4] The Father, Son and Spirit,

---

3 H. Bavinck, J. Bolt, and J. Vriend, *Reformed Dogmatics, Volume 2: God and Creation* (Grand Rapids, MI: Baker Academic 2004), 577.

4 H. Bavinck, J. Bolt, and J. Vriend, *Reformed Dogmatics, Volume 2: God and Creation* (Grand Rapids, MI: Baker Academic 2004), 557.

who eternally exist in the perfection of covenant community, is imaged in the creation of humanity in covenant community.

So, what happens when sin enters the world? Just what we would expect. The marring of the image includes the fracture of covenantal relationships. This extends far beyond marital problems between husband and wife (Gen. 3:16). It includes fratricide (Gen. 4:8) and extends to the decline of humanity into corruption and violence (Gen. 6:11).

Even when there is unity among humanity after the Fall, it is unity in our rebellion and rejection of our covenantal Lord's commands. We're told in Genesis 11 that there was a time in human history when everyone had the same language and spoke the same words. Humanity was in solidarity. Moses tells us that everyone could speak and understand each other. Everyone is on the same page, but it's in their rejection of God's command. They're on the same page in their rebellion against what God has explicitly commanded them to do. After the Flood, God again commanded humanity to be fruitful and multiply, to fill the earth (Gen. 9:1). Yet, in direct and conscious rebellion, humans determine they don't want to fill the earth, they want to settle where they are. There is no serpent in Shinar tempting humanity to disobey God's word. An external tempter isn't necessary. Humanity is one big happy family against the Lord.

God's response in Genesis 11:7 included judgment and mercy. Our language was confused so that we could not understand one another, and we were forced to fill the earth. The willful rebellion of humanity against God's explicit command resulted in the use of all our faculties united for an impossible goal. We were joined together to establish ourselves as God, with all authority and power. God mercifully moved to restrain our sin by confusing our language.

Yet, there was still the issue of the confusion of our language. We now had the creation of "ghetto living." From Babel onward we are still in solidarity against God, yet this solidarity is expressed in isolated communities. These ghettos, because they are in rebellion against God, are also naturally against each other.

Thus, what happens far too often is that we understand our human dignity and value as coming from isolated community. And we love our ghettos: our ethnic ghettos, our social ghettos, our cultural ghettos, our economic ghettos, our academic ghettos. And we love them to a fault. When we see cultural and ethnic differences, we don't embrace our God-given, creational dissimilarity.

Instead of rejoicing in how God made us, we immediately distrust others. We instinctively reject others and often mock them because we're still confused and don't understand each other.

Community restored

When Christ came, he proclaimed far more than individual salvation. He proclaimed the coming of the kingdom. Integral to that is the restoration and renewal of community, the reversal of Babel. Jesus said that his Father assigned to him a kingdom, and he assigns this kingdom to his Apostles (Luke 22:28–29).

After his resurrection, our Lord spent forty days speaking to his disciples about the kingdom of God (Acts 1:3). When the Spirit came and filled the disciples for kingdom proclamation and work, the first thing they do is declare the mighty works of God. Men from what Luke calls every nation under heaven —Parthia, Media, Elam, Mesopotamia, Judea, Cappadocia, Pontus, Asia, Phrygia, Pamphylia, Egypt, Libya, Crete, Arabia, Rome—were able to hear, understand, and respond to the message (Acts 2:5). The work of bringing people from every tribe, tongue, people, and nation under the banner of the Lamb of God had begun.

That is the work God continues today and that will not be complete until the consummation of the kingdom. The day is coming when the redeemed will fully reflect the image of our Creator as one family, summed up under our single head, Jesus Christ. This is the biblical, covenantal vision that fuels my passion for ministry in the local church.

Dr. Martin Luther King Jr. said, "For so many years we had to face the tragic fact that eleven o'clock on Sunday morning, when we stood to sing, 'In Christ There Is No East or West,' we stood in the most segregated hour of Christian America."[5] His words still ring true about the church in America almost sixty years after he spoke them. So now we must ask: How's it going? What does it look like in practice?

---

5 Martin Luther King Jr., "Some Things We Must Do," 2nd Annual Institute on Nonviolence, December 5, 1957. Accessed March 3, 2016, http://kingencyclopedia.stanford.edu/encyclopedia/documentsentry/
some_things_we_must_do_address_delivered_at_the_second_annual_institute_on_/index.html.

The church I serve is City of Hope Presbyterian Church, in Columbia, Maryland. Columbia is a suburban community in Howard County, which was founded forty-five years ago. It is located midway between Baltimore and Washington, DC. The vision for Columbia was to create a city that was diverse in every way. Columbia's founder James Rouse explained his vision for a complete city by saying, "Columbia will be economically diverse, polycultural [sic], multi-faith, and inter-racial."[6]

This vision has in large part been attained. By all accounts, Columbia has achieved economic, racial, ethnic, and religious diversity. But not in the church! By and large, the quote above from Dr. King is true among most of the churches in our community. Sunday morning is still the most segregated hour, and that is tragic.

Thus, when I'm asked how things are going, I'll give this tongue-and-cheek answer, "It's going."

If I were not convinced that God's vision as he builds his kingdom is to gather people from diverse backgrounds, cultures, and ethnicities into the local church, I would be quite satisfied to stay in my cultural comfort zone. The ministry of reconciliation is hard. Everyone comes with preferences. If you intentionally pursue ministry in such a way that the makeup of the local church reflects its community, you are forced to deal with the issues that relate to power dynamics. We rarely think of the issues that way, but discussions about liturgy, worship music, Bible study groups, preaching style, service length, and more all relate in some way to the question of power.

I praise God that often he provides an *"apple of gold in a setting of silver"* (Prov. 25:11) at just the right time. The Lord loves to send a word of encouragement to enable his servant to keep pressing on.

One of these much-needed golden apples came to me when a woman said, "Pastor Irwyn, City of Hope has to make it. Our family needs this church." As we were again facing the financial challenges of church planting, that dear woman told me our church had to survive. She's Caucasian. Her husband is of Middle Eastern descent. They have two biological children and two adopted African American children.

---

6 Columbia Archives, "History of Columbia: A Story of a Planned Community," http://www.columbiaarchives.org/?action=content.sub&page=history_community3&oid=1.

They've been members of the typical majority White church. Why does she feel as though her family needs our church? It is because we are striving intentionally to live out the Gospel imperative of redemptive ethnic unity in Christ. She explained that, in addition to her family's need, she personally needs the challenge of a racially diverse church. She is embracing the need to have her values, preferences, and preoccupations reassessed in light of the Bible.

What we have learned is that the answer to the question of power is not how we end up after we ask "Who wins?" or "Who loses?" but rather "Who dies?" In this difficult pursuit, we should keep asking the question, "Is this thing that's offending me a kingdom issue, or is it simply a preference that the Lord would have me die to for the sake of unity in the body?" I don't want to die to my preferences, and some would say that I shouldn't have to. Yet, the practice of Christian liberty calls me to be ready and willing to do just that.

Through the first eight years of City of Hope, I have seen the Lord take us through the controversies and challenges of how we ought to go about pursuing multiethnic ministry. One example was in the development of our music ministry. When the church began, we hired an African American trio of Gospel musicians two Sundays every month to be very intentional about having a Black Gospel sound regularly. We had to deal with the question of whether or not we should be hiring outside musicians for worship. Even though having musical diversity was and is a high value, that did not prevent the topic of paying such a high price to bring in people who were not committed to our church.

Staying the course turned out to be a blessing because the value and pursuit of diversity in our worship music has become an integral part of our identity. Our own musicians developed with this value. With those early conversations now in the past, our music team leaders organized a Christmas Chorale for the Advent season. What a blessing it was to be led in song through Negro spirituals, traditional hymns, and contemporary Christian music. That chorale was a microcosm of our current dynamic. If you worship with us, you'll find that the musical genre changes from week to week, and even within a single service.

Our most difficult challenge to date struck at the core of our ministry vision. We planted the church with an ethnically diverse pastoral team. For both financial and functional reasons, it didn't work out. We had to wrestle with whether or not a multiethnic pastoral team was essential to the ministry vision or was just "nice to have."

The dissolution of the pastoral team was hard. Some of the dear people who began with us left the church, and those who remained had to go through a period of recovery and healing. Thankfully, that recovery and healing has largely taken place. It has been painful but good.

In a recent gathering with a handful of brothers from City of Hope, I asked them to evaluate how the church was doing. The conversation that followed was outstanding. Here are some of the things they shared:

> "Because the Gospel shows me my sin... it allows me also to look at my culture and some of the things that are wrong with my culture and not be afraid to point it out or try to safeguard it."

> "For me, the process of coming to an awareness of my own culture and its benefits and its sinfulness and the necessity of me as a Christian to be willing to step outside of that and learn that my understanding of God is limited because I can't grasp his image in other cultures, that was a painful process."

> "I just realized five minutes ago that I'm the only White guy in the room! It doesn't even cross my mind.... How do we cultivate the multicultural ministry? I'm actually not sure. That's why I'm so focused on outreach; because I want to draw in the community so that we are the community."
> "Generally when a White person in a homogenous White community says, 'I'm colorblind,' it means, 'You're White, too. You're equal with me. I'm only going to engage you on my own terms.' It means, 'I'm blind to your culture.'"

> "When we engage others in the community, my culture, my family's culture, begins to change and reflect those others in my community. It begins to take on aspects of Black community. It begins to take on aspects of Latino community. Because we're doing life together. So I change. My culture transforms. It's not just a bunch of different people coming together and going back and being our own different people."

The combination of the specific challenges I mentioned earlier (music and staff) along with the normal "mess" of ministry (shepherding people through loneliness, marital issues, parenting, health crises, etc.) makes this an intense pursuit. At the same time, hearing from these brothers enabled me to get out of the trees and see the forest.

Not everyone who comes through our doors on a Sunday morning gets excited and encouraged by our ministry vision. Yet we rejoice because the Lord is painting a beautiful picture at City of Hope. His Spirit is at work confirming the vision by actually bringing it to pass! I am humbled by the love, hospitality, accountability, and fellowship that have become defining characteristics of the church.

We know that we will never "arrive" until glory. Ministry will always be messy. But just like we don't wait until glory to pursue righteousness and holiness, to put to death that which is earthly in us, we ought not be content to wait until glory to see the nations gathered together under the banner of Christ pursuing the unity of the Spirit and the bond of peace.

Reconciling out of love

My denomination—the PCA—and many other majority-White denominations need more diverse, Gospel churches. In 2010, the PCA published a strategic plan to address challenges to overcome in order to grow. The report lists the transition from Anglo-majority culture in the United States as an external challenge. Two of the denomination's internal challenges are "maintaining biblical worship with cultural diversity" and "ethnic homogeneity both in general membership and denominational leadership."[7]

David Livermore explains the challenge when he says:

> We have to learn to be the people who become culturally accessible, living messages of Jesus and his love. Embodying Jesus cross-culturally is a messy, complicated process. This is what often splits churches, divides families, and erodes Christian fellowship.[8]

Are majority-White denominations ready to reject ethnic homogeneity and learn how to love those who have not historically been members of our churches? Are we wrestling with how to become more ethnically and culturally

---

7 Presbyterian Church in America Cooperative Ministries Committee, PCA Strategic Plan (http://pcahistory.org/ga/38th_pcaga_2010.pdf: 2010), 14. Accessed August 17, 2015.

8 David A. Livermore, *Cultural Intelligence: Improving Your CQ to Engage Our Multicultural World. Youth, Family, and Culture Series* (Grand Rapids, MI: Baker Academic, 2009), 34.

diverse as a whole, attempting to discover what it looks like to love those around us?

The answers to these questions involve actions by and attitudes of churches. They involve choices by individuals. In my case, I am one of the few African American pastors in the PCA, and I've chosen to commit to and love my denomination.

When the PCA began in 1973, the founders declared the denomination to be the Continuing Presbyterian Church. Therefore, as a denomination, we own that church's history, both its virtues and its wickedness. Recent work by Stephen R. Hayes in *The Last Segregated Hour* and by Sean Michael Lucas in his book on the history of the PCA have helped to make us aware of the specific sins that were committed. Whether we like it or not, the perception by many minorities that the PCA is a White, socially conservative, Right-wing, racist denomination is connected to this history.

This is why, when we began our church in 2007, we named it City of Hope Church. We didn't want the "Presbyterian" hump to be the first hump people had to overcome when they considered our church. We are now, officially, City of Hope Presbyterian Church. The Presbyterian hump is still real. However, what is more real is the grace of Christ, enabling us to engage openly and honestly about who we are, where we've come from, and where we desire to see the Lord take us.

The Lord appears to be moving in the hearts of leaders in the PCA to once again testify to his reconciling grace through confession and repentance. For this, I am thankful. My prayer is that all of Christ's church will embrace a "reconciliation or bust" commitment to living out the implications of God's Gospel.

Chapter 24

Why We Must Confess Corporately

Rev. Duke L. Kwon

Duke Kwon is the pastor of Grace Meridian Hill, in Washington, DC. He has degrees from Brown University (AB) and Gordon-Conwell Theological Seminary (MDiv, ThM). Duke and his wife, Paula, have two children.

How can I repent of racial sins I did not personally commit? This is a critical question to grapple with in the pursuit of racial harmony. After all, reconciliation and justice always involves groups—i.e., people who share a common ethnicity or nationality or denominational identity—as well as individuals.

I would argue there is clear biblical precedent for the practice of corporate repentance and confession. Ezra, praying as a "we" (rather than an "I" or "me"), confesses "our" guilt (Ezra 9:6–16). The Levites lead the Israelites in grief over "our sins" (Neh. 9:35). Daniel ponders the transgressions of no smaller a group than "all Israel" (Dan. 9:11) and famously confesses, *"We have sinned … we have been wicked … we have turned away … we have not listened"* (Dan. 9:5–6). Evidently, the repentance of the righteous must not be limited to one's individual sins alone but must include the corporate sins of the covenant community. Yes, must. The Lord commands it (Lev. 26:40).

These prayers are properly described as "corporate," not simply because they are prayed in unison, but because they are prayed on behalf of one another. The grammar of these acts of confession is profound and revealing.

But how can this be so? Upon what logical and theological basis is such corporate repentance—confessing sins I did not personally commit—permissible or possible?

Imputation argument

One popular approach is to appeal to the principle of imputation vis-à-vis the doctrine of original sin. The argument goes something like this: "We are held responsible for Adam's sin though we did not personally commit it, and Christ paid for our sin though he did not personally commit it. Therefore, we likewise should be willing to confess sins we are associated with but did not personally commit."

But here's the problem: While the imputation of Adam's sin to us and ours to Christ is helpful as analogy, it is imprecise as theology. Imputation, strictly speaking, assumes federal headship. Adam's sin is credited to me because he is the covenantal representative of the human race—and for no other reason (Rom. 5:12–21). The same could be said of Christ's relationship to the new humanity recreated in him (Eph. 2:15). Most importantly, this arrangement is presented in Scripture as a once-for-all exchange in redemptive-history. It was legally and morally unique, and thus cannot form the theological basis for confessions of sin practiced by "ordinary" members of Christ's church.

Of course, this is not to say that the category of imputation cannot be helpful by way of analogy. Perhaps one could appeal to it in a situation like this: A church apologizes to its neighbors for the racist remarks of its pastor or some other delegate serving as a (quasi-covenantal) representative. Or an elder, who is covenantally bound to his congregation, publicly repents for his church's historic exclusion of African Americans from its pews. Or a mayor, on behalf of the town she represents, issues a similar apology on the basis of the (covenantal) civil relationship she shares with her constituents.

One could partially apply this principle in a variety of contexts. But let's be clear: Even in the aforementioned scenarios, strictly speaking, neither the guilt of one individual nor the obligation to repent of that guilt can be "imputed" to another. My personal racial sins cannot be individually imputed to you; therefore, you cannot be morally responsible for them or obligated to repent of them on that basis alone. As Scripture testifies, *"Everyone shall die for his own iniquity"* (Jer. 31:29–30; cf. Deut. 24:16; Ezek. 17b–22).

Is there, then, a different theological basis for corporate repentance? I believe there is. The strongest theological basis for the practice of corporate repentance, in my opinion, is not the principle of imputation, but rather, the principle of corporate identification.

Corporate identification

God has always dealt with humanity covenantally as both a "me" and a "we"—that is, both individually and corporately. Throughout Scripture, moral responsibility is assigned for sins on both these levels, albeit in different ways. Indeed, many in Israel were held accountable for sins they did not personally commit. By virtue of their shared identity as God's people, bound together by covenant (Jer. 30:22; cf. 1 Pet. 2:10), the Israelites suffered the afflictions of exile, even physical death, as a form of temporal judgment for their sins, transgressions for which they shared joint, covenantal responsibility (Neh. 9:32).

This included (don't miss it!) even those who had exercised saving faith and personal "repentance unto life." Some were simultaneously personally righteous and corporately responsible; we could name Ezra, Nehemiah, Daniel, along with many others, as examples. The "wheat" and "tares" were treated as a covenantal unit. They sinned together; they suffered for sin together; they were called to repent together (Jer. 15:19; Ezek. 14:6; Hos. 14:1; 1 Kings 8:46–51). And the righteous would repent of sins, even those they had not committed personally (Lev. 26:40–45; Ezra 9:6–16; Neh. 9:16–37; Dan. 9:4–11).

Some may argue that times have changed under the New Covenant, which ostensibly deemphasizes the corporate dimensions of the Old. I would simply point out that Jesus himself regularly issued corporate calls for this "wicked and unbelieving generation" to repent (e.g., Matt. 12:39–45; 17:17), as did his Apostles (Acts 2:40). In the letters to the seven churches in Revelation 2–3, he does more of the same, inviting entire churches to repent, it appears, irrespective of which individuals were responsible for the enumerated sins (Rev. 2:5, 16; 3:3). Evidently, the principle of corporate identification with respect to repentance endures in the New Covenant.

Therefore, it is proper to repent for sins of those with whom you share a covenantal identity—not because God legally credits other individuals' sins to you individually, but because God holds the covenant community responsible for their collective sins collectively. Of course, these two dimensions of repentance —individual/personal and corporate/communal—are not morally equivalent. It is important to note that many Israelites regularly participated in acts of corporate confession—for example, on the Day of Atonement (Lev. 16)— without having "circumcised their hearts" (Jer. 4:4), which is to say, they did not exercise saving faith and had not received the grace of repentance unto life. This highlights the enduring necessity (primacy!) of repentance for personal sin for eternal life (Ps. 51:1–12; Acts 2:38–39). Again, individual and corporate repentance are not morally equivalent, but they are both morally necessary.

My need to confess corporately

Where does this leave us? All that's preceded is more than mere theology. It is not only biblical; it is also practical and deeply personal. You see, I am a Korean-American, a minister of color in a denomination grappling with its racial failures, both past and present. And this covenantal principle of corporate identification is one reason why, though I wasn't alive during the days of Jim Crow and the founding of the Presbyterian Church in America, and though I am neither White nor Black, and though I did not personally bar African Americans from my pews, nor preach in support of segregation (or slavery), nor participate in White supremacist organizations, I, on behalf of—and, Lord willing, together with—my denomination, do repent of our racial sins of commission and omission during the Civil Rights Era.

I did not personally commit them; nevertheless, they are mine.

Chapter 25

A Path I Never Considered

Rev. Dr. Mike Khandjian

Mike Khandjian serves as pastor of Chapelgate Presbyterian Church in the suburbs of Baltimore, Maryland. He studied at Belhaven College (BA) and Reformed Theological Seminary (MDiv) and received an honorary degree from Miami International Seminary (DMin). Mike has pastored three churches during his thirty-plus-year ministry, each considered a "renewal" project. He and his wife, Katherine, have three adult children.

> In contending with the problem of evil, it is useless to try to escape either from the bad past or into the good past. The only way to deal with the past is to accept the whole past, and by accepting it, to change its meaning.—Dorothy Sayers[1]

I was raised in Miami, Florida, a largely metropolitan, racially diverse and ethnically mixed city. However, when I was born it was more like Andy Griffith's Mayberry. When Cuban immigrants entered into the mix in the late '50s (when I was born) and early '60s, tensions flared—between Black, White, and Hispanic. Suddenly this city that already lived in a painfully settled and unspoken racial détente was thrown into a new struggle. Tensions could no longer be masked by unspoken understandings. Neighborhoods were abandoned, people's homes burned, and people died, yet the church was largely indifferent.

---

1 Dorothy Sayers, *Letters to a Diminished Church* (Nashville, TN: W Publishing Group, 2004), 72.

And me? I lived in a safe, insulated White "Christian" world, oblivious to the injustices and sorrows of the racial struggle and Civil Rights Movement. It wasn't until college that I began to understand that my upbringing was sadly defined by a broken worldview that stressed a passion for souls, while protecting what Francis Schaeffer referred to as, "personal peace and affluence," at the expense of actually caring about the plight of the weak and oppressed or my role in God's work of renewing all things.[2] Caring outside of my own context was a path I never considered.

Through the influence of people like Dr. Martin Luther King Jr. (his writings), Jeff White in Harlem, Nicholas Wolterstorff, Louis Wilson, Irwyn Ince, and others, I have been graced with a slowly growing understanding of my role as a pastor and Christ-follower with regard to promoting justice and peace. As my awareness of injustices in our broken world increases, I more readily can acknowledge my part in the sins of the past and present and gain clarity on what I believe I am being called to do moving forward.

Called to care

I have been called to embrace the reality of my spiritual lineage in Adam. In Adam we have all sinned and are sinners. We teach this, and it is true. *"Therefore, just as sin came into the world through one man, and death through sin, and so death spread to all me because all sinned."* (Rom. 5:12).

By virtue of Adam's failure, I am connected to everyone who is, has been, and will be part of the story of this nation's racial struggle, and every other, as we are to all sin. For me, the starting point is to embrace and accept this reality. I don't have to knowingly or consciously have entered into the actual sins of the past in order to bear responsibility for them (though on some level I have).

I have been called to embrace others' sins as my own. After all, I belong to a Redeemer—Jesus—who died for sins that someone else committed. *"God made him who knew no sin to become sin for us, that we might become the righteousness of God"* (2 Cor. 5:21). It isn't rocket science.

---

2 Francis A. Schaeffer, *How Should We Then Live?* (Grand Rapids, MI: Fleming H. Revell Company, 1976), 205.

In "owning" a particular sin, we participate in the substitutionary physics of the Gospel. Personally, I like that. Our fellowship with Jesus begins with his suffering, and the flashpoint for his suffering is my sin. I am called to no less, because truly, in Jesus "justice and peace embrace." (Psalm 85:10)

I have been called out of the darkness of my own self-deception. When I say, "Why should I repent for sins I haven't committed," I deceive myself in the way Peter did when he refused to eat with Gentiles. What is so striking about Peter is that from his messages, we know he knew in his mind that the Gospel was free to all. His problem wasn't what he knew, it was that in his heart he was unwilling to accept it. He even arrogantly attempted to use the Law to undermine God's leading (Acts 11:8)!

The reality is that I have participated in the sin of racism, whether in thought, deed, unwarranted fear, ignorance, or inaction. I didn't have to be alive at the time of the Civil Rights Movement, or before, to have benefited from the advantages gained from others' being treated unjustly. Therefore, I am called to repent.

I have been called to listen. While every instinct within me is to respond and fix, right now I believe God is calling me and others like me to simply listen, because in some way there is, within my fallen and White thinking, a tendency to want to reframe issues in terms that I like and am comfortable with, even at the expense of reshaping a narrative that belongs to others.

Put another way, often without even realizing it, I want to take over a discussion because this enables me to make the narrative less threatening and uncomfortable, less demanding and less convicting. Taking over makes me an insider rather than a listener and a leader rather than a disciple. It puts me on the "us" side rather than the "them" side. It is my way of finding a place above the fray, safe from the convicting work of the Spirit in my own heart. But it clogs arteries of healing in others because it insulates me from admitting my own sin and becomes yet another expression of my tendency to invalidate others. So for now, the Father wants me to listen, because in listening I love, and I learn what I have been deaf to for much of my life.

I have been called to love. One of my favorite quotes is from Dr. King's *Strength to Love*, where he writes, "… there is a deep longing for the bread of love. Everybody wishes to love and to be loved. He who feels that he is not loved feels that he does not count."[3]

Currently, in our country, and in the ecclesiastical "universe," our African American brothers and sisters are asking us to join hands in affirming the sins of the past, while validating their oft-disregarded personhood. Why would it not be enough for those of us who are White to support this simply because our African American brothers and sisters need or want us to? Do I need more of a reason?

I know that some could argue that just because someone tells us to do something is not a good enough reason to always do it. But how many times have we been asked to support something like this? For most of us, never. And I would argue that because our brothers and sisters have asked us to stand with them is, in fact, a good enough reason and is an opportunity to show love. When they face repeated injustices and could understandably choose to lash out, they simply ask us to stand with them in the fight. How can we refuse?

I have been called to love those I don't want to love. Here is what I mean: There is a dimension of this cause that is about people who have overtly said and written things that are offensive, sinful, and destructive. Against every instinct within me to find comfort in distancing myself out of some twisted form of comparison, out of my own innate self-righteousness, I am called to love those with whom I fiercely disagree—I am called to love my enemies. Without my willingness to do so, rather than be a vessel of healing, I will have disintegrated into every tyrant, every society, and every horrid movement in which power and advantage are obtained through injustice, oppression, and annihilation, rather than through the conquest of love. This is the lovely, invasive, disturbing, reconciling beauty of the Gospel. What is it that brings us together when we've been torn apart theologically, ideologically, socially, racially, ethnically? Jesus, our one true sacrifice.

---

3 James M. Washington, ed., *A Testament of Hope: The Essential Writings and Speeches of Martin Luther King Jr.*, (New York: HarperOne, 1986), 500.

A blessed path

Each February I have the privilege of announcing to our congregation that it is Black History Month. With this announcement I encourage our folks to read and learn of the Civil Rights Movement and the story of Black America. Shamelessly and unapologetically, I also ask our Black brothers and sisters that if they would be willing to cook up some soul food, that my wife and I would gladly eat with them! We have been the beneficiaries of some amazing meals, and more importantly, beautiful stories.

One year, an older-than-us couple had us over. They not only cooked a magnificent feast that included sweet potato pie, corn, barbecue ribs, mustard greens, chitlins, and cornbread, but they also told us the story behind each plate all the way back to the days of slavery. Then they told their stories. The wife, a high school principal in Miami, was raised in Alabama, and with her sister rode the Freedom Bus during the Civil Rights Movement. Her sister was arrested and jailed in Gadsden, Alabama, during a peaceful protest. The husband is an insurance agent that served in Vietnam. He told of how he and other Black soldiers were constantly given the most dangerous front-line assignments and put into harm's way during the war. They were neither defiant nor apologetic; they were just telling their stories. What a sweet evening.

By the time President Obama was elected to office, we lived in Maryland, and late on the evening of the election, after the results were in and America had voted for her first African American president, I called that couple. They got on the phone, weeping and saying, "We thought this day would never come."

I long for this to be the cry of our brothers and sisters in the church. Amen.

Chapter 26

Hallowed Be Your Name

Rev. Kenneth Foster

Kenneth Foster has served as Associate Pastor at Grace Presbyterian Church in Dover, Delaware, since 2006. He was called by his presbytery to assist a monoethnic church pursue its vision of becoming multiethnic. Kenny and his wife, Connie, have two sons and one daughter-in-law.

> *Our Father in heaven,*
> *hallowed be your name.*
> *Your kingdom come,*
> *your will be done,*
> *on earth as it is in heaven.*
> *Give us this day our daily bread,*
> *and forgive us our debts,*
> *as we also have forgiven our debtors.*
> *And lead us not into temptation,*
> *but deliver us from evil.* (Matt. 6:9–13)

My father said, "You have got to give the White man what he wants." My father's words were like the fingers of a potter shaping the formless lump of clay that was my perception of the world as a nine-year-old boy. But it was only one of the hands.

The other hand that worked in the clay of my childish perception was the Lord's Prayer.

My Father, who couldn't read, would make us recite a Bible verse each week. My siblings and I would argue over who would get to use John 11:35, *"Jesus wept."* We knew it was the shortest verse in the Bible, and our hope was that he wouldn't remember who recited which verse the last time we were before him. We also learned the Lord's Prayer, so we used it often.

My Father was a fallible man, but by making me learn Scripture he was doing a wise thing. Now decades later, I am still mining the caverns of beauty and probing the depths in the prayer Jesus taught his disciples to pray. It is most profound!

A recent gem I've discovered in this pattern of prayer laid down by the Lord is the connection between the first petition of the prayer and racial reconciliation. I had never considered before that ethnic separation and ignoring matters of racial division, including separate but equal thinking, is dishonoring the name of the Father.

God is our Father, so we know our position with him is as his children. Through prayer we learn to acknowledge that he is to be hallowed. And this hallowing of the name of the Father is something that keeps us at peace with him and in sync with what he is doing.

Moreover, our prayer leads to actions. We pray, and we work. Consequently, this Prayer of Prayers is instructive for the family of God's living. We should recognize then that this is a kingdom-building prayer.

The splendor of God's holiness

We hallow the name of the Father when we recognize we have a holy deficit that is filled as we experience God's holy love in Christ. This then gives us a corporate identity, which translates the splendor of God's holiness to a watching world. When we worship the Lord in the splendor of his holiness, we fuel this continued hallowing of his name.

The word "hallowed" is usually only heard in relationship to Halloween, and most folks couldn't tell you what the word "Halloween" means. There is no understanding that it means hallowed evening. It is just a time to dress up and get candy. Furthermore, if anyone speaks of something being holy, it is usually in a derogatory way. For most people "holy" means someone is being self-righteous and holier than everyone else. We are deficient when it comes to understanding the words "hallowed" or "holy." Most people today don't take holiness seriously.

"Hallowed" means "to consecrate, to sanctify, to separate from profane things, to dedicate to God." "Holy" is purity and has a quality that is completely other. It is unlike anything or anyone. Holiness is splendorous and immense in its beauty. It is to be celebrated. The word "holy" appears in the Bible 551 times. It describes things that God says are his, from the Sabbath day in Genesis 2:3, to the ground on which Moses stood when he was in the presence of the Lord at the burning bush. God calls Israel his holy nation in Exodus 19:6. The dwelling place of God is holy. Zion is his holy mountain, offerings were to be holy, certain days were holy, the temple had the holy place and then the Most Holy Place, the priest and his family line were holy to the Lord. In other words, everything that God has anything to do with is holy.

This is because God himself is holy. He is a holy Father. His love is holy love. His anger is holy anger. His kindness is holy kindness. His people are holy people. His kingdom is a holy kingdom. His home is holy. His angels are holy. When he acts he does so out of his holy character. He is holy in his love; he is holy in his wrath. He is not tolerant of anything that is unholy.

You might say, "How can he be holy in his love, holy in his wrath, and not tolerate anything unholy, yet love people who are not holy?" This holy God makes up for our lack of holiness. We experience God's holy love through faith in Christ. We cannot have salvation apart from the holy love of God. There is no standing as the children of God apart from this holy love of God being applied to us. Holiness would not and could not leave us in our unholy state. God in his holiness could not tolerate our unholy being and in his love he could not tolerate our destruction. Instead he gives us both his holiness and his love, in Christ.

That the holiness of God issues to mankind as love is amazing! Holiness is not running away from sin and demanding its punishment. Rather it runs toward the sinner and seeks to convert him or her into family. That is what Jesus did for us! This encounter should then lead us to repentance and faith.

A corporate identity

As Christians, we have a new identity that is shaped by hallowing our Father's name. We—the whole family of God—translate the Father's holy name to the watching world. Paul describes the size of the family in Ephesians 3:14–15, *"For this reason I kneel before the Father, from whom his whole family in heaven and earth derives its name."* Paul's prayer is that the uncommon wisdom of God is made known to the rulers and authorities in the heavenly realms through this family of God. That uncommon, holy wisdom is what God showed in revealing the mystery of his will to bring all things in heaven and on earth together under one head, even Christ (Eph. 1:10).

I suspect Paul's understanding of the Gospel was rooted in the prayer that Jesus teaches us to pray, the Lord's Prayer. Paul saw this new corporate identity as Jesus taught us to pray, *"Our Father in heaven, hallowed be your name."* Since the pronouns used in the prayer are first person plural, it reminds us that our prayers are not just about our personal well-being.

The context of the prayer is looking at the practice of the family that is to hallow the name of the Father. In my truck driving days, my coworkers and I were constantly reminded that the truck and trailer had a logo on the side, BI-LO. We were reminded that people would connect the way we drove with the way the company did business. I didn't have a separate identity apart from the truck when I was driving it. The truck, the company, and I were one. That is what it means to have a corporate identity. The way we interact with one another, love each other, and reach across lines of ethnicity, disabilities, and class are all ways that we share in the corporate identity we have in Christ.

We are not Black Christians, White Christians, Korean Christians, Latino Christians, etc. We are Christians who happen to be Black, White, Korean, or Latino. The color of our skin doesn't enhance or modify our identity in Christ. Our identity is not derived from our ethnicity, class, or ability. Our identity is derived from the Father and his name. Hallowing his name is related to my relationship with my fellow Christians.

This means their struggle is my struggle as we are commanded to "bear one another's burdens and thus fulfill the law of Christ" (Gal. 6:2). That is why it is important for Christians to stand up with other Christians and all those who are oppressed. Holiness is not merely personal—it is communal. The healing of the ethnicities begins with hallowing the Father's name within his family.

P.T. Forsyth, a theologian writing during WWI, said this about holiness and unity:

That moral certainty of God's conquering holiness is the only foundation of any faith in man's unity, when the last pinch comes. It is not in himself but in his God as his Savior. It is his unity in a Redeemer and a Redemption, a unity not natural but supernatural, not by evolutionary career but by mortal crisis, not in the first creation but the second, not in generation but regeneration. Nothing can give us footing or hope amid the degeneration of man but his regeneration by God. God's method with evil is not prevention but cure. And this is the note of the church, moral reconciliation, holy regeneration, upon a world scale—the new Humanity. This faith is the only condition, nay, the only creator, of church unity; and it is the only creator, through the church's Gospel, of the unity of the race and its peace.[1]

Have you ever considered that the key to racial unity and peace is the holiness of God? God's conquering holiness is the ignition point of the whole family deriving its name from the Father!

If I place my ethnicity as that which defines me, I am not treating the name of the Father as holy. If I am deriving my identity from my social status, then I am not treating the name of God as holy. If I use sexuality as the basis for my identity, then I am not hallowing the name of the Father.

What are you using as your identity? If you are defining yourself by something other than the Father's holy name, you are mistreating the name. You are seeking to be individualistic when holiness is calling you to unity.

Hallowing the name of the Father is tied to the way we love, serve, forgive, and supply for each other's well-being. This is something the Israelites were indicted for by God in Ezekiel 36:23 when he says, *"I will show the holiness of my great name, which has been profaned among the nations, the name you have profaned among them."* It was not just their personal holiness that led to the chastisement of the nation, but it was their disregard for the injustices of their neighbors. The self-righteousness of the nation was an idol that blinded them to the suffering of others. By ignoring the oppression around them, they profaned God's holy name.

The reason you don't ask for your own daily bread is because you are part of a family. You should want every member of the family to have food. The reason you don't ask only for your sins to be forgiven is because you have a corporate

---

1 P. T. Forsyth, *Justification of God: Lectures for War Time On A Christian Theodicy* (London: Duckworth & Company, 1916), 14.

responsibility to seek and give forgiveness to other people in the family. If hallowing the name of the Father were only about personal standards of holiness, then Jesus would have been applauding and celebrating the Pharisees!

In fact the Bible teaches us that holiness and peace go together. Hebrews 12:14 says, *"Strive for peace with everyone, and for the holiness without which no one will see the Lord."* We are commanded in First Peter 1:15–16, *"But as he who called you is holy, you also be holy in all your conduct, since it is written 'You shall be holy, for I am holy.'"*

Hallowing the name of the Father means embracing our new corporate identity in Christ. We translate the splendor of the holiness of the Father to a watching world with our uncommon love for each other. If holiness sounds like too hard a thing to achieve, this is why Jesus said to pray!

Christ makes people holy

Psalm 29:1–2 says, *"Ascribe to the LORD, O mighty ones, ascribe to the LORD glory and strength. Ascribe to the LORD the glory due his name; worship the LORD in the splendor of his holiness."* As we ascribe the glory due his name, we find that he who is holy provides the means for you and me to be holy as we take in the splendor of his holiness as we worship.

For instance, we know the sun will shine. We don't have to make the sun do its work; it just does it. You don't have to think about the way plants derive their nourishment from the sunlight. Photosynthesis doesn't have to be understood in order to appreciate the splendor of the sun. You just know that the sun will do its work as it shines. If the sun doesn't shine, all of life on earth will cease. Accept the sunshine!

Likewise, worship the Lord with other believers across the lines of race and class. Let your worship of the Lord do its work in you! The Lord's holiness will transform you from one degree of glory to the next as you worship. And just as the sun gives light and life to everything on the planet, everything about us depends on the name of our Father being hallowed. It is the Father who will change us.

How can we help but be changed when we are in the presence of such impressive beauty?

"Woe to me!" I cried. "I am ruined! For I am a man of unclean lips, and I live among a people of unclean lips, and my eyes have seen the King, the LORD Almighty." Then one of the seraphs flew to me with a live coal in his hand, which he had taken with tongs from the altar. With it he touched my mouth and said, "See, this has touched your lips; your guilt is taken away and your sin atoned for." Then I heard the voice of the LORD saying, "Whom shall I send? And who will go for us?" And I said, "Here am I. Send me!" (Isa. 6:5–8)

Grasping these truths will unmask us and free us from the burden of hiding our guilt and shame. We all want to be loved and accepted in the presence of someone who is greater than we are. That is what hallowing the Father's name will do for us.

P.T. Forsyth says it well, "Unless there is within us that which is above us, we shall soon yield to that which is about us." This is why we need to hallow the Father's name! He sees us unmasked and loves us enough to change us![2]

As individuals, churches, and denominations, we need to repent of the ways we have failed to hallow the name of the Father in loving our neighbors across the lines of ethnicity. We need to repent of the ways we have failed to pursue the poor or stand up for the oppressed and the alien. We need to repent of how we do not hallow God's name before the watching world because we are too busy trying to remain separated as the family of God! As a consequence, we have no credibility to speak to the sins of racism and classism or discrimination within the culture.

I, as a Black Christian, by the grace and sovereign will of God, remain in a White-majority denomination in order to fight against the perception that my earthly father taught me when I was very young. I am convinced that our prayers to hallow the Father's name will yield the praise that is to be ascribed to his name. I am convinced that this will reflect the splendor of his holiness.

These are actions we can take to complement our prayers:

1. Recognize that we have a holy deficit. None of us are holy on our own. We are not holy individually or collectively.
2. We understand that we experience God's holy love through faith in Christ and this makes up for our deficit. Believe the Gospel individually and corporately. This is the first step in hallowing the Father's name.

---

2 P. T. Forsyth, GoodReads 2016, http://www.goodreads.com/author/show/377389.

3. Embrace the new corporate identity we have as members of the Father's family. Remember the family in both heaven and earth derives its name from the Father. In the name of the Father, defend the oppressed and serve the poor, for in so doing we honor God (Prov. 17:5). Know that God is answering our prayer in the way we love, serve, forgive, live in unity, and supply for each other's physical needs.

4. We are not intimidated by holiness, but worshipping the Lord, basking in the splendor of his holiness, we celebrate the Father! For just as everything living derives nourishment from the sun, worshipping the Lord in all of his holy beauty, with all our diversity, will provide the nourishment for our souls to be holy as he is holy.

No one can be holy without Jesus, and it takes all of us to comprehend and express the holiness of God. As Jesus instructs us to pray and to act upon the truth that the Father's name is hallowed above all things, for everyone, everywhere. Amen?

A Way Forward

Chapter 27

Meet My African American Mentor

Rev. Scott Sauls

Scott Sauls has served as the Senior Minister of Christ Presbyterian Church in Nashville, Tennessee, since 2012. Previously, Scott was a lead pastor at Redeemer Presbyterian Church in New York City. He has also planted churches in Kansas City and St. Louis and is a frequent speaker at conferences and leadership retreats. He has degrees from Furman University (BA) and Covenant Theological Seminary (MDiv) as well as the author of Jesus Outside the Lines. *He and his wife, Patti, have two daughters.*

I have a confession to make.

Not long ago, I was naïve enough to believe that electing a Black president would go a long way in solving the race problem. And yet, fifty years post–Civil Rights Era, it has become clear that we are not yet ready to call ourselves a post-racial people. I was painfully reminded of this when a friend sent me a New York Times essay written by George Yancy, a Black philosophy professor at Emory, called "Dear White America."

In his essay, Dr. Yancy laments the state of things for people of color in Western society. In his view, when the history books, the evening news, entertainment, business, education, politics, theology, and church cultures are shaped predominantly by the White perspective, people of color have little choice but to live under what he calls "the yoke of Whiteness."

To White Americans, the use of this phrase may seem unfair. The word "yoke" feels inflammatory because it hearkens back to the days of slavery. And we in the modern West are against slavery and the racism that supported it, right? The public schools are racially integrated now. Lynching and mobs and violence, these are all now punishable by law. White ministers like me quote Black thinkers such as Dr. Martin Luther King Jr. in our sermons. We read books and essays by John Perkins and Cornel West, and we speak out and tweet for racial equality. It is not uncommon for a White person to marry a person of color these days or to adopt a child of another race.

Most White people would say they deplore racism and are sickened by the shedding of Black blood by White bigots. Our hearts hurt over Black casualties in Selma, Ferguson, Charleston, New York City, and all the other places where racial violence has occurred. Where there is injustice, most White Americans would say they stand with the victims and against the perpetrators. But do people of color feel these things are true?

The reality is we still have a race problem. We know this because the subject of race still hurts for many people of color. Dr. Yancy writes:

> Don't tell me about how many Black friends you have. Don't tell me that you are married to someone of color. Don't tell me that you voted for Obama. Don't tell me that I'm the racist. Don't tell me that you don't see color. Don't tell me that I'm blaming Whites for everything. To do so is to hide yet again. You may have never used the N-word in your life, you may hate the KKK, but that does not mean that you don't harbor racism and benefit from racism. After all, you are part of a system that allows you to walk into stores where you are not followed, where you get to go for a bank loan and your skin does not count against you, where you don't need to engage in "the talk" that Black people and people of color must tell their children.... As you reap comfort from being White, we suffer for being Black and people of color.[1]

Are we listening to each other?

Ten years ago, Dr. Yancy's words would have bothered me. I might have even dismissed them as unfair and unreasonable. I would have assumed, wrongly, that his chief goal was to make White people feel guilty for being White.

---

1 George Yancy, "Dear White America," *The New York Times*, December 24, 2015, http://opinionator.blogs.nytimes.com/2015/12/24/dear-White-america/?emc=edit_ty_20151224&nl=opinion&nlid=54716909&_r=0.

But over time, and because of the courage and truthfulness of friends whose skin is darker than mine, my perspective has changed. These days, I find myself more sympathetic toward, and not offended by, words like the ones written by Dr. Yancy. Largely through friendship and a lot of personal mistakes along the way, I hope that I am growing in my understanding of the minority experience in the modern West.

The love, patience, and candor of mostly Black and Asian men and women in my life has given me a new set of ears for Dr. Yancy's outcry. When I listen to him, I do not see a chip on the shoulder, unfounded anger, guilt mongering, or some sort of "reverse racism." Rather, I see a man representing the minority voice, appropriately fatigued from feeling unseen, unheard, misunderstood, misjudged, and in many ways written off by a White majority.

Recently, a Black friend shared an insight with me about people who riot (which, by the way, is not something unique to people of color). He said that rioting is a terrible and damaging thing, and yet it comes from a place of feeling helpless in a system that dooms you, by virtue of your situation and the color of your skin, to be disadvantaged and overlooked. "Rioting," my friend said from a place of tenderness and concern, "is helplessness acted out. It is trying to give a voice to something without a voice."

In describing the act of rioting this way, my friend put his finger on a widely known truth: Hurting people hurt people. Ugly behavior can stem from a place of being treated as ugly. Destructive behavior can stem from a place of feeling destroyed. Dismissive behavior can stem from a place of feeling dismissed. Diminishing behavior can stem from a place of feeling diminished.

Pause here. Go back and re-read the statement from Dr. Yancy.

Can you hear the pain in his words? Are you listening carefully to the alienation and marginalization and "otherness" that he feels?

Am I?

Stuff White people like

There is a satirical website called Stuff White People Like that is written by and about White people. For the most part, it is a "poke fun at ourselves" commentary on the blind spots and deficiencies of White culture. One section describes how White people "like" ethnic diversity:

White people love ethnic diversity, but only as it relates to restaurants. Many White people... will spend hours talking about how great it is that they can get sushi and tacos on the same street. But then they send their kids to private school with other rich White kids and live in neighborhoods like Santa Monica or Pacific Palisades. But it's important to note that White people do not like to be called out on this fact. If you run an ethnic restaurant you can be guaranteed repeat business and huge tips if you act like your White customers are adventurous and cultured for eating food that isn't sandwiches or pasta.[2]

As a White person, I can read a paragraph like this and laugh. But I wonder if such a paragraph, while poking fun at how misinformed White people can be about true diversity, rubs salt in the wound for a non-White reader?

The kind of "diversity" described above is more cosmetic than real, more recreational than relational, more token than authentic. In fact, it is not true diversity because it requires zero self-reflection or change from the ethnic majority. On the other hand, cosmetic, recreational, and token "diversity" is costly to minorities because it requires them to do all the bending, all the adjusting, all the adapting, all the sidelining and sacrificing of their own culture and heritage and uniqueness, to assimilate into a White world where things are done in the "White way."

One time I gave a sermon on diversity at Redeemer Presbyterian Church in New York City where I was serving as a preaching pastor. At the time, Redeemer was about half White and half Asian. In my sermon, I said something that I thought would resonate with my Asian brothers and sisters, and maybe even cause them to stand up and cheer. I said:

The kingdom of God is as diverse as humanity is diverse. God has called people to himself, and into his church, from every nation, tribe, and tongue. He has called us to be one body, with one Lord, one faith, and one baptism. Therefore, there should be no White church and no Black church and no Asian church and no Latino church... because there is only one church.

---

2 Christian Lander, "#7 Diversity," *Stuff White People Like*, January 19, 2008, http://stuffwhitepeoplelike.com/2008/01/19/7–diversity.

As I said these words, I had no idea how much hurt they would cause.

Afterward, an African American friend approached me to give feedback. Looking at me with sorrow in his eyes, he said, "Brother, you don't get it." This felt jarring and left me wondering what I had done wrong. But sometimes, a simple and direct statement of fact is what's needed to get us listening.

Soon after this, an Asian friend approached me, also wanting to give feedback. He humbly and courageously offered the following (this is a paraphrase):

> Scott, since your sermon yesterday, I have heard from several friends who, like me, are ethnic minorities. All of them, to one degree or another, felt hurt by your words. Many of them grew up in minority-specific churches and felt that you de-legitimized those churches in your sermon. It felt like you were saying that those churches shouldn't even exist. Scott, I really believe that you meant well and that you sincerely value the diversity God desires for his church. But I'm afraid your sermon moved us backward instead of forward. In a White-dominated society, sometimes the only place that ethnic minorities can freely celebrate the beauty and uniqueness of their cultures, the only place that people of color are free to fully be themselves, is in churches where their ethnicity is the majority. Your words about ethnically diverse churches may be helpful for a White audience. But for ethnic minorities, your words reinforced the alienation that many of us feel in a White-led world and also in White-led churches. I'm afraid that your sermon added to, rather than taking away from, that feeling of alienation.

As this friend spoke these things, I felt thankful and sorrowful. I felt thankful because he had exposed a blind spot in me. He had given me a glimpse of my inability to understand the minority experience and of how much growing I have to do with regard to my awareness of issues of race. I felt sorrowful because, in an attempt to build some bridges, I burned them instead.

Appreciating minority-culture voices

More recently, I was invited to participate in a national discussion on race. It was an all-day discussion, and there were about twenty people present. The group was about half White and half Black, and included authors, musicians, social workers, pastors, politicians, nonprofit leaders, and a Freedom Rider.

Although I was invited several times to contribute to the discussion, I stayed silent for most of the day. Instead of talking a lot, which is a preacher's natural default, I decided instead to listen and take a lot of notes. Here are some of the things we heard from our Black friends. Rather, what I mean to say is, here are some of the things we heard from our friends:

> "Please don't call me your Black friend. This kind of label actually reveals the poverty of our friendship. Not until I am seen as simply your friend will it start to feel like you regard me as your equal."

> "Imagine if the goal of your whole life was proving to White people, who have all the power, that you are not a threat because of the color of your skin."

> "I am a dark-skinned man married to a White woman. Our light-skinned children have a much easier 'race experience' than our dark-skinned children do, even though they share the same DNA."

> "White gentrification is taking over Black neighborhoods in virtually every major city. Gentrification is when the haves displace the have-nots without regard for the have-nots."

> "White privilege is our institutional muscle memory. Privilege is when you can be successful without ever having to touch base with any other culture."

> "There seems to be a lot of fear among Whites in today's climate. Fear of giving up privilege. Fear of listening more and of speaking less."

> "Pain and lament aren't often taught in White Evangelical books. Learning to deal with pain is a gift that people of color can give to White people."

> "We never hear about the big scary White man, only the big scary Black man."

> "Race is not an 'issue' for people of color. For us, it's our whole lives."

> "As a former Freedom Rider, I speak mostly to Caucasian groups. I'm rarely asked any more to speak to African American groups. They have lost hope. They think, 'What's the point?'"

"As a Black man, I don't need people feeling sorry for me. Help me believe I can be somebody. Raise the bar on me, don't coddle me."

What I am learning is how important it is for me as part of the majority to talk less and to listen more to the minority voice. I'm starting to see that because I haven't lived the minority experience and because I have for all my life "reaped comfort from being White" in a White-dominated society, I should be quick to listen and slow to speak. I should presume less, offer fewer solutions, and ask a lot more questions. For only when I listen to the pain of the minority am I able to love across the lines of difference in ways that are helpful and not hurtful.

Racial justice in the New Testament

The pain associated with cultural inequality, and also with minority versus majority dynamics, is not new. In fact, an overlooked minority was one of the earliest problems in the New Testament church.

The church in Acts began with an all-Hebrew (Aramaic-speaking) leadership. However, it didn't take long before a complaint arose from Hellenist (Greek-speaking) minorities against the Hebrew majority, because the all-Hebrew leaders were not hearing the cries of the suffering, underserved and overlooked Hellenist widows.

With all the privilege and power in their favor, the Hebrews had the luxury of not being required to respond. As the majority, they could have simply dismissed the concerns of the Hellenist minority rather than going through the trouble, inconvenience, costliness, and awkwardness of addressing their complaint. They could have easily responded to their Hellenist brothers and sisters, "Can't you just be grateful that we are allowing you to be part of our community? Don't you realize that it's not a very 'Christian' thing to complain? Why can't you just appreciate what you do have?"

Or, they could have simply showed the offended Hellenists the door, sending them down the street, perhaps, to start a community of their own. "Since you're not happy here, since you don't seem to like our culture or the way we are running things, why don't you just go somewhere else and start your own church?"

In a million ways, the Hebrew majority could have dismissed the minority complaint. But that's not what they did. Rather than responding defensively, rather than writing off the concerns of the minority, the all-Hebrew leaders handed the entire widow-care system over to the offended minority. Seven people were chosen to correct the issue of racial inequality in the church—Stephen, Philip, Prochorus, Nicanor, Timon, Parmenas, and Nicolas—all of whom were Hellenists.[3]

You might say that the Hebrew leaders of the early church were among the first to take "affirmative action" to ensure that minority concerns were addressed and solutions were discovered and implemented by the minorities themselves.

A first step toward true diversity—whether cultural, economic, political, ethnic, or otherwise—is to recognize that charity toward minorities, by itself, is not enough. Charity, to be truly charitable and biblical, must also result in empowerment, where the majority humbles and positions itself to follow the minority voice regularly. Especially where injustice and inequality exist, the majority must proactively seek out ways to surrender microphone and gavel rights to the minority. Invitations to give "input" must be replaced with opportunities to lead. Crumbs from the table must be replaced with a seat at the table. Otherwise, we remain stuck with an anemic, counterfeit diversity. Otherwise, particularly as pertains to race, we remain stuck with only stuff that White people like.

An unexpected invitation

My friend Ronnie Mitchell is more than a friend. He is also a mentor to me.

Pastor Ronnie calls me his "brother from another mother," and yet, we are different. He has lived in the same neighborhood his entire life. He is nearly two decades my senior and has been married to the same woman for almost as long as I have been alive. While also working a second job, he has pastored one African American congregation, New Livingstone Church, for close to forty years. He is also a Black man.

In our time together, Pastor Ronnie has taught me more about life in Jesus than the books I've read or sermons I've heard. He has opened my eyes to pain

---

3 See the whole story in Acts 6:1–7.

associated with being Black in a White man's world, but never for a moment from a place of resentment or self-pity. In this, he has been to me a picture of grace and longsuffering. He has taught me how gentrification helps some while it hurts others, and how as neighborhoods get "better" for one people group, they tend to get worse—no longer accessible, that is—for another. He has shown me, in the presence of his granddaughter, what it looks like for a grown man to be wrapped around a little girl's finger. He has spoken twice at my church, both times bringing his whole church with him as a demonstration of unity and solidarity. In one breath, he is a model of dependent, childlike prayer. In the next breath, he shows what it looks like to storm the gates of heaven in power.

Ronnie has taught me how sometimes the poorest people in the world are the ones at the top of the organizational charts and pecking orders and the richest people are sometimes at the bottom. He has taught me, in ways that nobody else has, that the kingdom of God is sometimes upside-down to our sensibilities. And man oh man, can Ronnie turn a phrase! But most importantly, when I'm close to Ronnie, I always sense that I am also close to Jesus. I need Pastor Ronnie for many reasons. I need him because in more ways than I can count, he makes me want to be a better man.

Recently, Pastor Ronnie honored me with an invitation to preach at New Livingstone's annual "Revival." Before this, I had never preached at a revival. I had also never before preached to an African American congregation. But after the fact, I can confidently say that this was one of the top three most heartening experiences I have ever had as a minister.

From the moment I stepped foot into their sanctuary, the New Livingstone family received me not as a guest preacher, but as one of their own. Their receptivity and hospitality toward me, toward the musicians from our church that Ronnie invited to lead the singing, and toward our church members that Ronnie invited to attend, was beyond welcoming, it was magnificent, a true taste of the kingdom of God.

As I left full from that beautiful church that night, I wondered why Pastor Ronnie had decided to invite someone like me to preach at his church revival. Why would this pastor, whose community knows what it's like to suffer under "the yoke of Whiteness," invite me into his pulpit? Why would he yield to me the sacred task of heralding a message of unity, love, reconciliation, and peace when the color of my skin, the zip code of my residence, and the history of my people in some ways represent the opposite of these things to his people? Why would Ronnie assume such a big risk for a leader in his shoes?

I think the answer is just that. The answer is that Ronnie is a leader.

For many years, Pastor Ronnie has taught his people, just as he teaches me, to see color not primarily through the eyes of cynicism and despair, but through the eyes of hope. He has taught his people, just as he teaches me, to see color not through the eyes of separation and alienation and otherness, but through the eyes of God's kingdom reflected in every race, nation, tribe, and tongue (Rev. 7:9). He has taught us all about how much we need each other, to learn from and listen to each other and share life together, in order for the image of God to be more fully formed in us. By treating me as one of his people, as a brother from another mother who is on his team, Ronnie reminds me that being united to Jesus also means being united to each other. It means that through Jesus, our definition of "us" must expand, and our definition of "them" must shrink.

This is only part of why I lean on Pastor Ronnie, not only as a friend but as a mentor. He is my mentor because he shows me what a real leader does in a racially fractured world. He did for me in his Black-majority church what early church leaders did for the Hellenists in their Hebrew-majority church.

That day Pastor Ronnie handed the microphone to me, a White minister from the other side of town. He did not bring the gavel down on me; instead, he put his gavel in my hand. He did not treat me as a foreigner; instead, he treated me as a friend. He did not belittle me; instead, he elevated my dignity. He did not ignore me; instead, he treated me like I had something important to say. He did not caricature me as one of them; instead, he welcomed me as part of his us. He did not give me crumbs from his table; instead, he gave me a seat at his table. He did not call me a White man from the other side of town; instead, he called me his brother from another mother.

Pastor Ronnie is my mentor. And from him, I still have a lot to learn.

Chapter 28

Moving Forward

Rev. Russ Whitfield

Russ Whitfield serves as the pastor of Grace Mosaic, a cross-cultural church in Northeast Washington, DC. He has degrees from New York University (BM) and Westminster Theological Seminary (MDiv). Russ has served in many ministry roles among diverse people groups. Russ and his wife, Vanessa, have three children.

You may be having a difficult time understanding the reactions of many people of color (and White allies) to the news of Black people dying at the hands of law enforcement. Maybe you are even a little bit frustrated with the emotional response and the cries of injustice against "the system."

Perhaps, you're on the other side of these events. You are angry, heartbroken, and feeling hopeless because you can't help but see injustice every time one of these all-too-familiar scenarios appears in news headlines. Either way, if you identify as a Christian, you have been called to be a reconciler, a peacemaker, and a light in this current darkness. It is imperative that you work through this distinctly Christian calling with wisdom, courage, and a mind to new obedience. The love of God constrains you. The grace of God teaches you. The Spirit of God empowers you to live an altogether different kind of life in light of the new age that has dawned in the death, burial, resurrection, and ascension of Jesus Christ.

The issues at hand deeply affect the lives of real people within your local church and real people outside of your local church whom you have been called to love faithfully. This is to say that our engagement or disengagement with these issues will shape the dynamics of our life together, along with our missionary encounter with the world. On these issues, our local churches will either testify to the glory of the risen Christ through mutual love and humble repentance, or we will obscure the glory of the risen Christ through hardness of heart and indifference.

One thing, however, must be made absolutely clear: passivity has never been a viable Christian response to divisive and destructive social dynamics, especially within the church. Most of us are already convinced of this. But we feel like we're stuck. We're unsure of how to participate in bringing the healing that is needed.

Story as guide

So how might we begin to proactively engage these issues? How can we begin to chart a course forward? I would invite you to consider the theme of story as a guiding paradigm for progress. All sides in this racial struggle tend to live within their own separate stories. These cultural narratives predetermine who our friends should be, who we can trust, and how we should relate to the world. These cultural narratives encourage us to find our deepest identities and alliances within our own ethnic, racial, and socioeconomic groups. However, I would propose that if we are to move forward together, then we must situate these tensions, our community, and our very lives within the same story—the story of God. No matter what truths may be found within these smaller cultural stories, we must give the greatest weight and the final say in our lives to God's story. To put it another way, the story of God must be our "true north," our greatest orienting factor. The story of God must dispel the cultural myths in which we have been living for far too long.

I'm intentionally resisting the typical "to-do" list, for real problems are rarely solved by checking the boxes. Rather, I'm proposing what I think will be a fruitful trajectory of thought as we try to move forward in mutual love and understanding. Admittedly, it takes much prayerful, humble, and communal reflection to figure out what this might look like in your context. The specifics will take different shape in different places. However, I would propose that if we are to be built up together in love (Eph. 4:16), then we must stay attuned to God's macro-level narrative for perspective.

Let's start with some important ideas. Each tragic, racialized event tends to take on a life that is much bigger than itself. Each of these events tap into a broader, more tragic, and more painful story for people of color. If this does not register for you, then the effect of all your preaching, Scripture quoting, and #praying tweets will be muted, at best. Please understand that every act of racial injustice, every episode of racism and race-based mistreatment takes on a symbolic status that brings to mind an entire network of historic injustices, sufferings, and the dehumanization of African Americans and other people of color. In the minds of many Black people, each racialized event serves as a heart-rending cipher for chattel slavery, Jim Crow, historic church bombings, Klan terrorism, redlining, and many other wounds received personally, and by living family members of former generations. Each event reads like another chapter in America's running commentary on my Blackness—my worth, my status, my place in society—and it's not a hopeful picture.

At one time, I did ministry in an affluent area in another part of the country, and I was often invited to large parties that were held in the beautiful homes of friends and church members. I was usually the only person of color in the place, except for "the help," of course. On more than one occasion, a fellow party-goer would come up to me and put their trash or empty glass on my plate, assuming I was "the help." I was clearly not expected to be in attendance as an equal or a friend. On another occasion, as I stood at the front of the house chatting with a friend and taking in the beautiful weather, a fellow party-goer tossed their car keys to me upon their arrival, assuming that I was the valet. Why did he toss the keys to me rather than my White friend? On each of these occasions, I heard America's commentary clearly: "We've already assigned a social role for people who look like you, and that role is beneath us."

Based on your current life situation, these events can carry slightly different, but equally painful messages. If I'm a Black achiever, I get the message that no matter how many letters I have behind my name (MDiv, PhD, JD), no matter how much money I have in the bank, no matter what gifts, talents, or job titles I hold, I will forever and always be subservient, even expendable. The dark clouds of stereotype, racialization, and essentialism will never lift.

I will never be able to walk through the world with the freedom and security of my White counterparts. The media stereotypes, fear-filled glances of passersby, and constant pressures to prove my virtue, decency, and value are a regular reminder that I don't get the benefit of the doubt so I must work that much harder to diffuse the doubts and fears. In certain situations, it could mean the difference between life and death. Each tragic episode tells me that I will be on the social treadmill indefinitely: The reality of motion with the illusion of progress.

If I'm a Black non-achiever, I get the message that if I ever entertained even the smallest notion of rising from my current situation, I should probably just forget about it. It's not worth the effort. I'm stuck and might as well stay put. If I try to rise, anyone with cultural power can put me back in my place of subjugation without any repercussions. Each racialized incident sounds like a ringing confirmation of the nihilistic chorus of voices that continually dance in my head. Sadly, many succumb to this bleak outlook.

If at this point you want to say, "Well just follow the law, and you don't have to worry about these things happening. You can take responsibility for your actions—look at Barack Obama!" I understand how this makes sense to you, and it is true that personal responsibility must be taken, but try to consider the countless Emmett Tills of America (and if you don't know who Emmett Till is —Google him!) For every Barack Obama, there have been thousands of Emmett Tills in American history. In addition, each incident is a reminder of the flood of personal experiences of racism and injustice that the particular individual has endured. Like that time when I was called a racial slur and that time when people expressed shock at my ability to speak "the king's English." Add in that day when my college friends suggested that I was granted acceptance because of "affirmative action" rather than personal merit (because I could not possibly have earned it...being Black and all). We could easily produce dozens of these microaggressions that have rubbed our souls raw through repeated abrasion.

None of these incidents that I or anyone go through happen in an emotional or historical vacuum. God made us as emotive, storied people, it's a fact of our anthropological hardwiring. So, often, when Black people experience America's commentary, it is an experience similar to the real, lived pain of seeing a mangled car on the roadside after having lost a dear loved one in an auto accident. Viewing that singular image on the side of the road instantly creates a tidal wave of emotions. Then, after this wave hits you, the rip tide of grief carries you out into the sea of anguish. You remember first hearing the news of the loss.

You remember watching your surrounding loved ones burst into tears. You remember the black suits and dresses at the wake. You remember the roses being thrown on the coffin as the undertaker prepared to lower your loved one six feet into the ground.

In a similar way, African Americans are reintroduced to a grief, pain, and sense of loss every time one of these tragedies occurs, and inasmuch as you refuse to acknowledge this and mourn with the mourner (Rom. 12:15), you exacerbate the pain and alienation. You stall healing and, sometimes, inflict deeper wounds.

We must realize that the optics of these events matter. Regardless of the particulars, the overriding truth, the loudest voice heard by African Americans is that another Black person's life has been extinguished because Black lives are invested with less value.

If you are always down in the weeds arguing "the facts," you will likely be harsh and insensitive. The worst part about this is that you may be "right" with regard to technicalities, but you will not be right with regard to Christian love. You may need to consider holding your tongue in certain moments. Many of the things that we think in our minds are not beneficial for public consumption (beware your Facebook and Twitter rants).

The question is not so simple as to ask, "Do the details of this particular case harmonize with the American justice system?" The bigger question is, "Does the American justice system harmonize with the true justice of God in this particular situation?" To conflate the American justice system with the true justice of God is naive and misguided. We have to acknowledge that the American justice system is failing Black people, brown people, White people, and law enforcement officers at any point where the American justice system departs from the principles of eternal justice. I'm not suggesting that we could or should pursue a theocracy in America. But what I am suggesting is that there must be an acknowledgment of the fallibility of our system and, at the very least, a fight to rid the American justice system of its glaring inadequacies, insofar as we are able to participate in this labor.

But it is also important for us to remember a number of other important facts as we aim to move forward.

First, there is a beautiful history of White people entering into solidarity and seeking justice for all. They have used their social, educational, and financial privileges to work for justice. People of color should encourage them and receive them as family and allies in this worthy struggle.

Second, there are many genuine, kind-hearted, White people who are doing their best to make sense of things. They do not see any injustice or why these incidents would warrant such strong reactions. They are honestly trying to work through it all. Let grace and the Golden Rule be your guide in dialogue. Try to give the same space and grace that you would need to see things from their angle, given their life experiences. If they ask you questions and the answers seem painfully obvious to you, don't assume or project malicious intent, lest you be guilty of the same kind of thinking that contributed to these tragedies in the first place.

Third, there will always be people who see emotional responses of pain and frustration in such situations as "race-baiting," "excuses," or "playing the race card." There will be trolls on the comment sections of digital newspapers and blogs that spew unspeakably awful, hateful things. I would simply encourage you to spend your emotional energies on your local context with real people, building real relationships of trust and honesty. Staying at the national level to the neglect of the local level will likely tend toward hopelessness and despair. Conversely, the small victories that happen around the kitchen table and in the neighborhood, born of prayer, love, and perseverance, will bless you more than you know. Celebrate this good fruit.

What's even more important than these practical pieces of advice is the more central need that we have to share the same overarching narrative. This is the truth: we need each other if we are going to break out of the dehumanizing narratives under which we each live. If there is any truth to the notion that we are deeply affected by the narratives under which we live, then we are confronted with a question: What does a narrative of untimely death, violence, criminalization, racialization, and inferiority do to a people group? When this historical narrative of subhumanity and expendability seems to be confirmed time and again, what happens to its beleaguered characters?

It has been said before that racism and the racialization of American culture is bad, not just for people of color, but for White people as well.[1] It is not true nor healthy for people of color to live under the narrative of inferiority and

1 Peggy McIntosh. "White privilege." *Race, Class and Gender: An Anthology,* (1998): 94–105.

dehumanization. In the same way, it is not true nor healthy for White people to live under the narrative of superiority and suprahumanization. You are in a dangerous and unhealthy position when your race, ethnicity, biology, and overall way of life is canonized and made to be anthropological holy writ. Adherence to this social orthodoxy will cloud your mind with a soul-stifling pride, which God opposes (James 4:6). No one people group should be so cast down below the rest, and no one people group should be so exalted above the rest—neither of these outlooks is a healthy way to be human. The conflicts we are witnessing result from the ways in which we have all lived out of these lesser narratives, allowing these mythologies to govern our lives and ruin our relationships.

However, there is a way in which all people can simultaneously acknowledge their lowliness, fallibility, and the vulnerability of their situation— but also the beauty, glory, and hope for their situation. This is the story of the Gospel, and it is this story that we must share together if we are to make progress in mutual love and understanding.

God's story

According to God's story, every human being was designed for glory and dignity in connection with God and the people around him or her. Every human being surrendered his or her glory in walking away from God. But the hope that God gives is that his story is all about affirming these twin truths: You and I are simultaneously sinners, yet accepted in the Beloved by grace alone through faith alone. We are ruined but rescued, awful but adopted, devious but delivered. God's story tells us that brokenness is not the sole proprietorship of any one ethnic group, and by God's grace, glory is not the sole inheritance of any one ethnic group. This is God's commentary on our shared identity in Christ; and it's infinitely better than America's commentary.

This story alone sets the stage for fruitful, healthy, restorative dialogue and true progress. This story tells me that my identity rests, not on being right, but on being loved. I am free to be wrong, to learn, and to change as I live in community with the other. I am free to acknowledge that my mind needs to be renewed, and that this renewal is possible. If what the Bible says about me is anywhere near the truth, then humility, teachability, and grace must govern the way I move forward.

Don't politicize this issue, gospelize it. The Gospel is the only story big enough to swallow up the grief of a ruined humanity, overcoming that ruin with the glory of a renewed humanity. Build this into your local church through every means available—pulpit, programming, community groups, and neighborhood gatherings. Explore the implications of God's story for the current racial conflicts that we are facing. In what ways do you need to embrace difficult changes personally and corporately? How does God's story encourage me to drop my defenses? Who should I be inviting to my dinner table in light of God's story? How should we rethink the power-dynamics of our church or organization in light of a glorious God who humbles himself in love in order to lift the other?

The story of God answers these questions and many more with life-giving and life-changing direction. But one thing is for sure, if you bury your head in the sand on important issues like these, your witness will be blunted and your missionary encounter with the world will ebb over time as America grows more diverse.

You have an opportunity to speak dignity over the disenfranchised—did not Christ do this for you (1 Pet. 2:9)? You have an opportunity to proclaim words that invite humility and gracious acceptance—did not Christ proclaim these words over you (1 Pet. 5:5)? You have an opportunity to participate in the formation of a cross-cultural community—is this not the community that God has already determined to bring to completion (Rev. 7:9)? In God's story, the poor are made rich because the rich One was made poor (2 Cor. 8–9). In God's story, the weak are made strong because the Almighty was pleased to enter into our weakness (Rom. 5:6, Phil. 2:5ff).

In God's story, there is hope for the hopeless, joy for the joyless, and power for the powerless. Christ, the King, will not suffer the status quo injustice and tragedy of this world to remain in place forever. But my question for you is this: Are you going to embrace your role as a participant in God's story of renewal? In Christ, we have an entire treasury of resources for living up into this bigger, more meaningful, and more beautiful story. I would invite you to reimagine your relationships in light of this story. Reimagine the final chapter of this story, allowing that vision to shape your life and relationships in the present. If you do, the mile markers on the side of the road will reveal that you are actually making progress in the journey toward racial healing and social flourishing. This story, shared among us, is our hopeful way forward.

Chapter 29

My Journey from Monoethnic to Multiethnic

Rev. Dr. Jonathan Seda

Jonathan Seda has served as Senior Pastor of Grace Church in Dover, Delaware, since 1983. He has served on the boards of Covenant Seminary, Young Life, and Mosaix Global Network and has a passion for multiethnic, cross-cultural worship and ministry. Jonathan has degrees from Houghton College (BA), Biblical Theological Seminary (MDiv), and Covenant Theological Seminary (DMin). He and his wife, Dale, have four children and six grandchildren.

It was a cool morning in Mérida, a colonial city in the northwest corner of the Yucatán Peninsula. I stood at the entrance of the hotel on the busy street where we were staying. The sound of motor scooters and motorcycles was interrupted by an occasional bus, lumbering by and leaving a vanishing trail of acrid diesel smoke. Then there was the ring-ring of bicycles with their thumb-pushed, high-pitched ringers warning pedestrians scurrying to the other side of the street. It was a déjà vu moment for me as I was suddenly transported to my early teens in Caracas, Venezuela. The sights and sounds were so familiar and brought with them such warm and familiar feelings. I stood there in Caracas, on the corner of Las Acacias and Avenida La Victoria, jostled by brown-skinned people like myself waiting for a break in traffic to scamper across. At the sound of a horn I awakened to my surroundings and stood there thinking, "What am I doing as a Latino pastor of a White, middle-class church in Dover, Delaware?"

I had never thought of it quite like that, but as I stood on that busy street in Mérida, early in 2000, my mind drifted back over the twenty-some years I had been a pastor. In particular, I thought about the recent years spent trying to lead Grace Church to become a multiethnic congregation. I stood there, disillusioned. "What am I doing as the pastor of a White, middle-class church?"

I confess that I had long been comfortable in Anglo churches. I have an Anglo mother (my father was born in Puerto Rico) and at age fifteen came to live on her brother's dairy farm in rural western New York, where I began the process of thorough enculturation. It was quite a culture shock to move from the world-class city of Caracas to a farming community, but I survived, went to college and seminary, and began my ministry at Faith Presbyterian Church in Wilmington, Delaware. Along the way, I attended completely White, monoethnic churches. I often thought about the churches of my early youth as a missionary kid, but they also were monoethnic—monoethnic Latino churches. I simply thought, "That was there and this is here."

The mystery of the Gospel

My awakening to the issue of race occurred in the spring of 1996, some four years before that day in Mérida. Somehow I was invited to be a part of a panel discussion at Delaware State University. I think it may have been because Grace Church is the closest church to the university, only a mile away. With shame, I confess that our church had never made even the feeblest effort to reach out to this campus. It is a historic Black university whose roots are in the wretched soil of segregation. How could we have been so blind? Why had we never seen the university as part of our mission? Whatever the reasons, I received a call from a department head asking me to participate in a panel discussion on the controversial book by Dinesh D'Souza, *The End of Racism*. A copy of the book would be given to me, he said. I accepted.

I read the book, and as I did, I increasingly wondered, "Where is the church in this issue of racism?" The answer was not pleasant. I began to study the Scriptures on the matter of race and began to see the scriptural imperative for ethnic reconciliation and unity in the church.

Along the way, I was pulled up short. I saw something in the book of Ephesians that I had never seen before. I heard Paul say to pray that *"words may be given me in opening my mouth boldly to proclaim the mystery of the gospel, for which I am an ambassador in chains, that I may declare it boldly, as I ought to speak"* (Eph. 6:19–20). The mystery of the Gospel? I had always thought Paul was in chains for being an ambassador of the Gospel! The mystery of the Gospel? What mystery?

As I re-read Ephesians, I was stunned to see what I had never seen before. I saw that the central message of Ephesians is "the mystery of the gospel" and that Paul tells us exactly what that mystery is: *"This mystery is that the Gentiles are fellow heirs, members of the same body, and partakers of the promise in Christ Jesus through the gospel"* (Eph.3:6). Paul's message in Ephesians is that Jesus is the Savior who unifies races and nations in his church!

Until I re-read Ephesians I would have said this passage, along with many others that teach Gentile inclusion in the church, taught the glories of Covenant Theology. And of course it does, and they do! But Gentile inclusion in the church does not only speak to Jew-Gentile hostility. It speaks to all racial hostility. Who knew that Covenant Theology was at the very heart of racial reconciliation and that it is the theological foundation of the multiethnic church! Why are Presbyterian churches not leading the way in diversity?

The night at Delaware State University began with each panelist giving an introductory statement. When it was my turn, I stood at the podium in the Martin Luther King Jr. Lecture Hall. Some six hundred people sat before me. It's possible there were some White folk there, but I don't recall seeing them. My brown skin may well have been the lightest of all. I began, "Dr. Martin Luther King declared in the sixties that eleven o'clock Sunday morning is the most segregated hour in America. It still is, and therefore, as a pastor, I have nothing to say to the culture at large. I can only speak to the church. So if you're a Christian, let me speak to you." I proceeded to make the argument that racism began at Babel, that Pentecost was the great reversal of Babel, and that God's plan is to unite all people in the church. I laid before them God's vision for the church as described in Revelation 5:9—a gathering of worshippers *"from every tribe and language and people and nation."*

That they may all be one

I went away from that night determined to dig deeper into the Scriptures on this matter. I came to see the prayer of Jesus in John 17 as having a particular application to the issue of outward, visible unity in the local church, a unity that is the great apologetic for the reality of the Gospel. I came to see that the model church of the New Testament was not the church in Jerusalem, but rather the multiethnic church in Antioch led by its multiethnic, cross-cultural leadership team. I came to the conviction that the homogenous unit principle of church growth that has infected the church is unbiblical. I came to the conviction that I could do nothing less than lead our congregation to embrace God's vision for his church, bringing people together across the lines of race and class to worship and follow Jesus.

And so my journey began. It would be a much longer journey than I imagined. There were times like that day in Mérida, four years down the road, when I came close to giving up. What was I doing as a pastor of a White, middle-class church? But the answer was clear! I was seeking to lead our church to embrace God's vision. It was this biblical conviction that would carry me forward and fuel my passion to this day.

God has been gracious to us at Grace Church. We have a long way to go, but he has brought into our congregation people from so many different ethnic and cultural backgrounds. We are becoming an ever more beautiful tapestry of people. We now have an African American pastor on our staff, and we fully share the preaching and pastoral ministry. We have a growing RUM Fellowship on the campus of Delaware State University. Did I mention that the university is only a mile away? The African American campus minister is in our church, and students are following him to worship with us. We are on the verge of bringing a Korean American pastor on board, thus deepening our multiethnic pastoral staff as we broaden our Gospel reach.

What else does the Lord have in mind for us? We don't know. But I'm praying that the Lord will work wonderfully and powerfully in our church and in the church at large. I pray that congregations all across the nation and world will catch God's vision for his church and make it their own. However long the journey may be, I long for the day when churches reflect more clearly God's vision for his church, a church of people from every nation, tribe, people, and language.

Chapter 30

Mission and Multiethnic Ministry

Rev. Joel St. Clair

Joel St. Clair is the pastor of a multiethnic church in Silver Spring, Maryland, inside the Beltway of metro Washington, DC. He has degrees from Texas Christian University (BSN) and Westminster Theological Seminary (MDiv). Joel and his wife, Stephanie, have four children.

Silver Spring, Maryland, experienced a boom in population during the 1960s. People purchased homes looking for the typical suburban life. The city sits on the northern edge of the District of Columbia, and at that time the demographics of the city were predominantly White. If you walked into a coffee shop then, nine out of ten patrons were likely to be White people.[1] But then things began to change.

Following 1960, each subsequent decade brought a gradual and steady shift in the ethnic makeup of Silver Spring. It became less vanilla and more Neapolitan. This growth stemmed from a variety of factors that include the Civil Rights Act (1964), Fair Housing Act (1968), and the positive flow of immigrants pursuing good schools and single-family homes to grow their families. This growth brought major demographic change. By 2010 if you walked into a Starbucks, four or five out of ten patrons were likely to be White people. The 2010 census results showed that for the first time the ethnic makeup

---

1 The 1970 Census Data reflects a growing population, up 16 percent from 1960 and approximately 94 percent White.

of Silver Spring was now majority-minority.[2] This change is not isolated to the metro DC area; it is a change that is ongoing across the United States.

Neighborhoods do not change at the same pace or at the same rate, but William Frey describes the significance of the overall population shift in his book *Diversity Explosion*.[3] He writes:

> The shorthand description of urban America as "chocolate cities and vanilla suburbs" still remains in the consciousness of many people, at least those of a certain age. [This book] emphatically puts that stereotype to rest by showing that white-only flight to the suburbs is a thing of the past.[4]

Frey points to a trend of minorities moving into the suburbs and White residents moving back into cities. Of course there are still many segregated neighborhoods across the United States, but Frey's contribution highlights a major shift in the big picture of the population. Minority groups are growing at a pace that will radically shift the majority-culture paradigm. Fifty years ago, many assumed a Caucasian majority with some remaining minority percent of the total population being divided among other ethnic groups. But if the current trends hold, there will soon be no ethnic majority in the United States.

Blessing to a different world

As Christians, God has called us to a particular mission that includes announcing the arrival of God's kingdom and sharing God's promises in the person of Jesus Christ. The changing demographics of our neighborhoods must be considered as part of our Christian mission. The new ethnic realities of our place will shape how we conduct church worship, live as Christians, and engage the pluralistic and secular world around us. This does not mean that the truth of God's salvation in Jesus Christ changes, but that majority-culture churches are called to consciously communicate this unchanging truth to a world that looks

---

2 The 2010 census data is available at http://factfinder.census.gov.

3 William H. Frey, *Diversity Explosion: How New Racial Demographics Are Remaking America* (Washington DC: Brookings Institution Press, 2014).

4 Frey, 16–17.

less and less like them.[5] Thanks be to God that he has provided us a story to shape how we move forward into this new reality.

God's mission to bring redemption for his people has always involved engagement with a changing world. Christopher Wright makes this case in *The Mission of God*, where he says the people and arena of God's mission extend beyond a single ethnicity. Wright writes:

> The bottom line of God's address to Abraham in Genesis 12:1–3 is universal. The outcome of God's blessing of Abraham and commanding Abraham himself to be a blessing would be blessing for "all the kinship groups of the earth." This universal scope of the Abrahamic promise is the clinching argument for recognizing the missiological centrality of this text, which is already explicit in the command "Be a blessing."[6]

Abraham's mission involved looking beyond his own ethnic identity. Subsequent generations were called to be a light to the nations. They were uniquely positioned to speak truth, show generosity, and give mercy to those in great need throughout the diverse nations around them. While they sometimes spent more time fighting their family members than they did blessing their neighbors, we catch glimpses of their mission taking them outside their front door through the lives of Rahab, Ruth, Naaman, and Jonah with the Ninevites. Yet God does not waver in his work to bless and care for the nations.

The prophet Isaiah shows us a picture of God's faithful servant who will come to deliver both Israel and their neighbors. He describes the justice and light that will come to all the nations through God's servant:

> *Behold my servant, whom I uphold, my chosen, in whom my soul delights; I have put my Spirit upon him; he will bring forth justice to the nations. He will not cry aloud or lift up his voice, or make it heard in the street; a bruised reed he will not break, and a faintly burning wick he will not quench; he will faithfully bring forth justice. He will not grow faint or be discouraged till he has established justice in the earth; and the coastlands wait for his law. Thus says God, the LORD, who created the heavens and stretched them out, who spread out the earth and what comes from it, who gives breath to the people on*

5 When the majority ethnicity of a broader culture or nation also composes the majority of a specific local church.

6 Christopher J. H. Wright, *The Mission of God* (Downers Grove, IL: InterVarsity, 2006), 216.

it and spirit to those who walk in it: "I am the LORD; I have called you in righteousness; I will take you by the hand and keep you; I will give you as a covenant for the people, a light for the nations, to open the eyes that are blind, to bring out the prisoners from the dungeon, from the prison those who sit in darkness. I am the LORD; that is my name; my glory I give to no other, nor my praise to carved idols. Behold, the former things have come to pass, and new things I now declare; before they spring forth I tell you of them. (Isa. 42:1–9)

This servant arrives in Jesus of Nazareth, the faithful son of Abraham (Matt. 1:1–16). He brings the Good News of God's salvation to Israel and to the world. With his arrival came the inauguration of God's kingdom, whose citizens would come from the ends of the earth. And so the mission of God extending to one's neighbors despite ethnic differences continues with the inauguration of this kingdom and the community extending outward from Jerusalem, Judea, Samaria, and to the ends of the earth.

This challenge met the early church head on in the ethnic confrontations of Jew and Gentile. The Apostle Paul worked this out in many of his letters by regularly reminding readers that all Christians regardless of ethnicity or social status are united to Christ through faith. The frequency of Paul pastoring early churches through conflict about ethnicity and identity demonstrates the difficulty of these issues.

The early church struggled to come to grips with the implications of their faith, especially as it entailed engagement with people outside their own common spheres. For example, when Peter withdrew from the Gentiles in Antioch, it carried vital implications. Paul writes to the Galatian church that this move threatened to undermine the entire community of faith (Gal. 2:11–14). Yet even with these difficulties, we see the power of God working. Just as God promised Abraham would be a blessing to all nations, this promise comes to fulfillment in Jesus Christ that all who are united to him in faith are blessed.

Finally, God gives us a picture of what heaven looks like. The promise made to Abraham and fulfilled in Jesus Christ has a consummation coming. We catch a glimpse of our destination when the Apostle John envisions the reality of the worshipping community by writing:

After this I looked, and behold, a great multitude that no one could number, from every nation, from all tribes and peoples and languages, standing before the throne and before the Lamb, clothed in white robes, with palm branches in their hands, and crying out with a loud voice, "Salvation belongs to our God who sits on the throne, and to the Lamb!" And all the angels were standing around the throne and around the elders and the four living creatures, and they fell on their faces before the throne and worshipped God, saying, "Amen! Blessing and glory and wisdom and thanksgiving and honor and power and might be to our God forever and ever! Amen. (Rev. 7:9–12)

When we work on a puzzle, we use the box cover to guide how the pieces will fit together. It gives us the full picture of what the discrete pieces will one day look like when properly connected. In this passage, God gives us the box cover of his people at the end of his story. It is a mosaic of people from all tribes and nations and languages united together in Christ and worshipping God. This gives us a picture to guide our work here and now.

Often, when we consider this biblical theological thread of God's mission of people from all nations and all tribes worshipping together, we think of world missions. We consider missionary work on a global scale. However, the changing demographics of our nation introduce another action that we should prioritize. Demographic changes in the US challenge us to think strategically about engaging across ethnic lines. God calls each of us to think of ourselves as missionaries to the global cities where we reside. This vision of cross-cultural ministry now begins in our own neighborhood.

The truth of Jesus's death, resurrection, and ascension calls us to go into the world and make disciples of all nations (Matt. 28:18–20). As we value the charge of Jesus, we must consider the changing demographics of our contexts and how to best communicate to the people around us. It is our turn to step out into the neighborhood, a place that is increasingly changing. In order to do that well, we need to respond individually and corporately. An effective response will involve large organizations considering their own stories and resources, churches engaging their local communities, and individuals building community together with their neighbors. The call from Jesus necessitates a full response on the organizational, regional/local, and individual levels.

Organizational response

The benefits of an organization include the size and resources available to carry out the Christian mission. The collective whole can accomplish what the discrete parts would be unable to do. How then do organizations think through the demographic changes that face them? God's truth does not change, but the cultural context of an organization does. Each organization needs to think through its story and resources. As part of its story, the organization may consider historic strengths and weaknesses in engaging their mission and how to move forward.

My ecclesiastical organization, the Presbyterian Church in America, took a serious step in 2002 to consider its own story in dealing with the changing demographics of the US.[7] The organization was founded with the purpose of maintaining faithfulness to Scripture, Reformed theology, and the Great Commission. But in the pursuit of biblical fidelity and theological rigor, there were missteps with regard to cross-cultural ministry.[8] As the organization reviewed its story in 2002 at their annual national gathering, they passed an overture (statement) on racial reconciliation.[9] This overture included repentance for the involvement of the church in the sin of racism.

Then in 2004 the denomination approved a Pastoral Letter on Racial Reconciliation to more fully describe the challenges and opportunities to pursue cross-cultural ministry.[10] These were not meant to be one-time pronouncements that allowed the church to put this issue to bed. Rather, these were part of an ongoing consideration of the church's past and its ability to move forward into the ever-changing world.

This process continues in 2016 as the PCA considers a denominational overture of repentance for actions during the Civil Rights Era. These types of self-examinations are critical for an organization that consciously works to bring

---

7 The PCA is international. So while I am focusing on the organizational response in the US, this is not intended to exclude the member churches in Canada.

8 It should be noted that the PCA intended to engage in cross-cultural ministry at the outset and was aware of its own shortcomings. See Sean Lucas, *For a Continuing Church* (Phillipsburg, NJ: P & R Publishing, 2015), 271, 307.

9 MGAPCA (2002): 261–66.

10 MGAPCA (2004): 427–58. Appendix H.

the Gospel to the world around it. They are critical in enabling an organization to work through the good and bad of its story as it looks ahead to engage a changing world. They are critical to prepare the church to move forward with the cost necessary to carry on the mission. There is a helpful illustration of this moving forward with prepared hearts from Dr. Martin Luther King Jr. in *Letter from a Birmingham Jail*. In his letter, Dr. King described the process of moving forward by intentionally understanding what it takes as an organization. He calls the process self-purification. He describes preparing for the hard road ahead this way:

> Mindful of the difficulties involved, we decided to undertake a process of self-purification. We began a series of workshops on nonviolence, and we repeatedly asked ourselves: "Are you able to accept blows without retaliating? Are you able to endure the ordeal of jail?"[11]

This process of preparing organizationally for what's ahead is necessary for all organizations. But the example of our Lord Jesus Christ and the power of the Holy Spirit compel us to move forward in a changing world to do what is necessary.

There is much work to do given our starting point as a denomination. Despite the organization's good intentions at its founding, there has not been much headway toward diversity in membership. Peter Slade introduces in his book, *Open Friendship in a Closed Society*, the metaphor of wineskins and multiethnic churches.[12] The lack of progress calls us to wrestle with the question: Are we working to put the new wine of multiethnic congregations into the old wineskins of a dominantly and disproportionately White denomination? Regardless of what happens to our organization, the Gospel compels us forward in the pursuit of reconciliation, unity, and representation. We do this not to accomplish a particular quota, but for the sake of fulfilling God's call to our changing world. We do this in faith, not knowing what the result will be.

---

11 Martin Luther King Jr., *Letter from Birmingham Jail*. April 16, 1963 (Philadelphia: University of Pennsylvania African Studies Center, 2010).

12 Peter Slade, *Open Friendship in a Closed Society* (New York: Oxford University Press, 2009), 169.

My prayer is that the growing ability to engage cross-culturally will enable my denomination to carry on its original mission of faithfulness to both Scripture and the Great Commission. I pray the same would be true for other ecclesiastical organizations.

Regional response

Local churches and regional networks have an opportunity to think consciously about the resources for cross-cultural ministry and where they are directed. Church planting may be the most effective tool in creating multiethnic congregations in that they are able to create a new church culture from the outset that intentionally addresses the demographics of a particular neighborhood. When considering church planting, assessment should be made of the changes in the target neighborhood as well as the ability of the planting pastor or team to engage a particular area.

Existing churches should consider the possibilities for their own cross-cultural ministry. Neighborhoods change and existing churches must avoid turning away from the demographic reality of their place. In the metro DC area, demographic changes have impacted churches in all Christian traditions. Alessandra Ram writes in *The Atlantic Monthly* about how particular neighborhood changes are impacting the Black church.[13] Not only does the changing neighborhood make it more difficult to connect locally with members, but it also opens ethnic diversity in a neighborhood where it may not have previously existed.

Other churches will continue to exist in monoethnic locations, but this does not make a church immune from considering a mission to work to the ends of the earth. In a culturally monolithic place, the Bible's theological direction toward multiethnic ministry may translate to both engagement with other monolithic neighborhoods of a different ethnicity as well as missions to other regions and nations.

---

13 Alessandra Ram, "In Changing Neighborhoods, Black Churches Face an Identity Crisis," *The Atlantic*, October 12, 2012. Accessed December 22, 2015. http://www.theatlantic.com/national/archive/2012/10/in-changing-neighborhoods-black-churches-face-an-identity-crisis/263305/. Of course the Black church is not monolithic, and not all churches are impacted in the same way.

Individual response

On an individual level, the way forward includes these steps: learn, meet, listen, and pray. First, learn the history of your city. When addressing the audience at the Areopagus, Paul declares:

> *He made from one man every nation of mankind to live on all the face of the earth, having determined allotted periods and the boundaries of their dwelling place that they should seek God, in the hope that they might feel their way toward him and find him.* (Acts 17:26–27)

Paul is reminding each of us, "Your place matters!" As God providentially locates us in a neighborhood, we respond. That response includes learning the story of our place. What is the history of my city? What events have most shaped its identity? What are the demographic changes taking place here? The answers to these questions provide a framework for considering how to best carry out the message of God's good news. Lesslie Newbigin spoke of this process as communicating changeless truth effectively to a changing place, so that people can actually understand why the news is good.[14]

Make it a priority to meet with people in the neighborhood. How well do you know your neighbors? There is an opportunity to engage with people that takes a conscious effort that can only be carried out by individuals. The decision to invite a neighbor over for dinner, welcome someone new to the community, and invite someone to church are all individual activities that radically shape the whole of a community or church. A full response to the changing world around us cannot be solely carried out by organizational events but also must include individual efforts to meet people.

We must listen. One of the most challenging things to living as part of the majority culture is that the concerns that are regularly on the minds of our minority neighbors are unknown to us. It's as if we wear blinders to the concerns of others with injustice we don't recognize. In order to faithfully minister to people, we must bring the Gospel to bear on their concerns. So our response involves listening to those around us with eyes to see and ears to hear what we may typically miss.

Soong-Chan Rah puts it this way in *The Next Evangelicalism*, "the call to listen and to gauge others before speaking and acting provides a model for

---

14 Lesslie Newbigin, *Foolishness to the Greeks: The Gospel and western culture* (Grand Rapids, MI: Wm. B. Eerdmans Publishing, 1986).

multiethnic ministry and dialogue."[15] The only way to see the world through your neighbors' eyes is to listen. This takes time, energy, and effort. But this is part of the Gospel calling. This listening guards against ethnocentricity and what gets defined as "normal."

We are all ethnic, but the majority culture has the luxury of forgetting this reality. So when we speak about grabbing some ethnic food, this can be a way in which we prioritize our food as normative but everyone else's as ethnic or different. This type of thinking can translate beyond food to aspects of church life. The way in which sermons are properly given may become culturally normalized against those other ethnic types of sermons. The way in which music may be culturally normalized against other ethnic types of music. The Gospel of Jesus Christ calls us to resist this prioritizing of our culture over others.

Prayer is one way to exercise resistance. Peter Slade in his book *Open Friendship in a Closed Society* comments on the way prayer became a gathering point for people from different ethnic backgrounds to safely be together without quick claims on a normalized form.[16] This effectively brought people together. In the life of our church plant in Silver Spring, prayer has been a vital part of our community and seeing the world through the eyes of others.

Engaging the world near us

The world is changing around us. These changes bring challenges for all of us. Christians are empowered by Jesus Christ to meet these challenges with the power of the Gospel. It is the power of God that brings unity to otherwise diverse neighbors. As the Apostle Paul writes:

> *But now in Christ Jesus you who once were far off have been brought near by the blood of Christ. For he himself is our peace, who has made us both one and has broken down in his flesh the dividing wall of hostility.* (Eph. 2:13–14)

This union with Christ—Jew and Gentile together—calls us to thoughtfully engage in cross-cultural ministry as the demographics of our neighborhoods change. In these challenges are the opportunities to continue God's story of redemption in Jesus Christ as a light to the nations.

---

15 Soong-Chan Rah. *The Next Evangelicalism* (Downers Grove: InterVarsity, 2009), 188.

16 Martin Luther King Jr., *Letter from Birmingham Jail.* April 16, 1963 (Philadelphia: University of Pennsylvania African Studies Center, 2010).

Acknowledgments

A hearty thank you goes to all who have contributed to this project. Thirty authors came together, no small feat. Rev. Robbie Schmidtberger helped to coordinate and corral submissions. Julie Serven is the most patient, expert editor of all time, and we owe her every piece of gratitude available for her hundreds of hours on this manuscript. Dr. Sean Benesh designed the cover and typeset the document. Thank you also to those who reviewed submissions and offered valuable insights.